AF593532

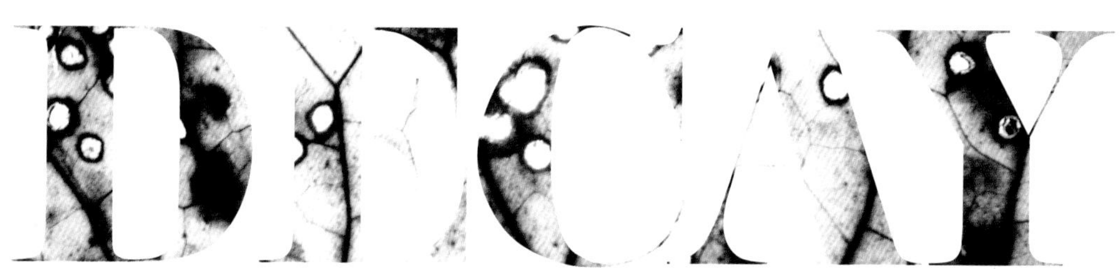

DECAY

NATHAN TROI ANDERSON & J.K. PUTNAM

Decay

Design: Christopher D Salyers
Editing: Buzz Poole
Typefaces used: Galeere, Didot

Library of Congress Control Number: 2007937351

Printed and bound through Asia Pacific Offset, China

10 9 8 7 6 5 4 3 2 1 First edition

Mark Batty Publisher
36 West 37th Street, Suite 409
New York, NY 10018
www.markbattypublisher.com

ISBN: 978-0-9795546-7-4

Distributed outside North America by:
Thames & Hudson Ltd
181A High Holborn
London WC1V 7QX
United Kingdom
Tel: 00 44 20 7845 5000
Fax: 00 44 20 7845 5055
www.thameshudson.co.uk

DECAY

MARK BATTY PUBLISHER NEW YORK CITY

NATHAN TROI AND

ON DECA

Pure decay is the living force inherent in every thing. It is the soil, the root, the blood that unites the greater body of ruin. Consuming the flesh in shadow, drawing a fossil to the sun, descending the earth by cover of night, the decay of light enters the body. The movement penetrates into stone. The flood of water begins the act of giving life then crushes the object down into a fine black substance. The body sleeps wrapped in this same irresistible force, day and night, falling toward itself. Decompose, disintegrate, burned away in the apparition of light, possessed in the embrace that breaks all body of its certain cast and releases those elements again in the water's return.

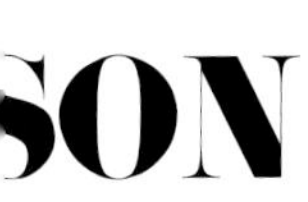

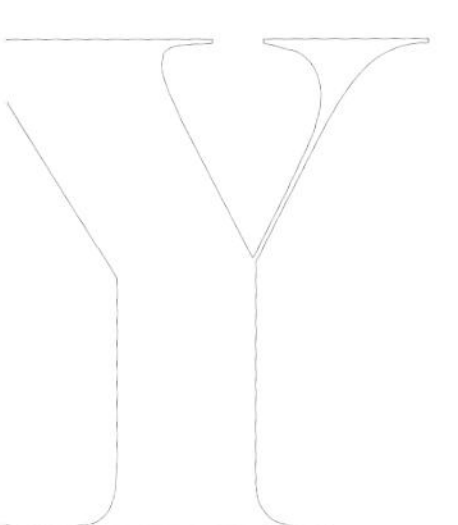

J.K. PUTNAM

ON DECA

I walked out through the waterless swamp toward what appeared to be the slender trunk of a tree. I could not tell if it had grown there or if someone had just stuck the thing end up in the muck. It had no branches and stood six feet over my head; it seemed solid in the mud. This was the first subject I shot for *Decay*.

The ground was sandy and wet and my feet sank whenever I stopped moving to take a picture. The rotted meat of the wood caught shadows from the November evening sun. When finished I made my way back through mud and weeds to the trail I had come in on. As I walked an itchy sensation moved up my legs. I ignored it until I got back to the car. Pulling up my pant legs I saw nothing at first. After closer inspection I noticed dozens of tiny, almost microscopic, black dots scattering around my legs. The dots had tiny features: tiny little legs and tiny little teeth. These wretched, tick-like bugs dug at my skin the whole way home. My first shower washed away any that were not holding on. The rest had burrowed their heads into my pores, forcing me to pick them out with my fingernail, one by one. Over the course of the following months the bites grew worse, they became impossible not to itch. The sensation of scratching my legs with fingernails was almost euphoric. The bites became dry, infected, bruised from scratching. My fingernails and the germs that ride them made visible the natural, silent decay of my skin.

The decay of my skin was the result of the bugs' bites, the dry winter air and my scratching. All of these factors aiding natural skin decay, which is inevitable. Once something is created it immediately begins to age. It is effected by environment, neglect, physical damage and time. Everything that begins in this world will end, and before it ends it will decay, but this can work both ways. Decay can bring new life. It removes one thing and makes room for another. In a city, an old building is demolished to make room for a new one. In the rainforest a tree dies, falls, rots and becomes host to new trees. In a rural countryside a house is abandoned; earth overcomes the foundation; vines grow up the walls. The land reclaims the house. Through creation and decay the world as we know it is changed. Take for example a glacier. It is formed from snow and ice. Gravity pulls. The ice deforms slowly and the glacier advances. It carves through rock like a river, uprooting everything before it. It stops and recedes, leaving rivers running high and a land that is changed forever. The result is beautiful to our eyes, but in recent years the picture has become ugly. Glaciers have become a symbol of humankind's affect on our environment.

There are no pictures of glaciers in this book. Other than the junk we leave to rot in the woods I did not photograph any real examples of ecological or environmental decay. There is no question that it is happening, however. The only question is whether or not humankind has sped up the process. I searched my archives for a photo showing our footprint on the environment. The example I found was a shot I had taken in the Olympic Mountains in Washington state: a thin hiking trail cutting across an alpine meadow. The trail was bare to the dirt. It was so kept and perfect one would think it was machine made. For as long as this trail is used it will never return to the way it was. One step off the path into the short, thick plants that survive there would be devastating. The damage caused from that footstep would take a century to repair. Looking at this photograph makes me wonder if getting to see such a breathtaking place makes the trail worthwhile. This is how I feel about most beautiful, secluded places. After I see them I wish them cut off from the world.

Environment is very important to me, whether it be the woods I walk in or the neighborhood I live in. In shooting for this book I was forced to take a closer look at the destruction of these places, whether it is natural or human-induced. The man-made structures and vehicles all exuded emptiness, as did the rotting bodies of animals. I am an avid photographer of wildlife, but I had never turned my lens on a dead animal. While working on this project I photographed swans, squirrels, rats, seals, newborn birds and insects: all dead, all rotting. I still saw no beauty in them. Only hints of what they used to be. The challenge was finding what was not there in a subject, and then using the camera to show that. In many cases decay was happening over such a long period of time that it became invisible.

Years ago, while hiking up the ridge of a mountain in New Hampshire, I found a small piece of granite loose in its bed. This rock was the weathering that one never sees. Wind, water and ice had separated the stone from the solid rock that made up all five-thousand feet of this mountain. The granite sliver rocked back and forth in its cradle with the help of my finger, bits of sand fell into the wind as it moved. It would not come out. In the seasons to follow, this speck of mountaintop will fall from its peak. These mountains are old. They are covered in trees, except at the tops where there is bare rock. In years to come the rock will weather and turn to sand. Trees will grow, covering the peaks just like the neighboring mountains to the west. Time will overcome the permanence of the Ice-Aged giant. How long until the whole mountain is nothing more than dirt? What if we use our fingernail? How long then?

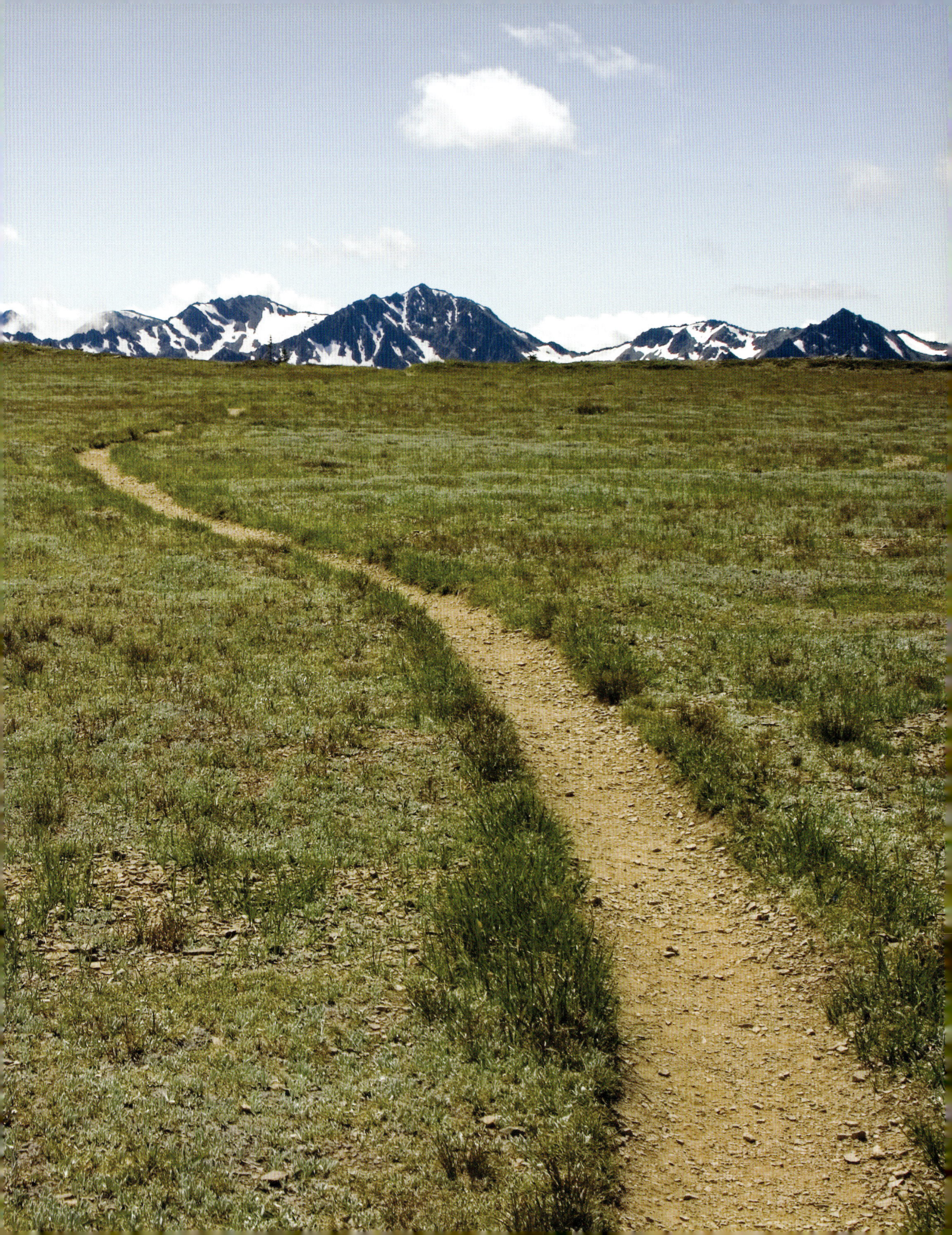

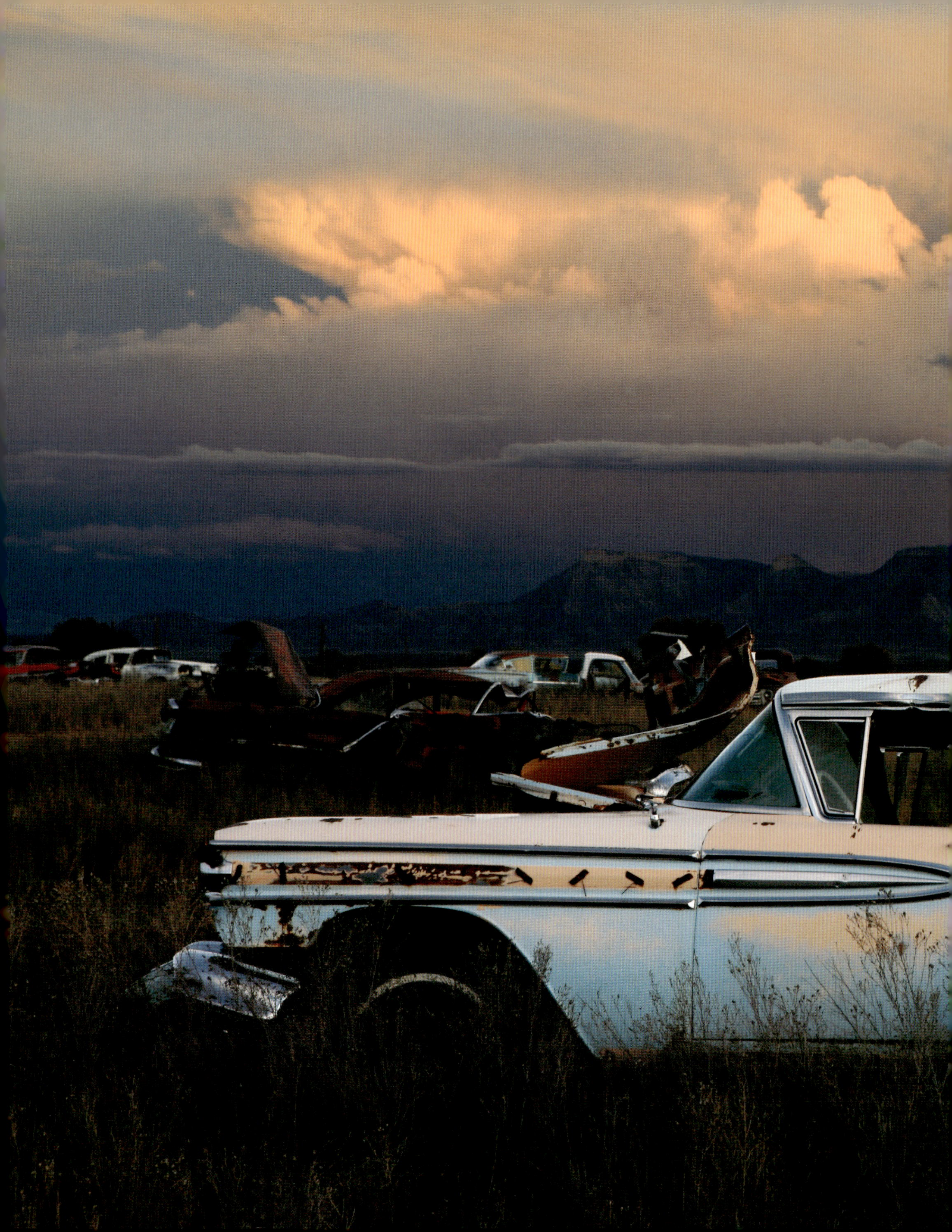

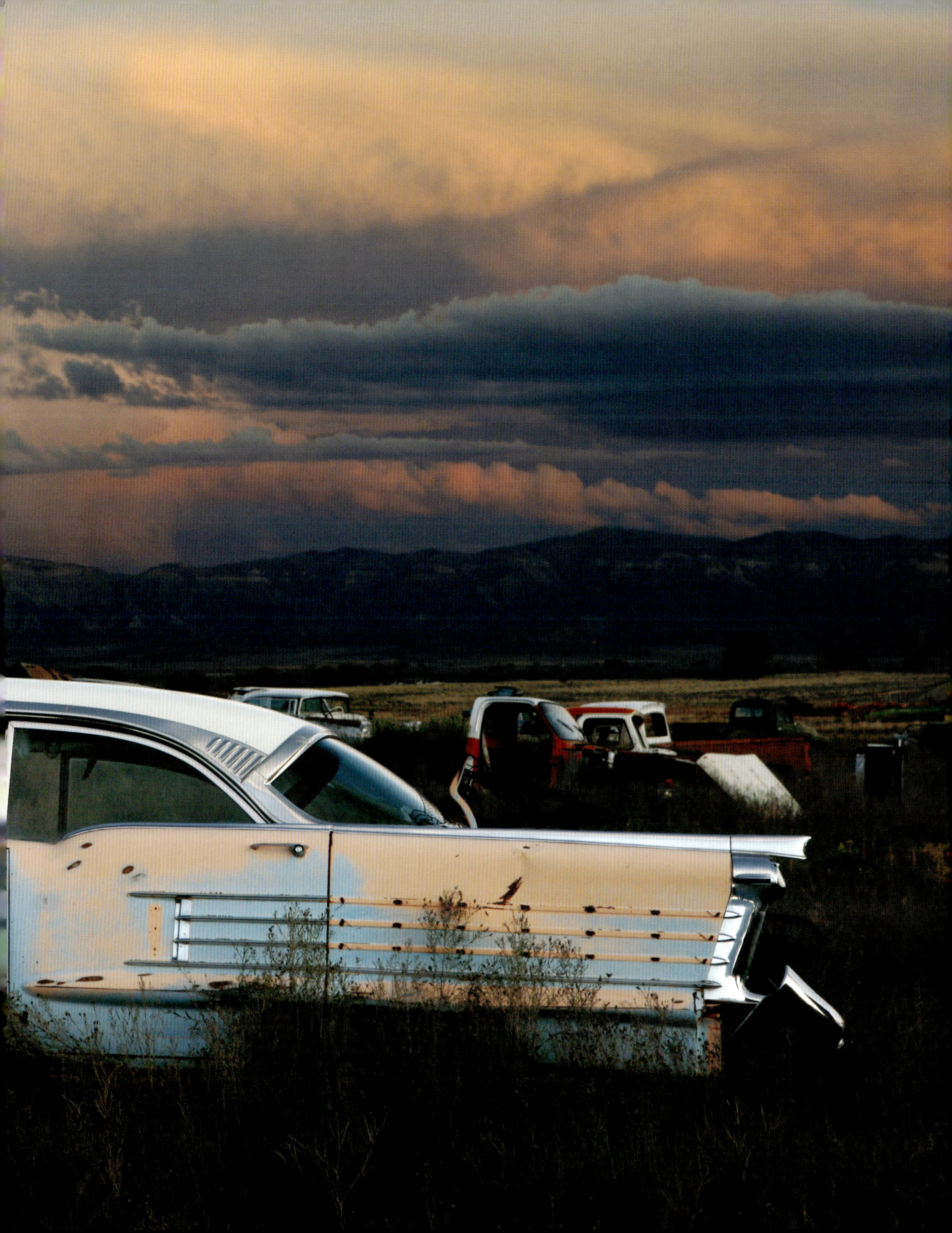

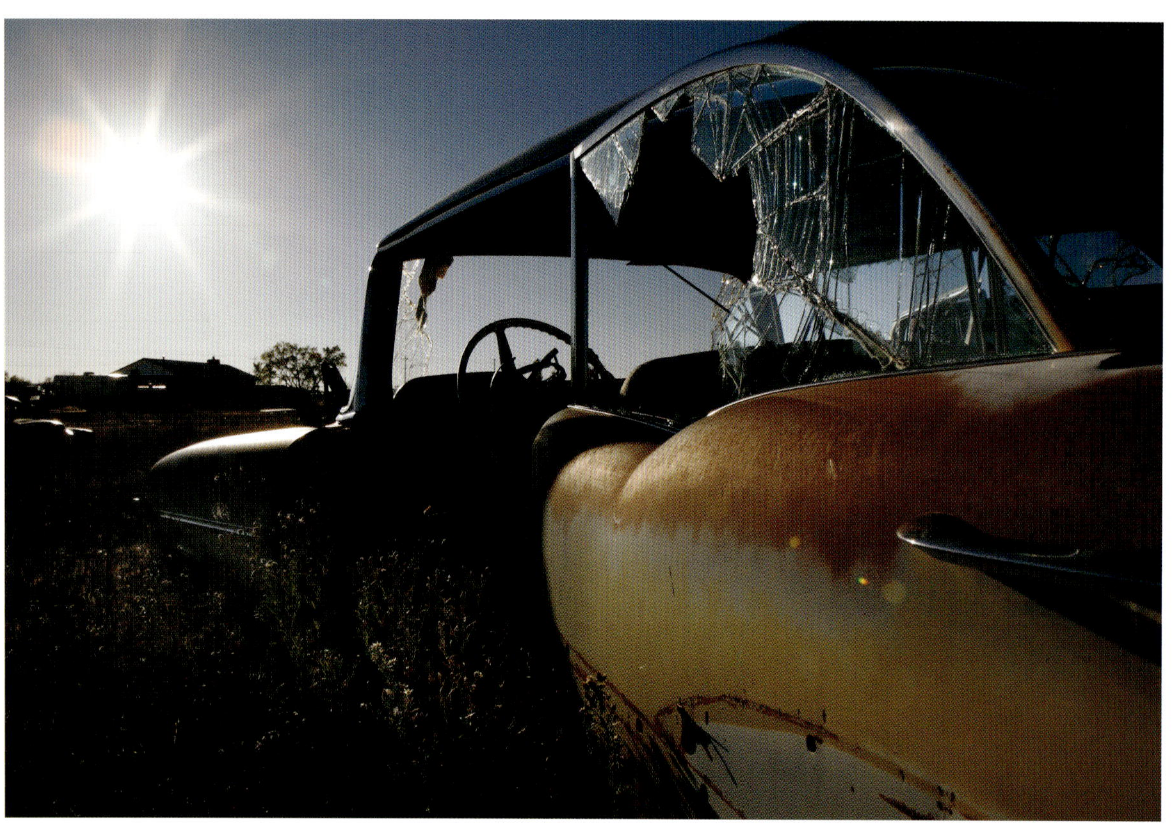

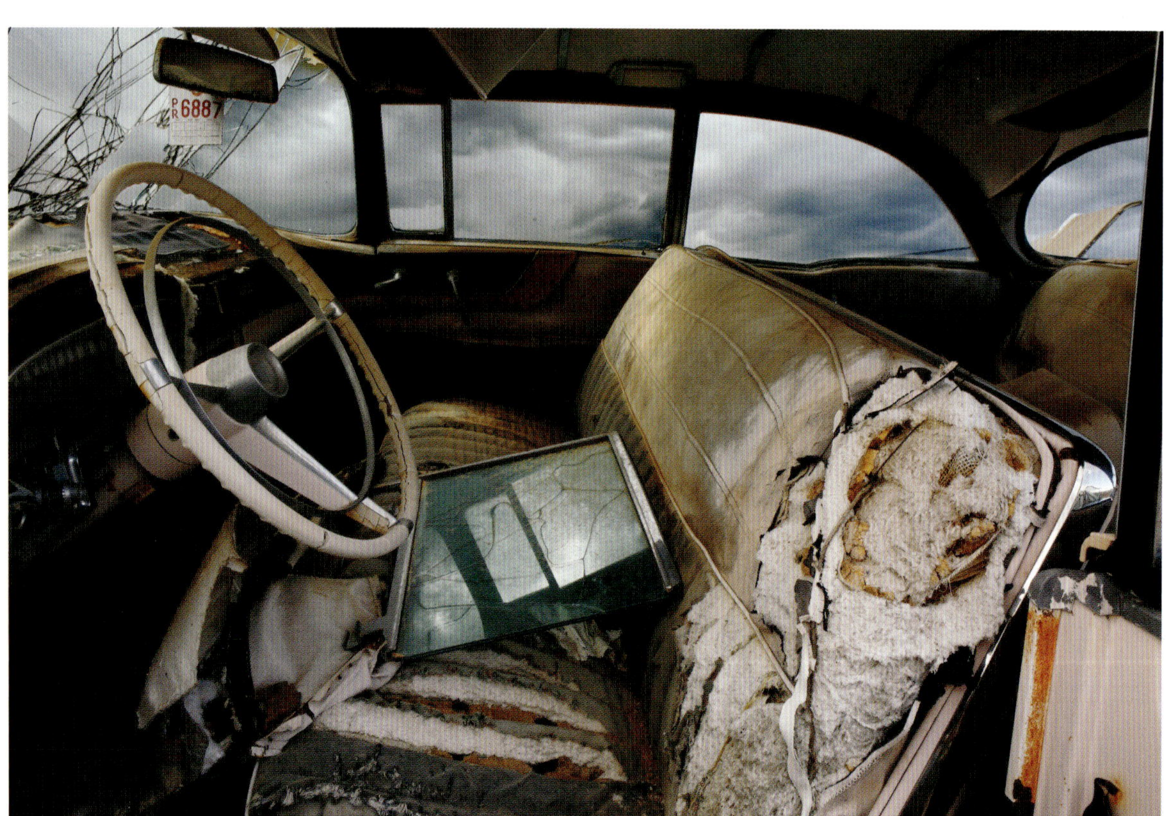
6887

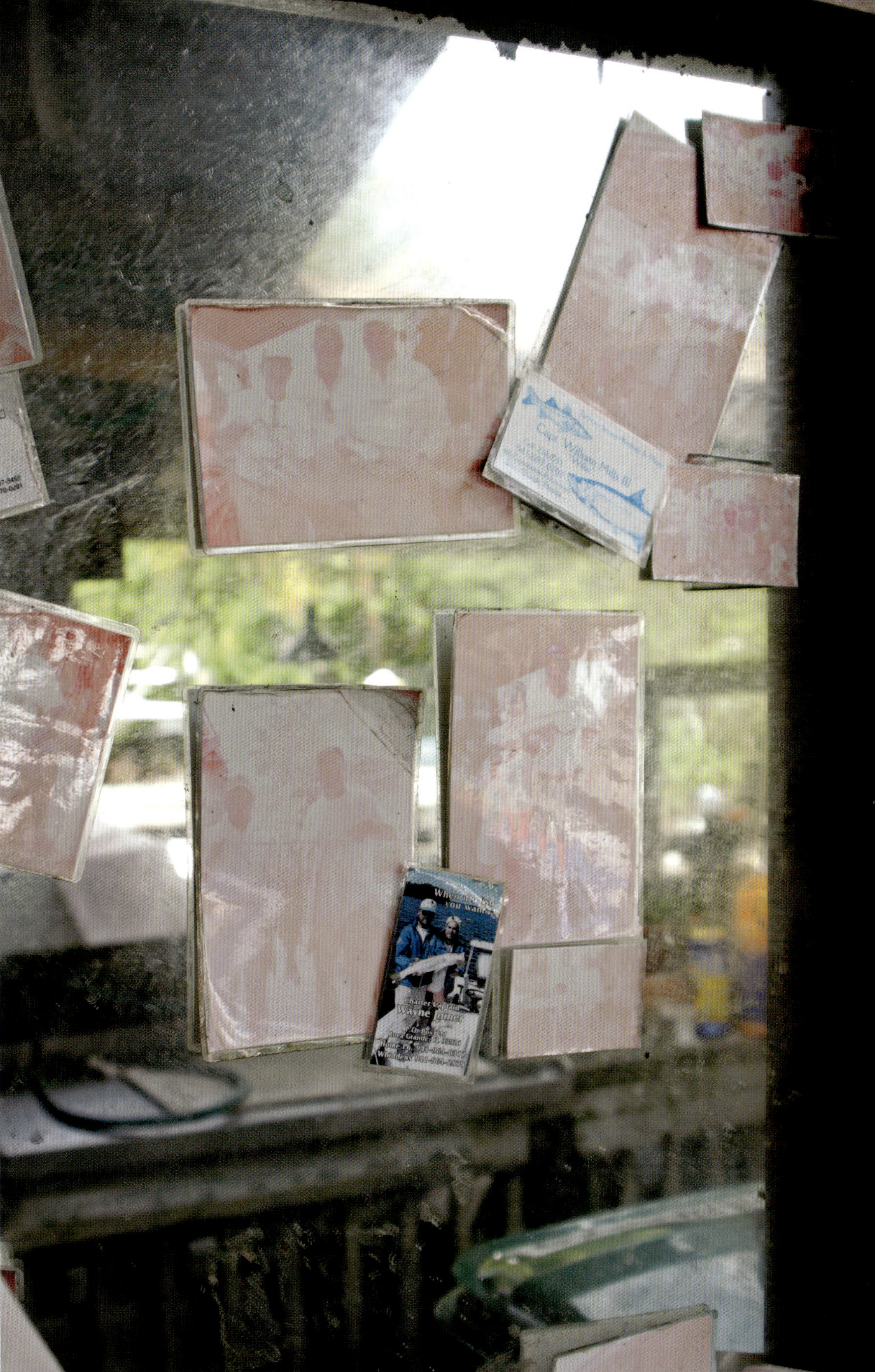
Capt. William Mills III
Charter Captain
Wayne Joiner

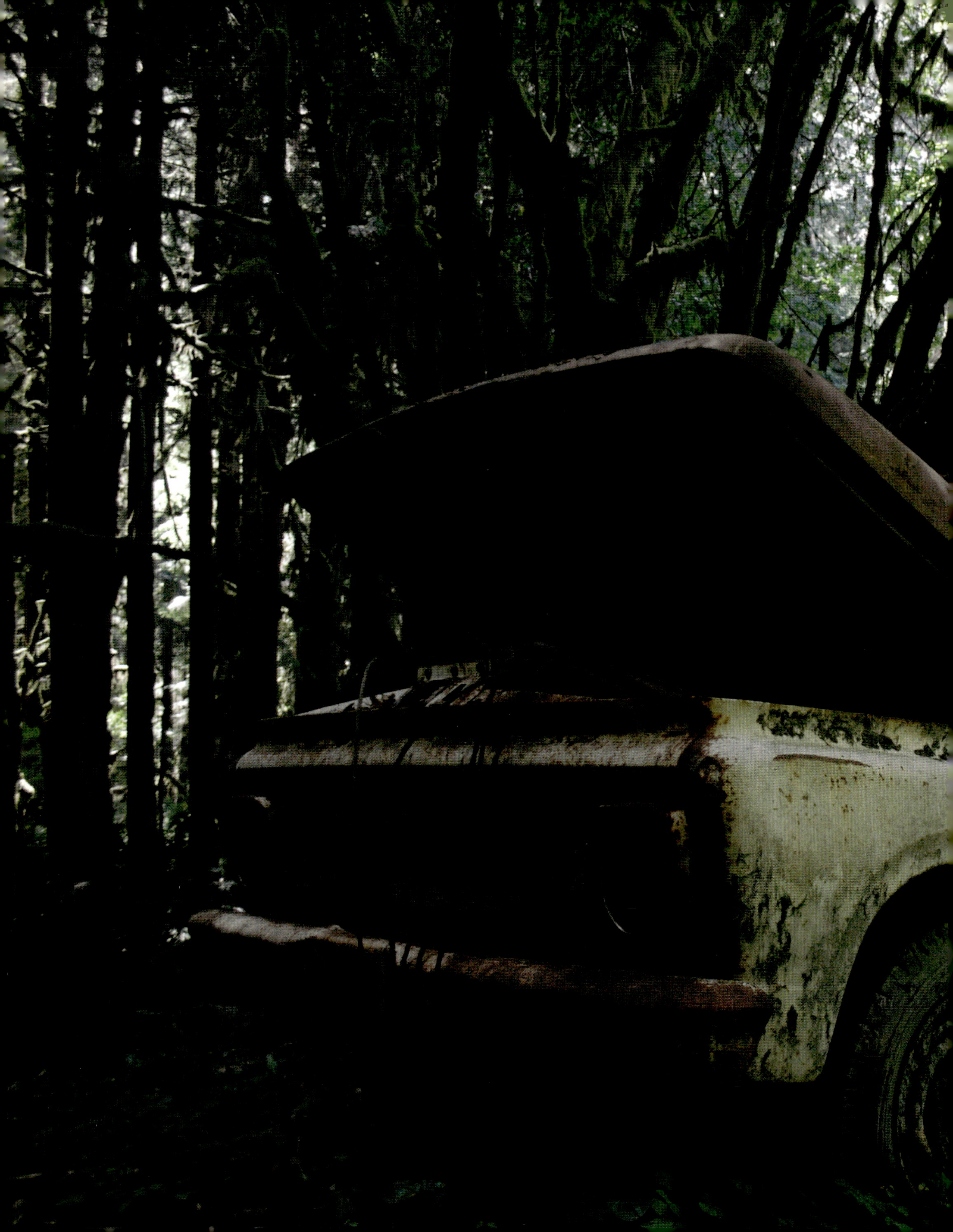

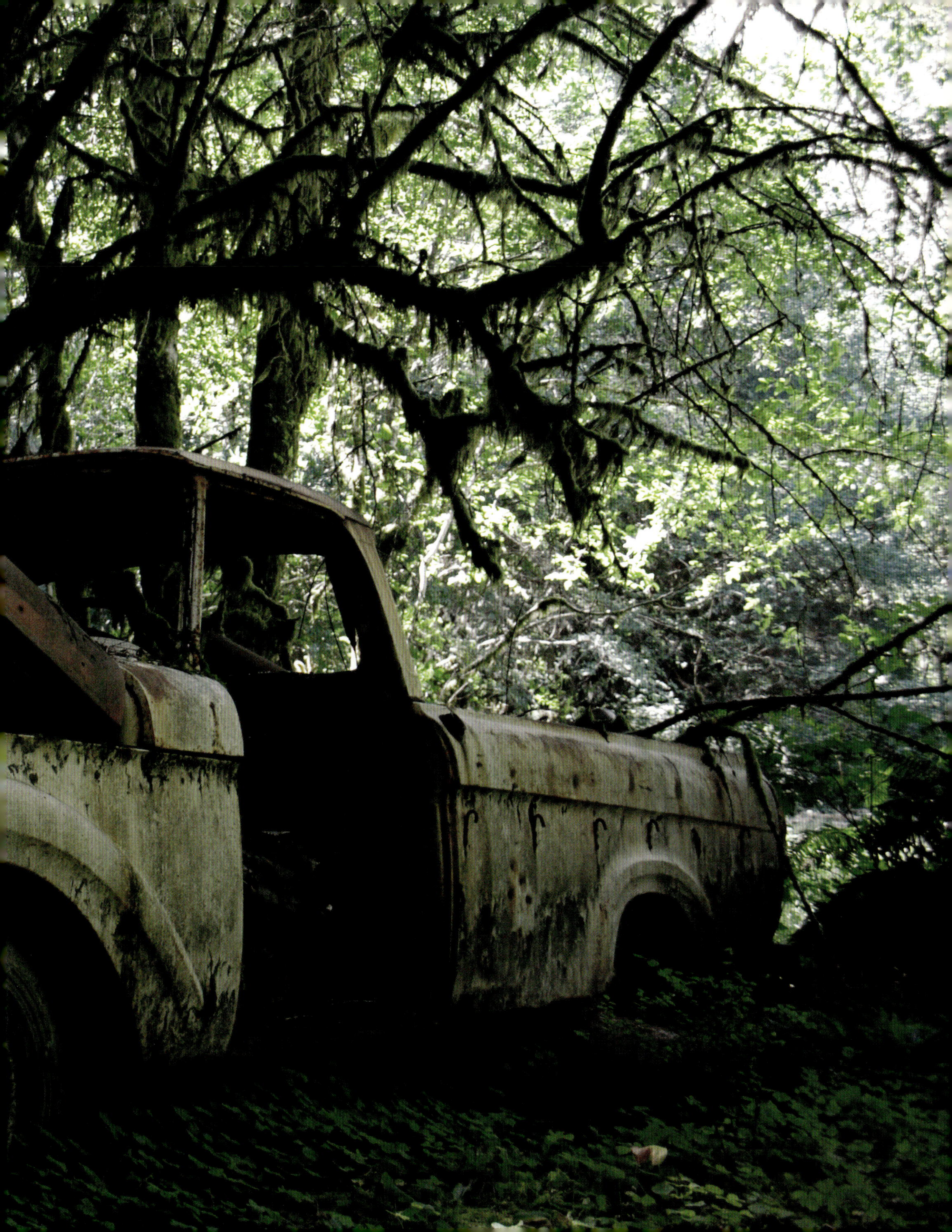

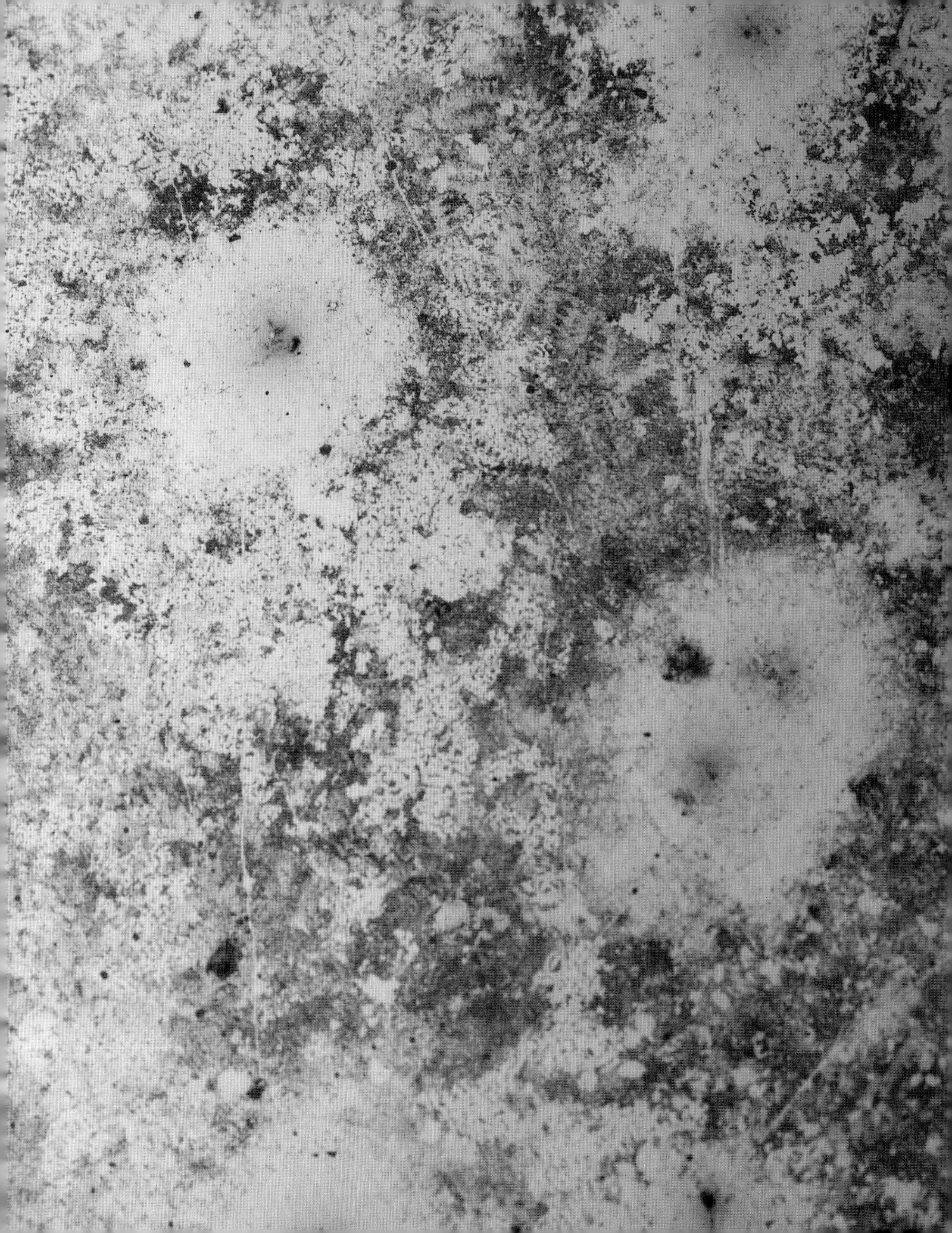

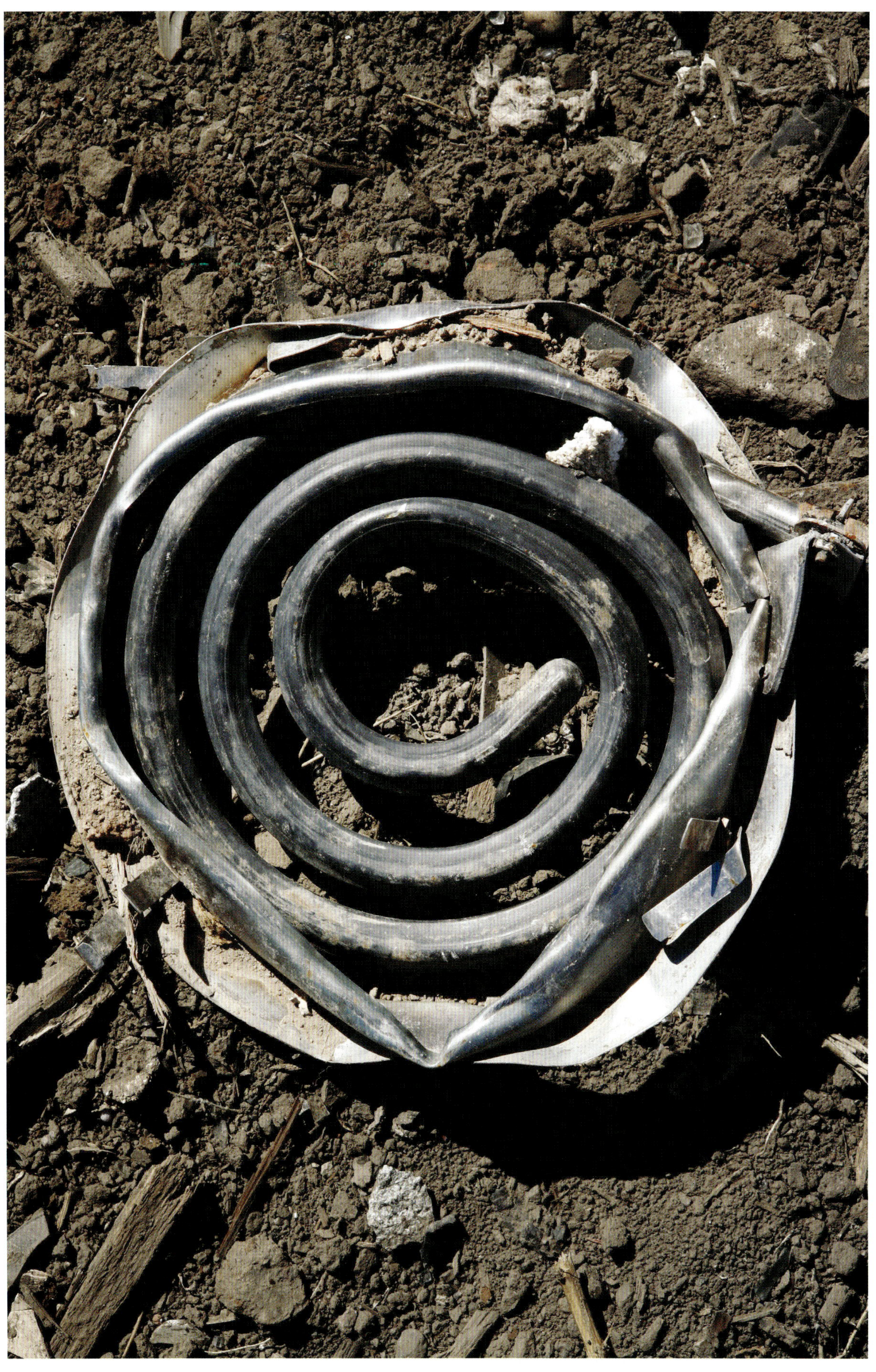

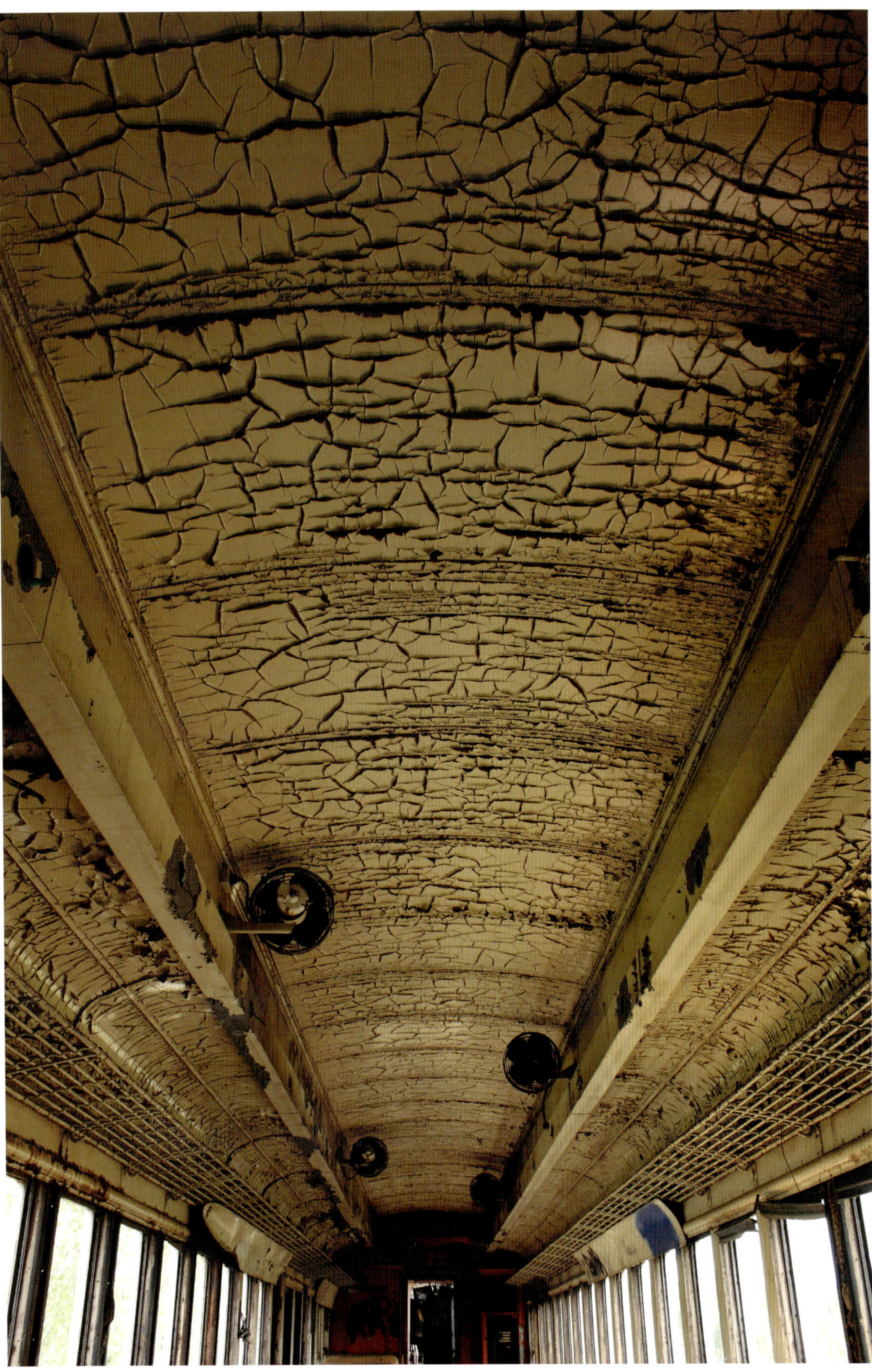

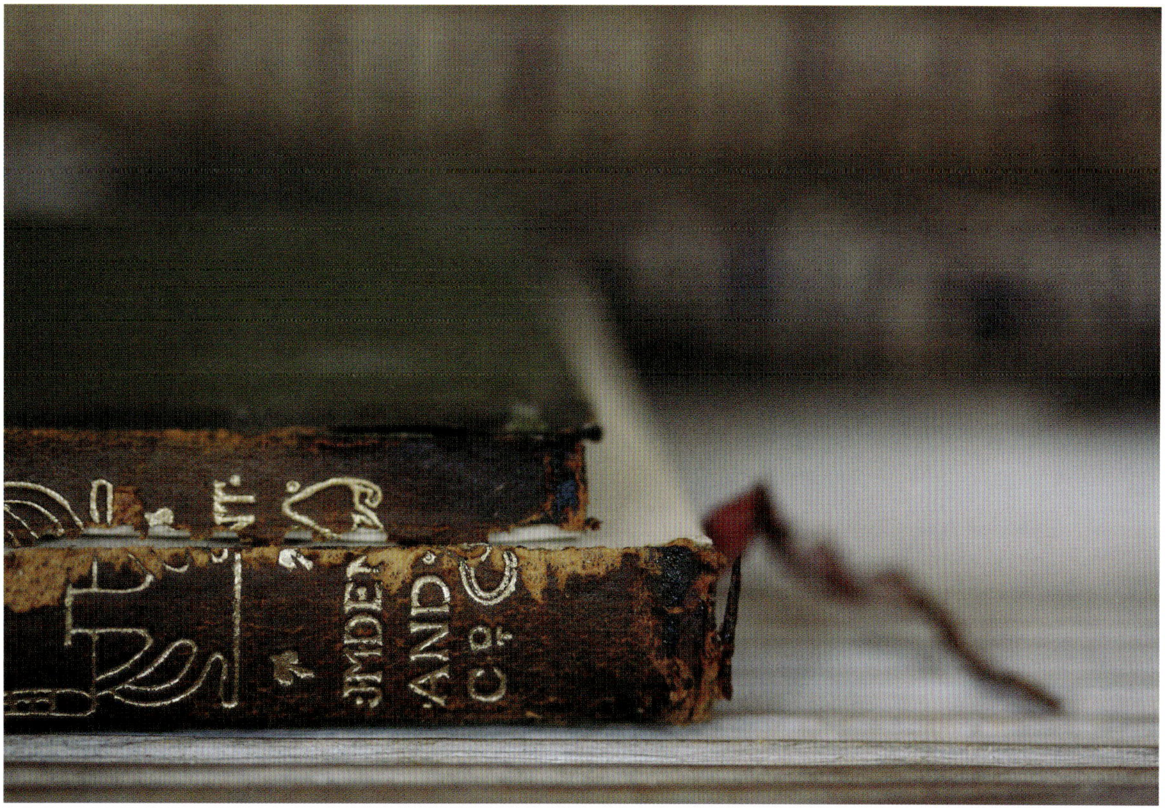

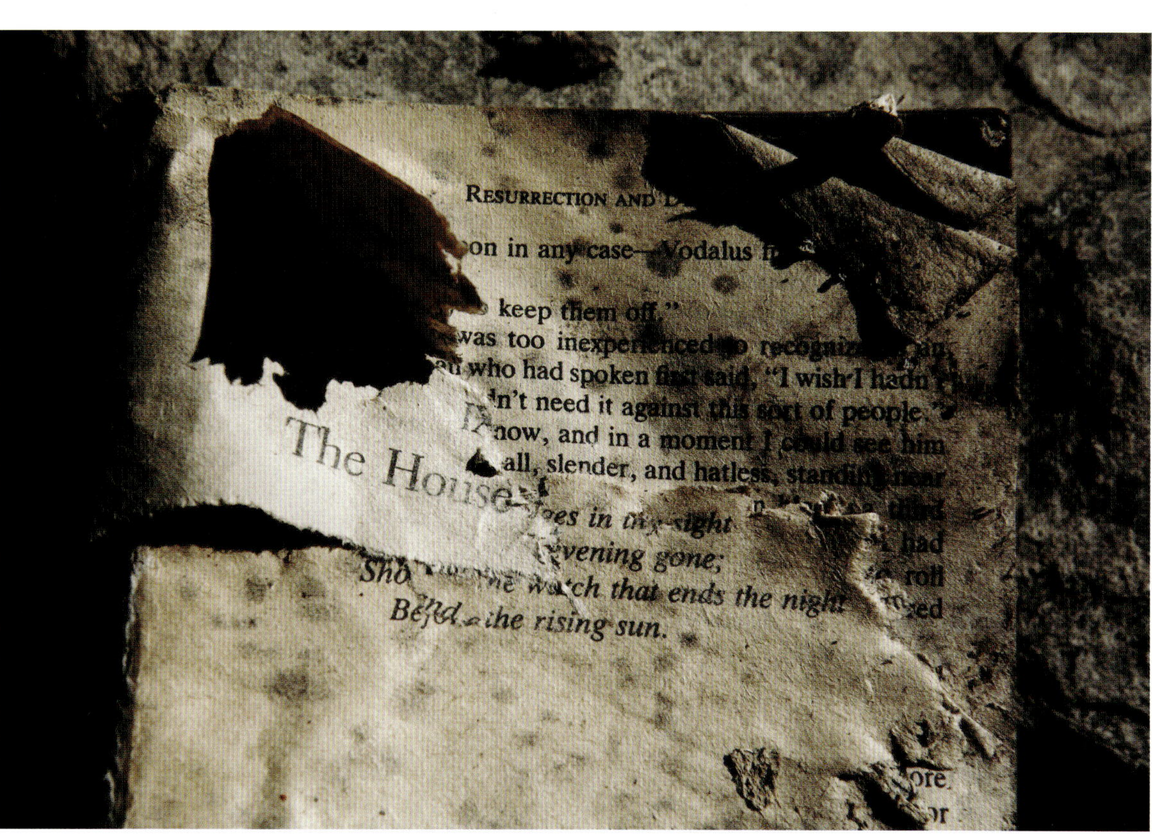
Resurrection and
on in any case—Vodalus
keep them off."
was too inexperienced to recogniz
who had spoken first said, "I wish I hadn
n't need it against this sort of people."
now, and in a moment I could see him
all, slender, and hatless, standing near
The House
es in thy sight
evening gone;
watch that ends the night
the rising sun.

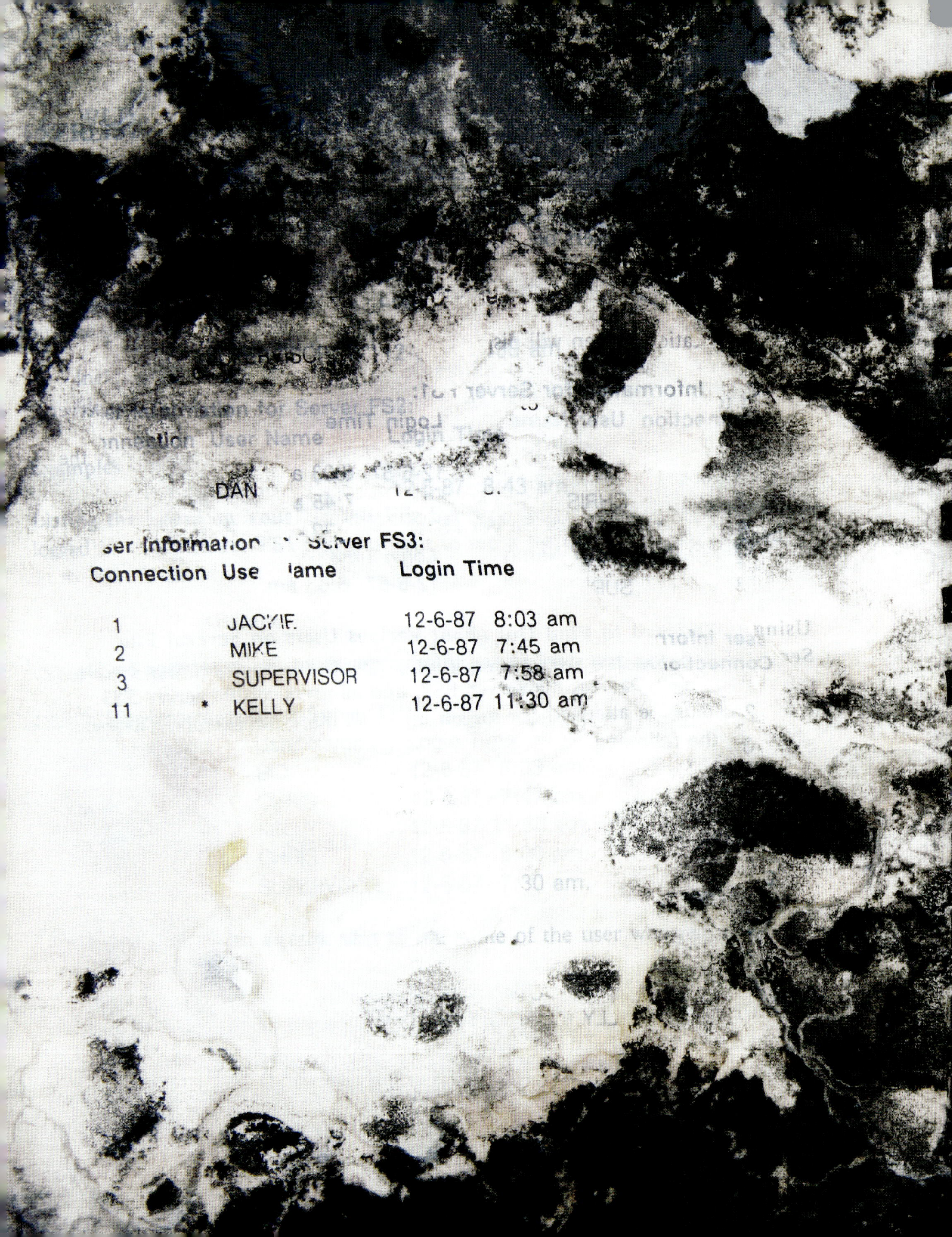

DAN

ser Informat.on ·· Server FS3:

Connection		User Name	Login Time
1		JACKIE	12-6-87 8:03 am
2		MIKE	12-6-87 7:45 am
3		SUPERVISOR	12-6-87 7:58 am
11	*	KELLY	12-6-87 11:30 am

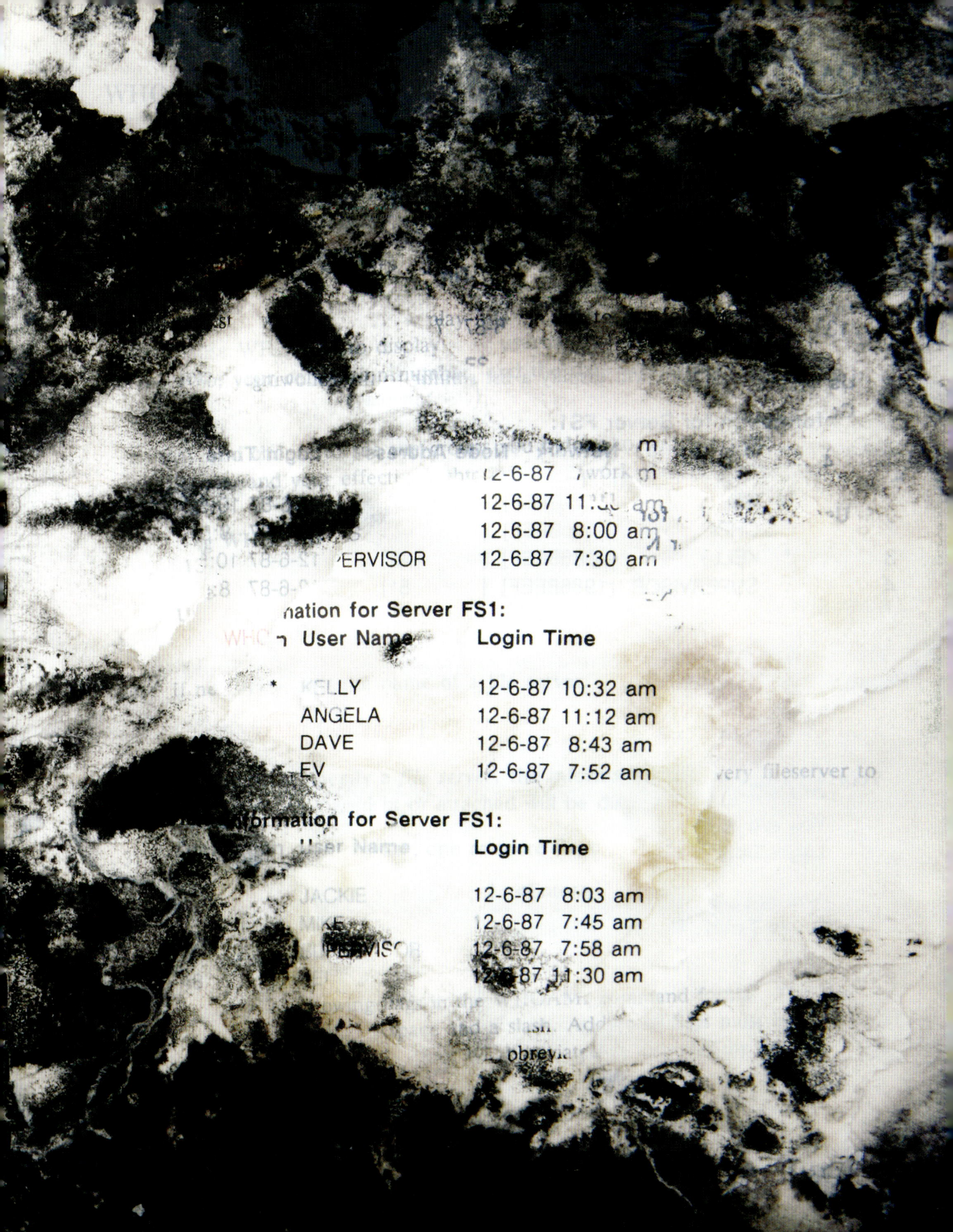

12-6-87 8:00 am
ERVISOR 12-6-87 7:30 am
nation for Server FS1:
User Name Login Time
KELLY 12-6-87 10:32 am
ANGELA 12-6-87 11:12 am
DAVE 12-6-87 8:43 am
EV 12-6-87 7:52 am
ormation for Server FS1:
Login Time
JACKIE 12-6-87 8:03 am
12-6-87 7:45 am
12-6-87 7:58 am
11:30 am

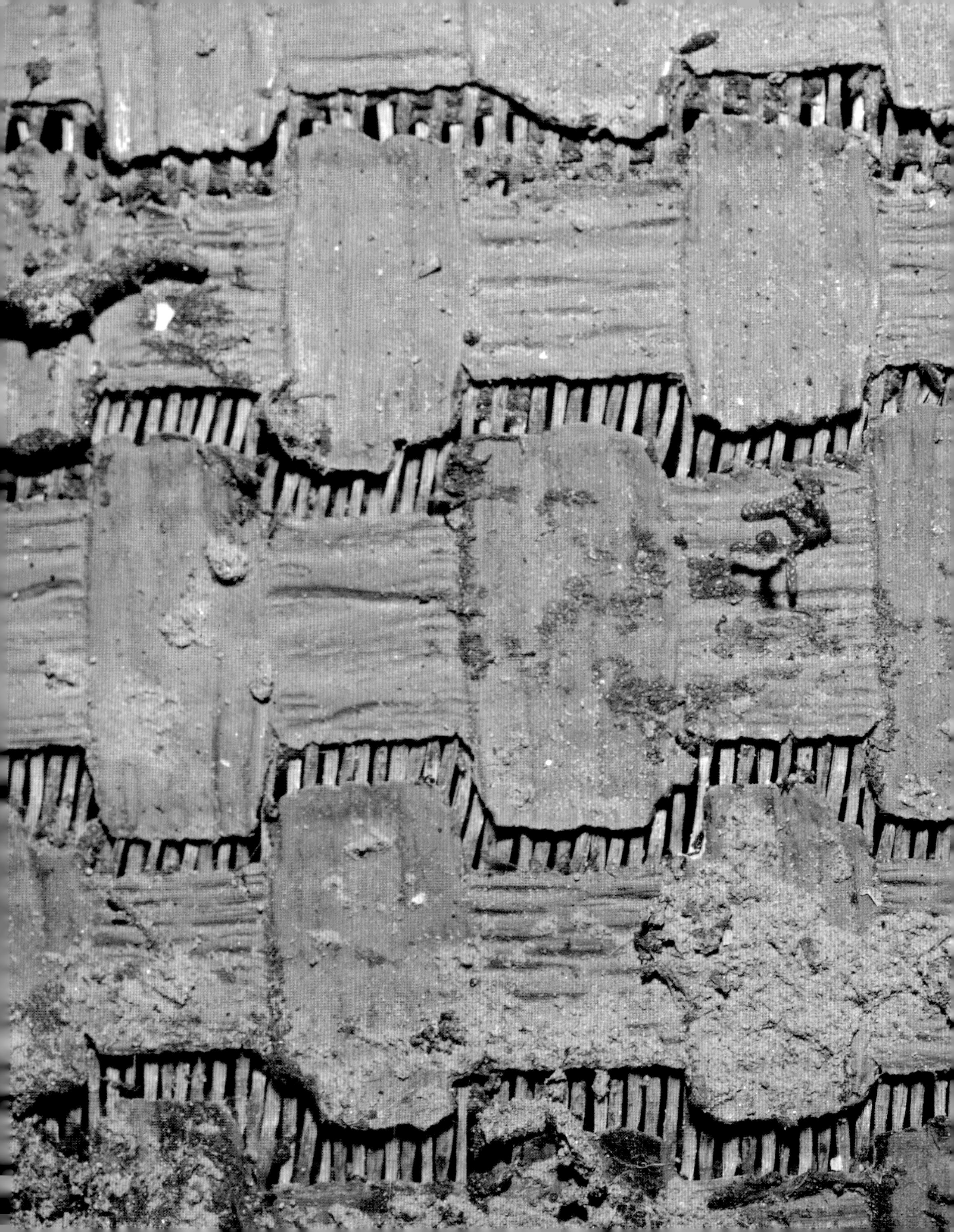

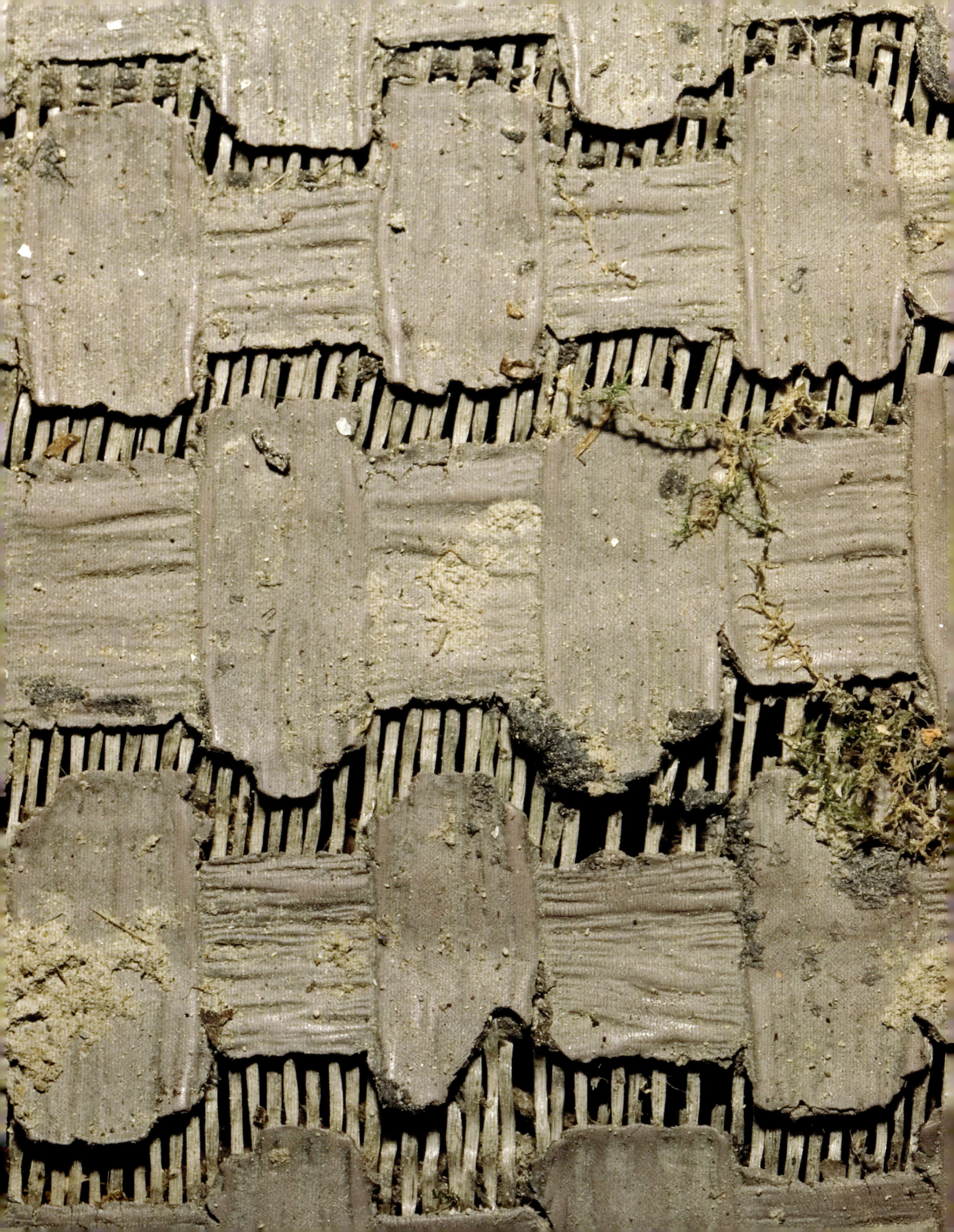

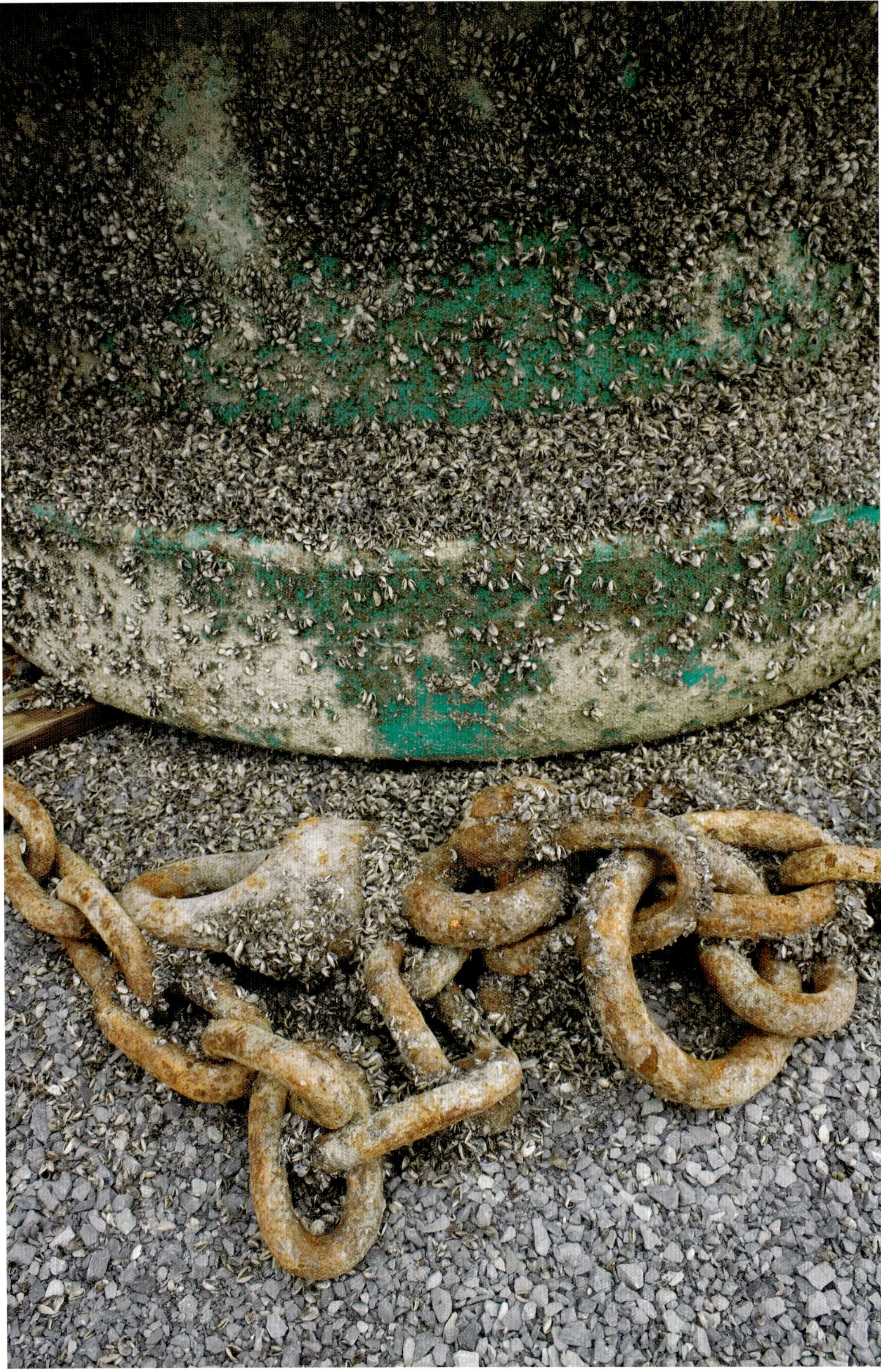

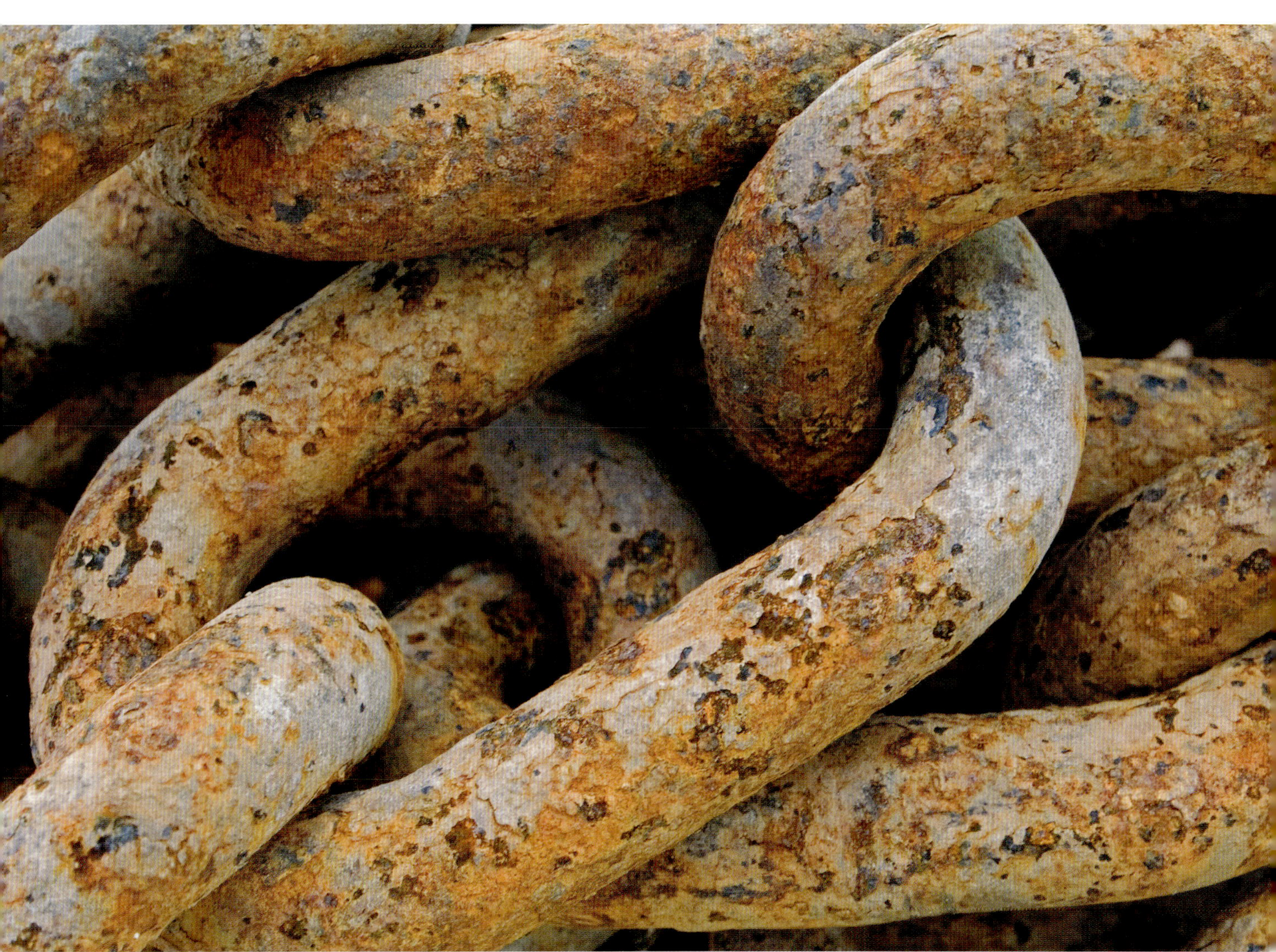

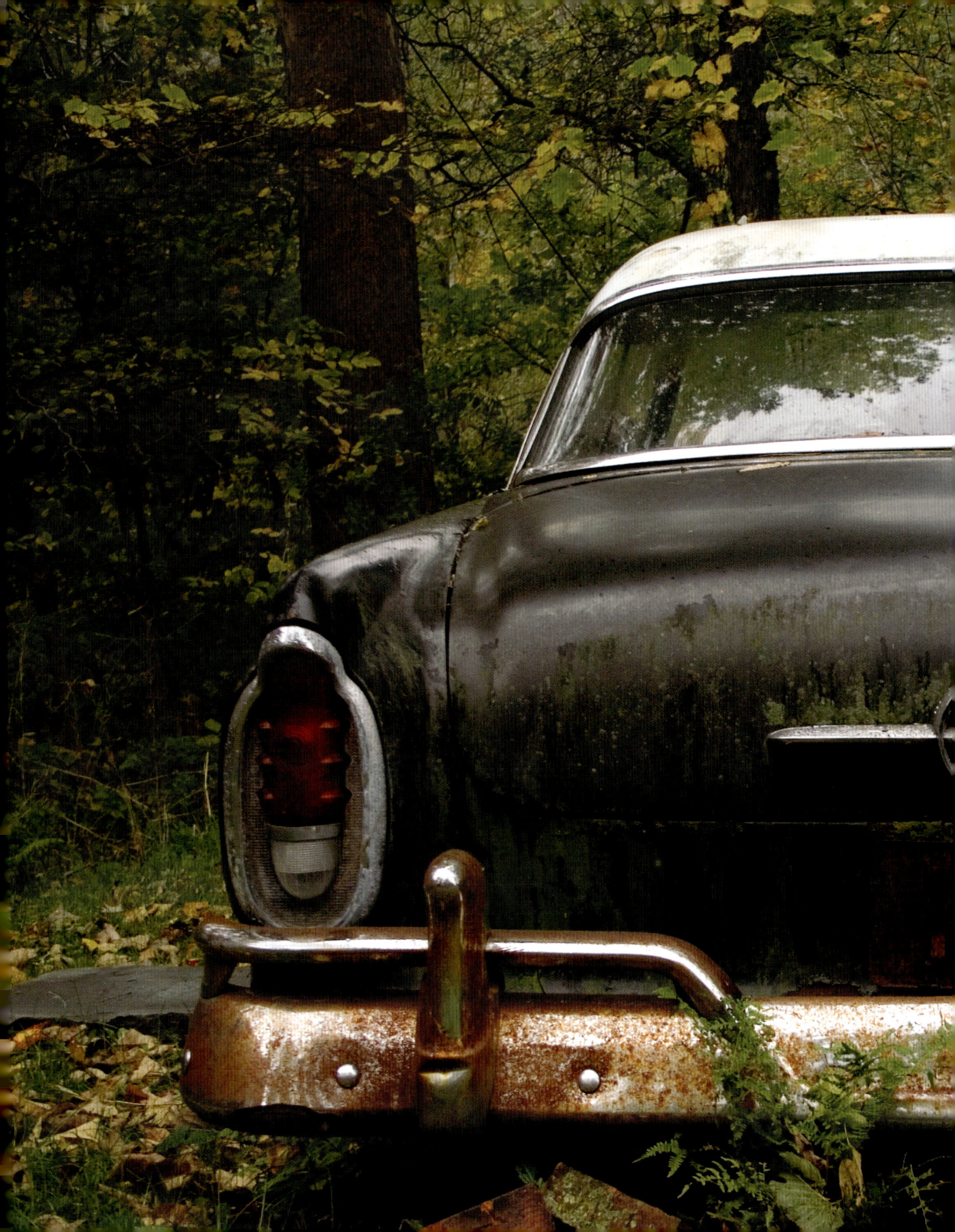

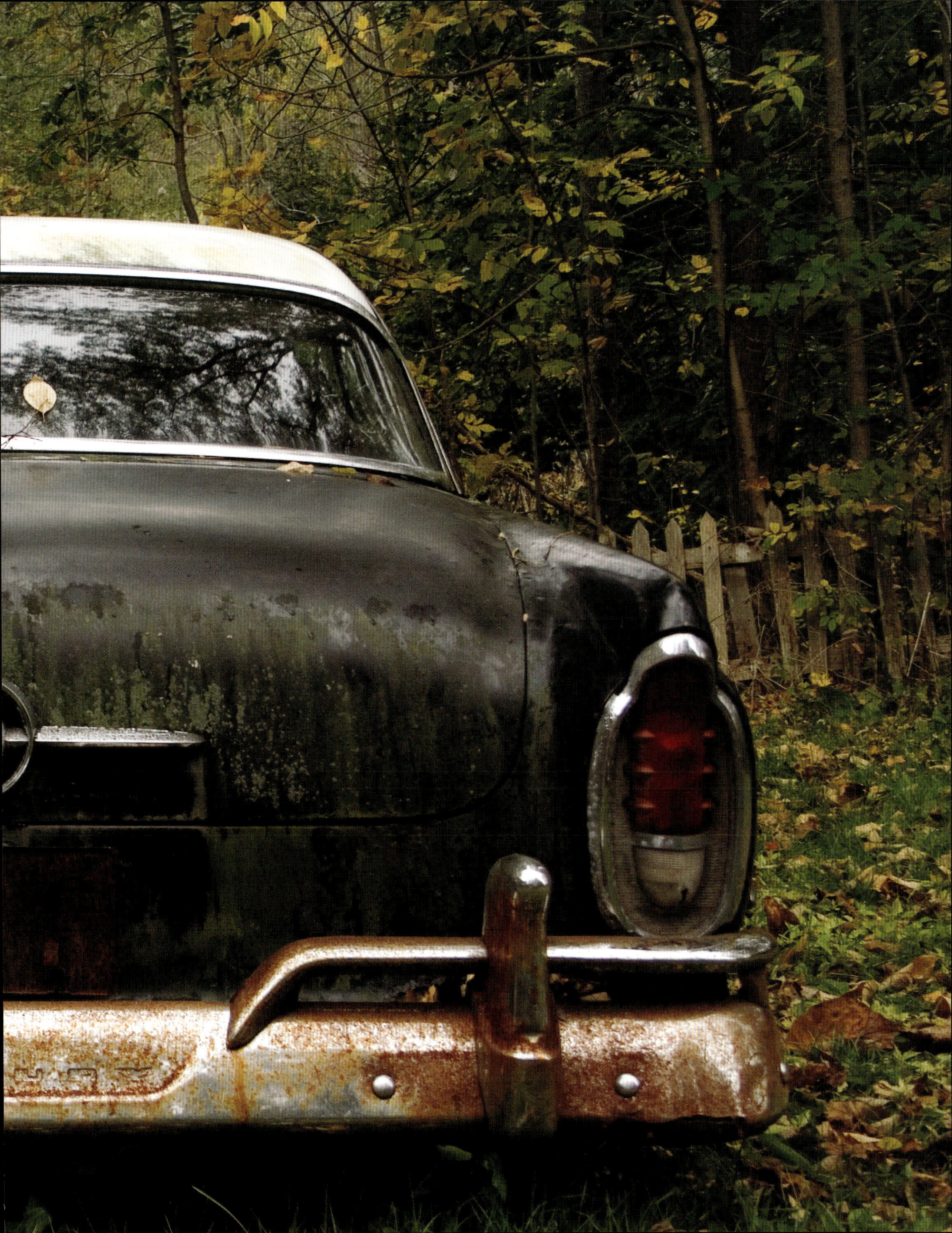

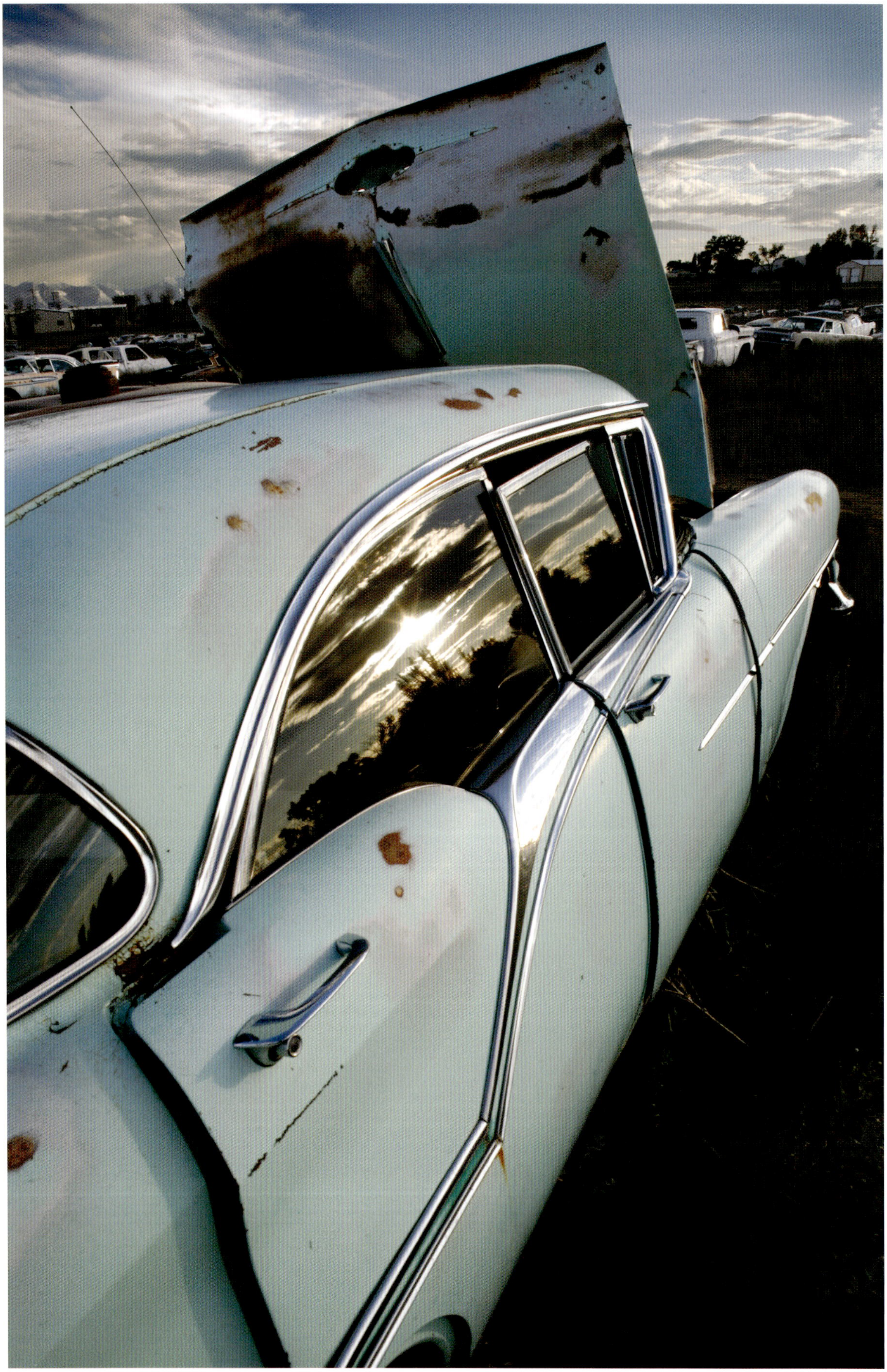

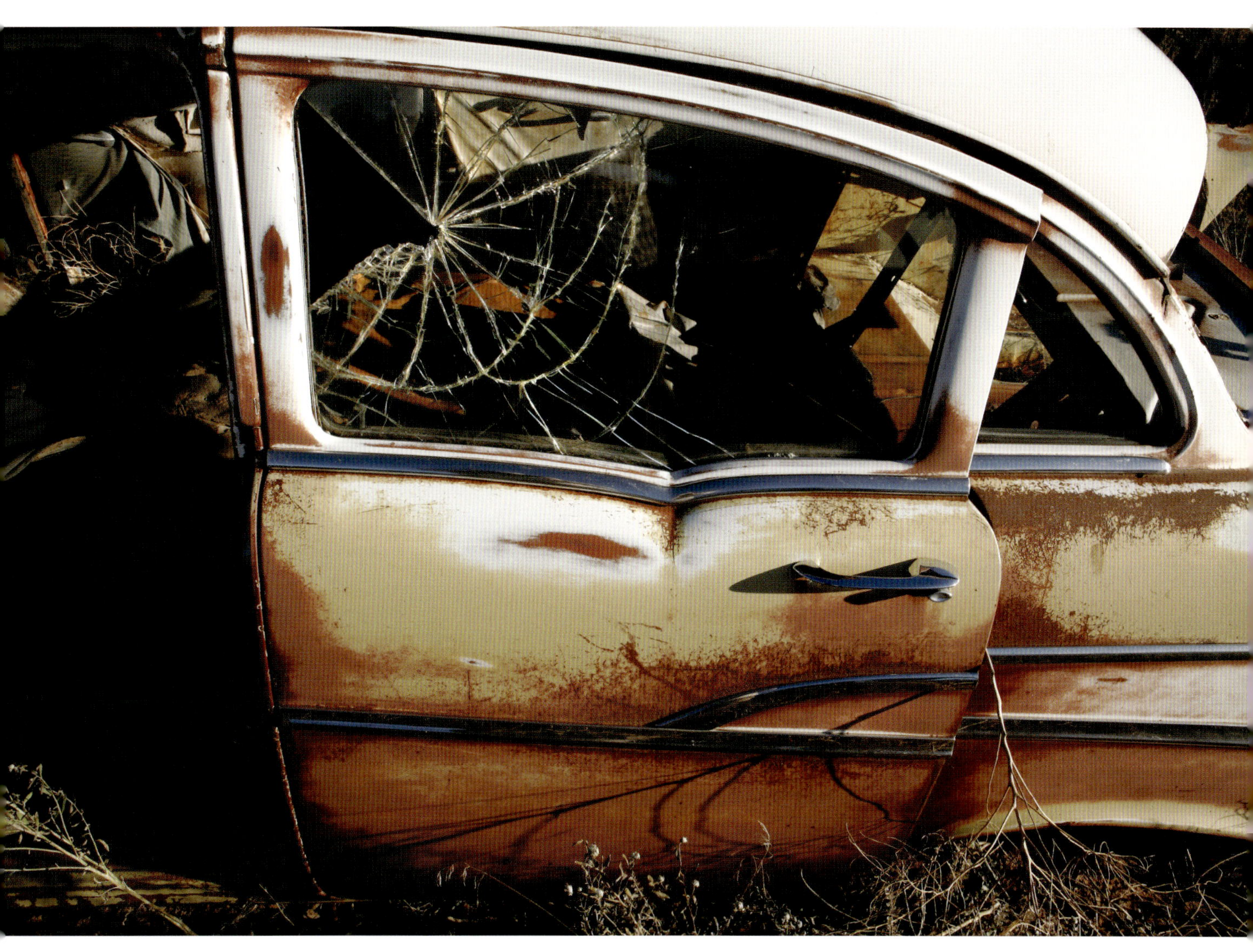

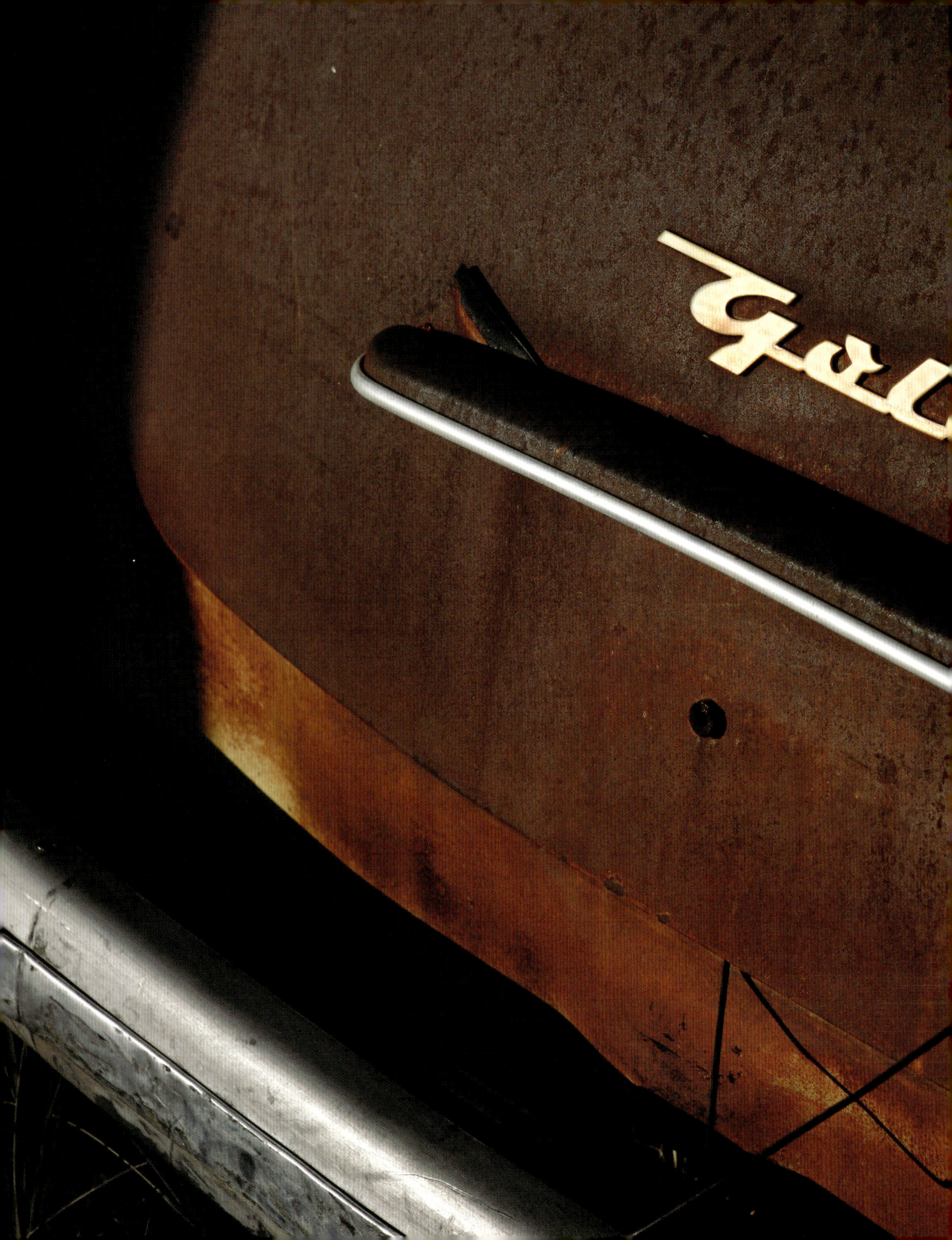

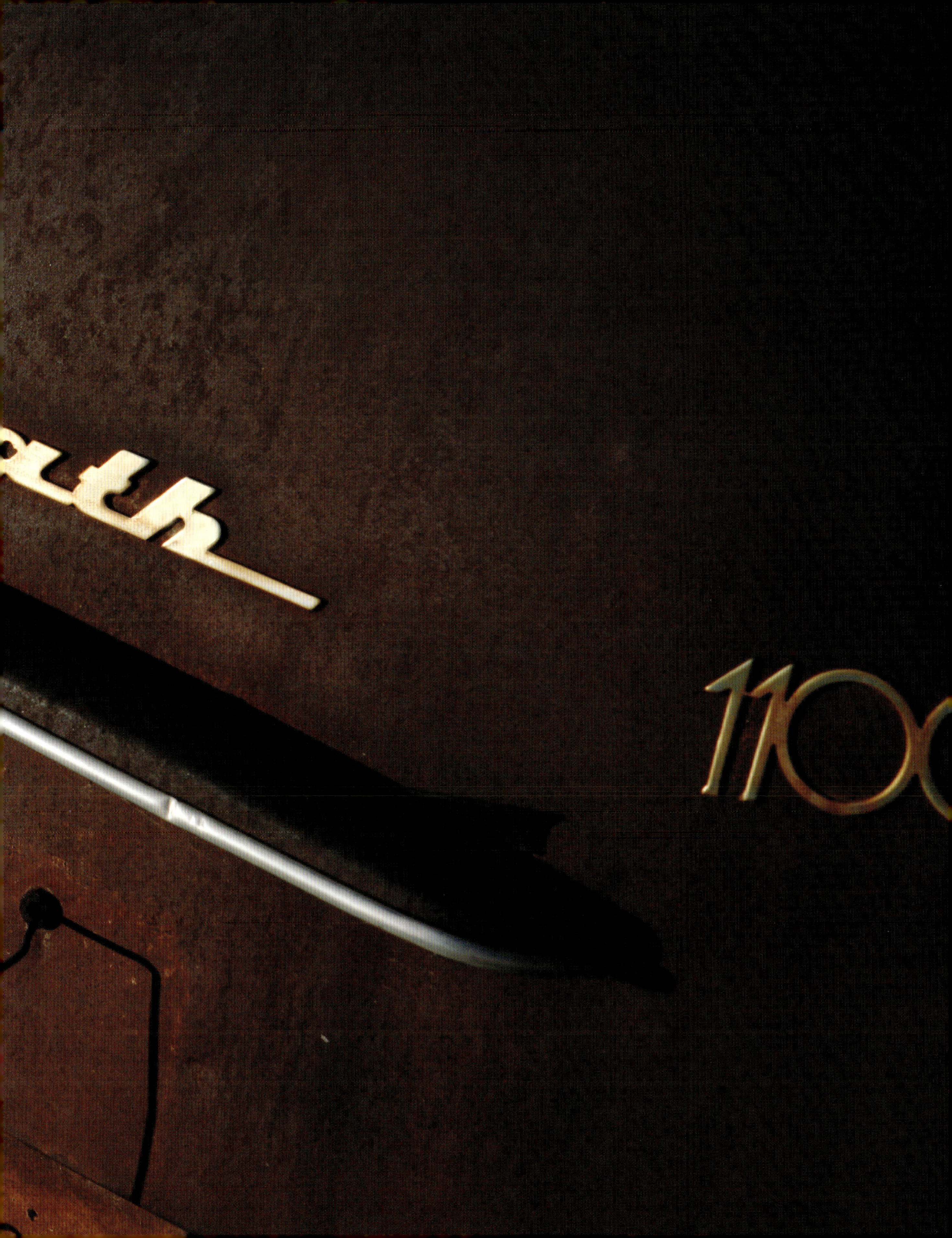

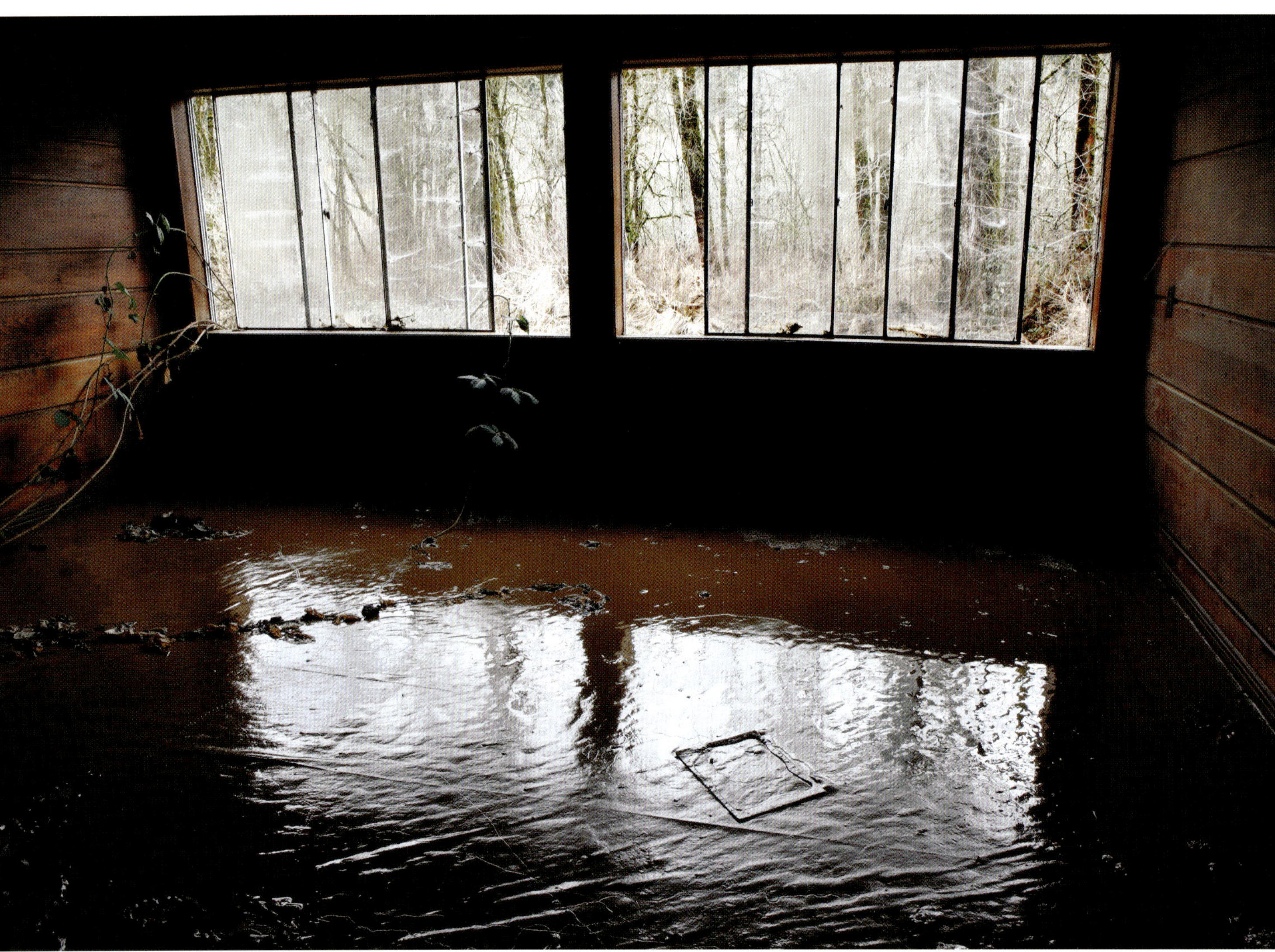

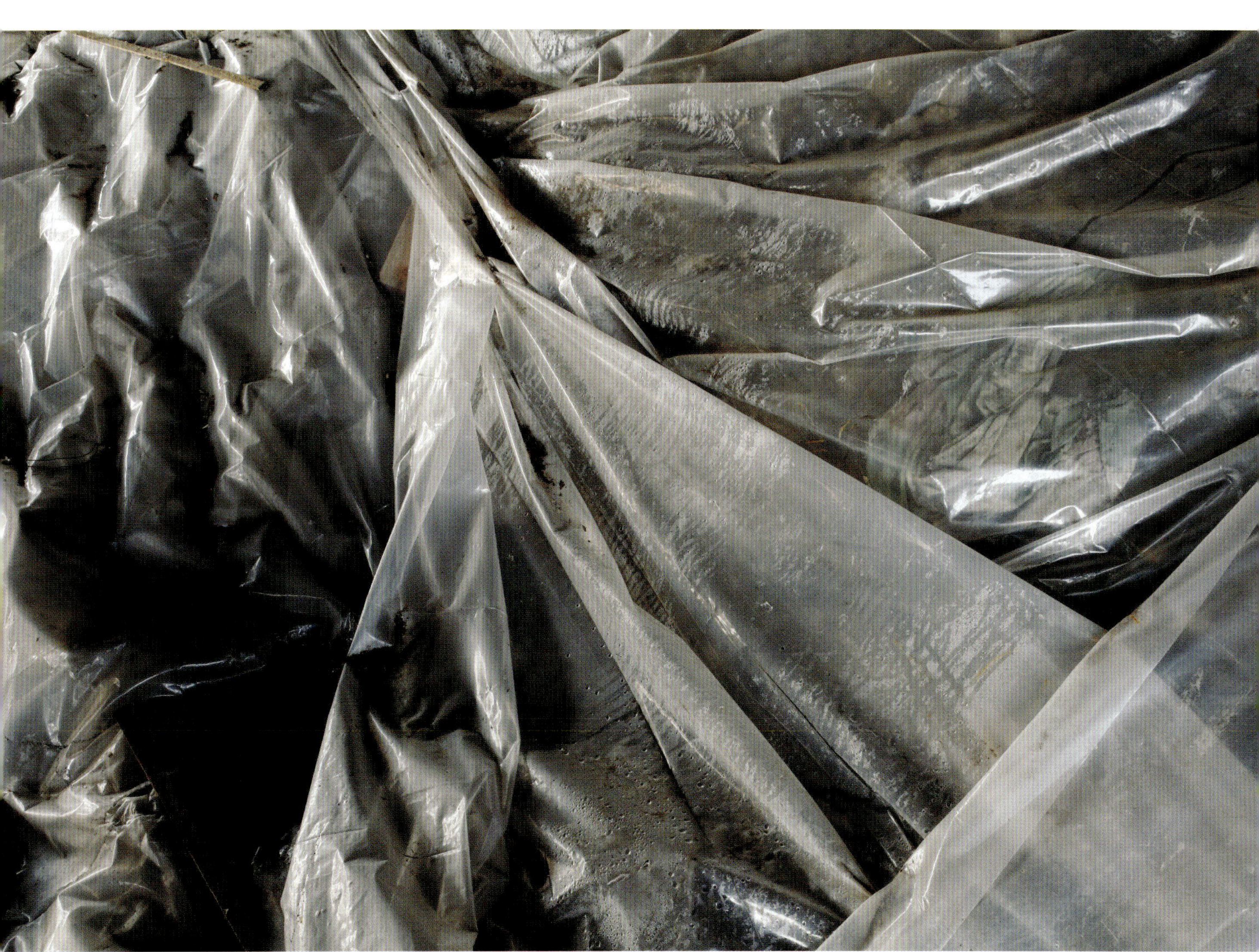

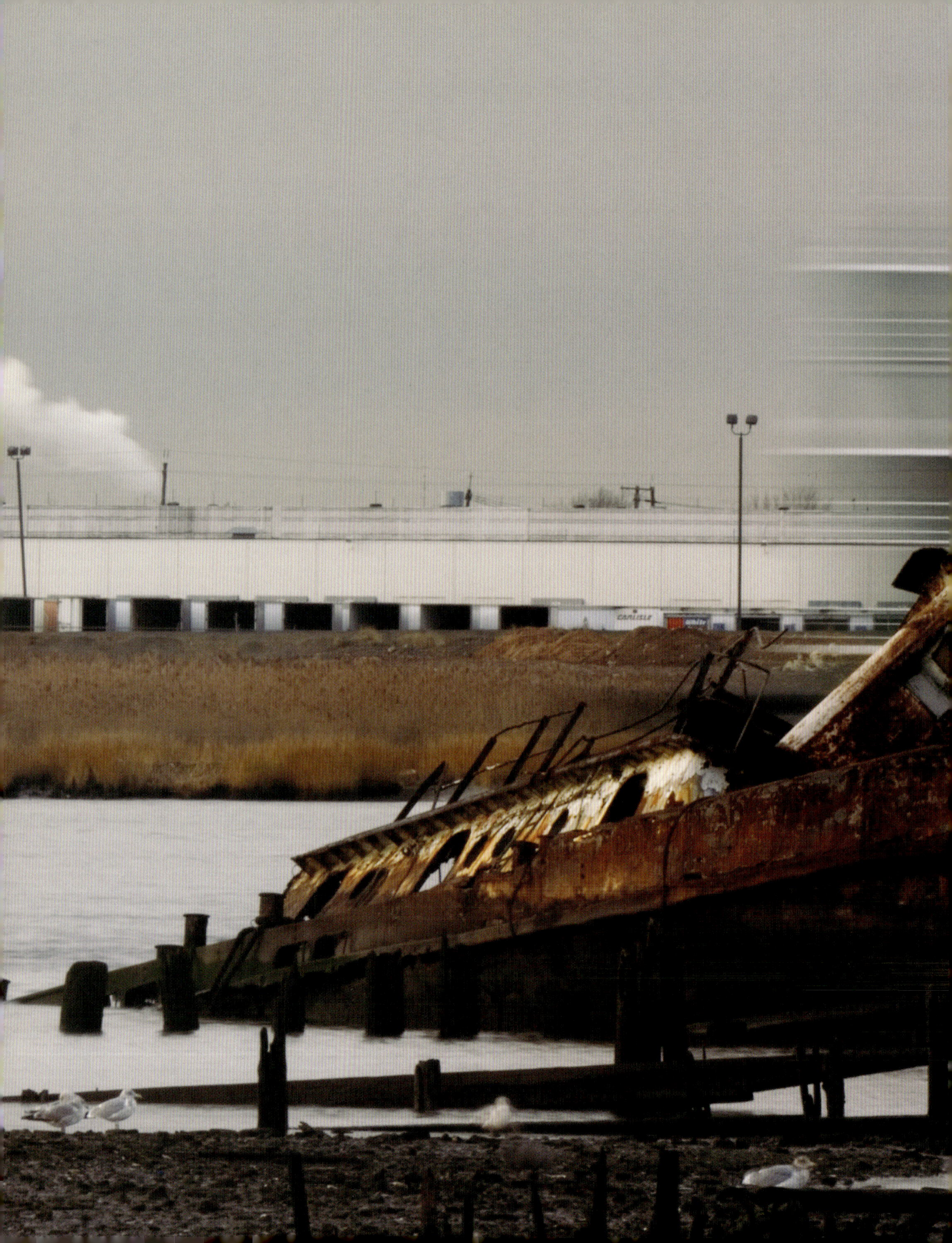

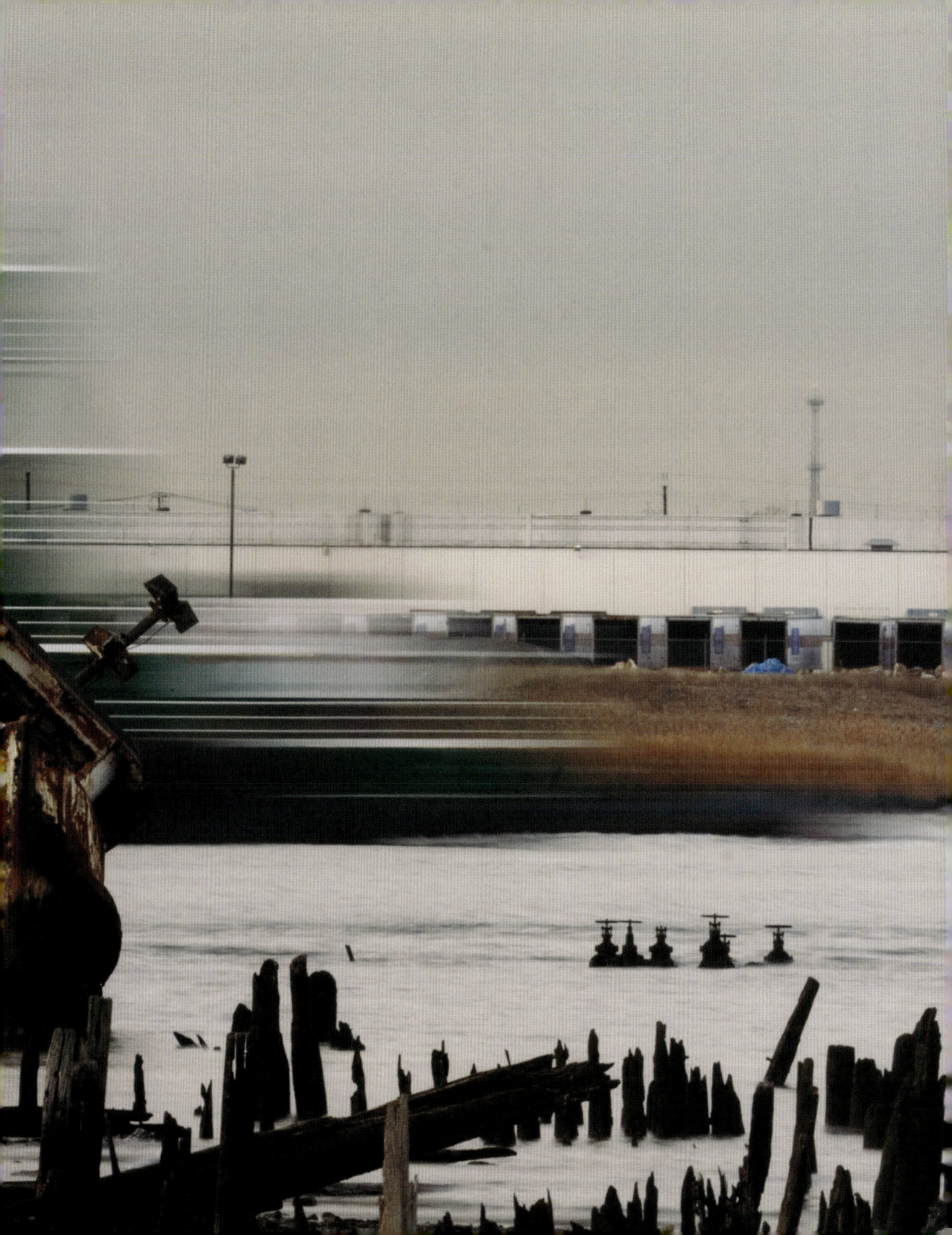

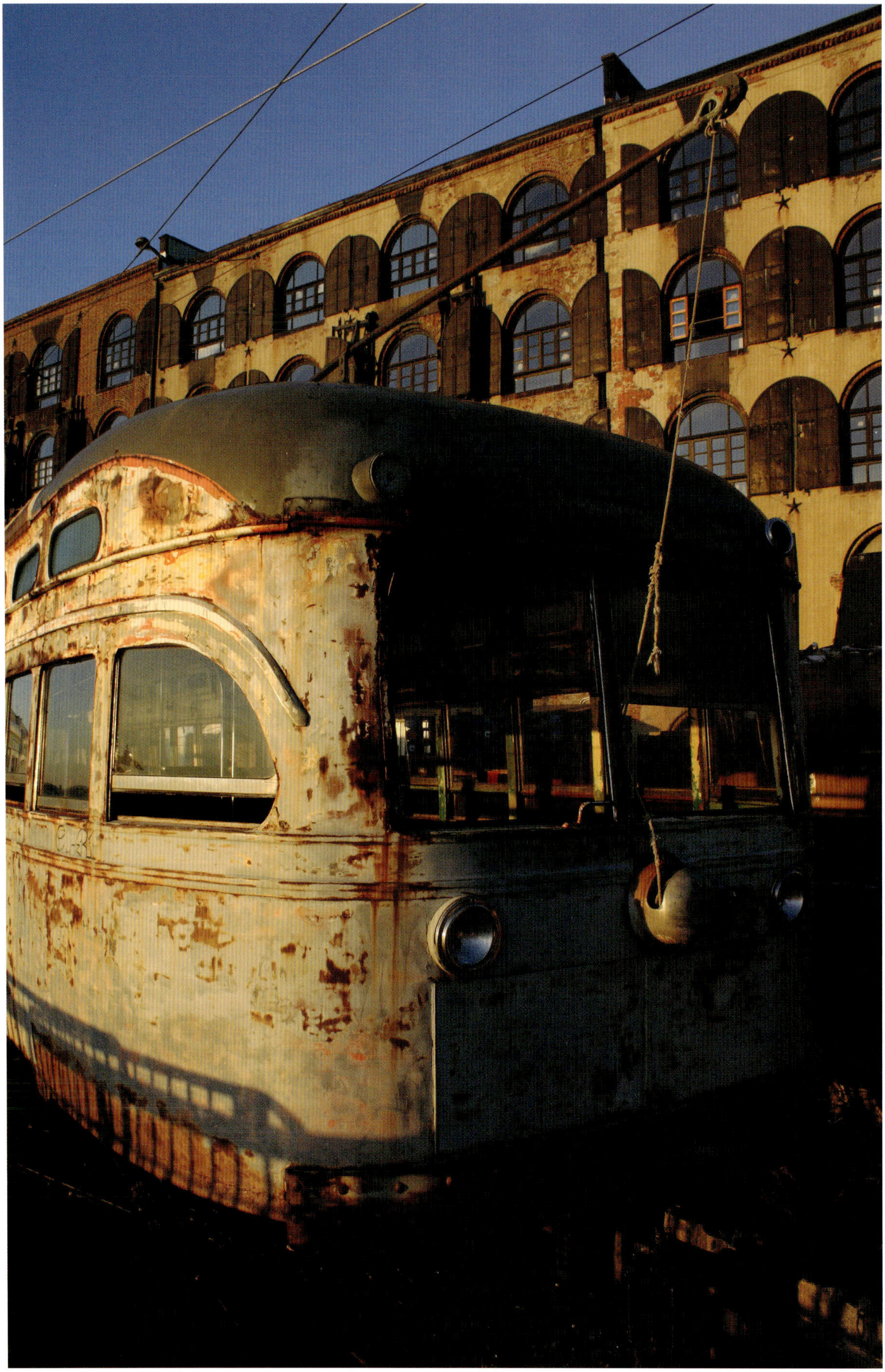

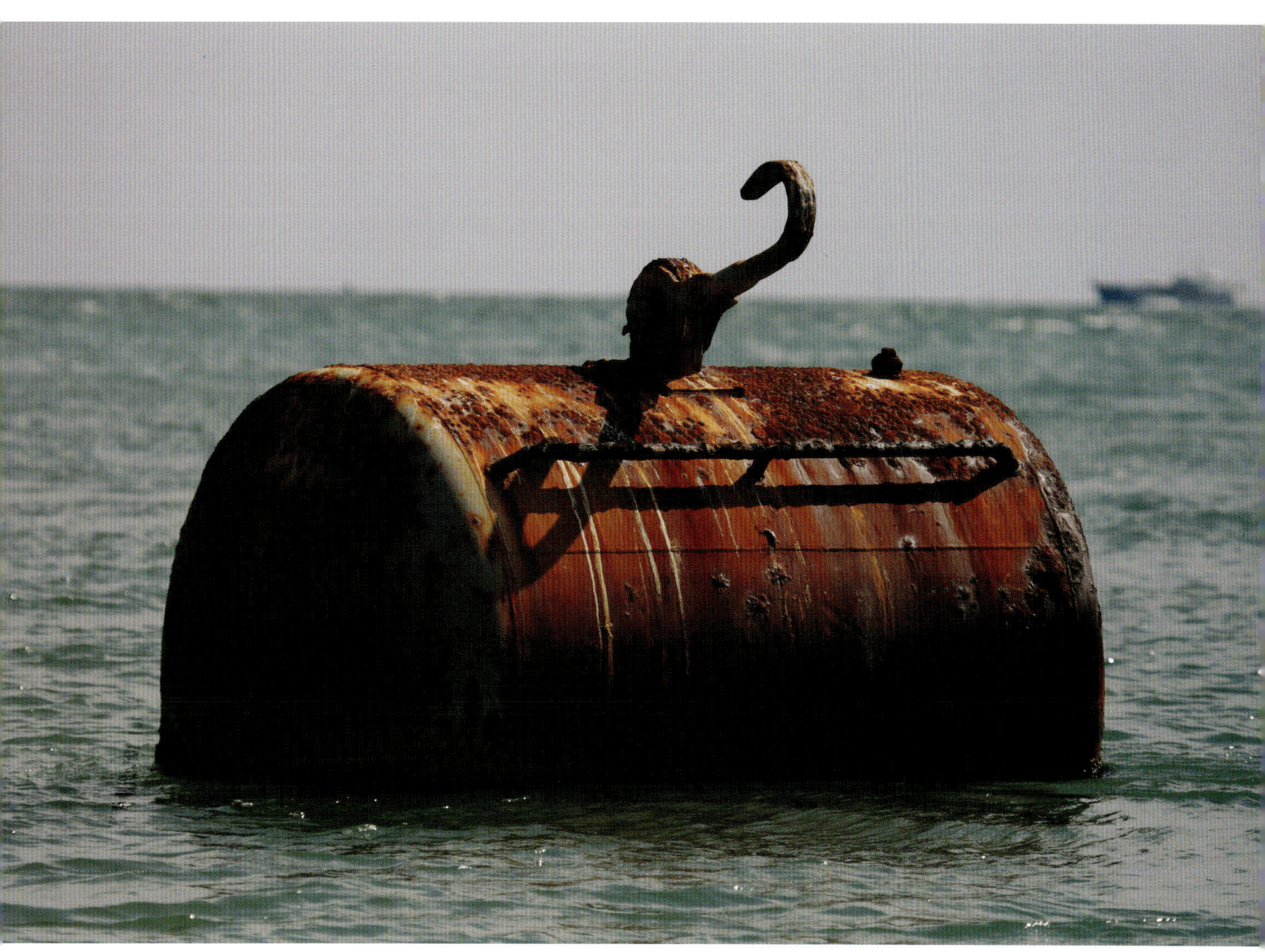

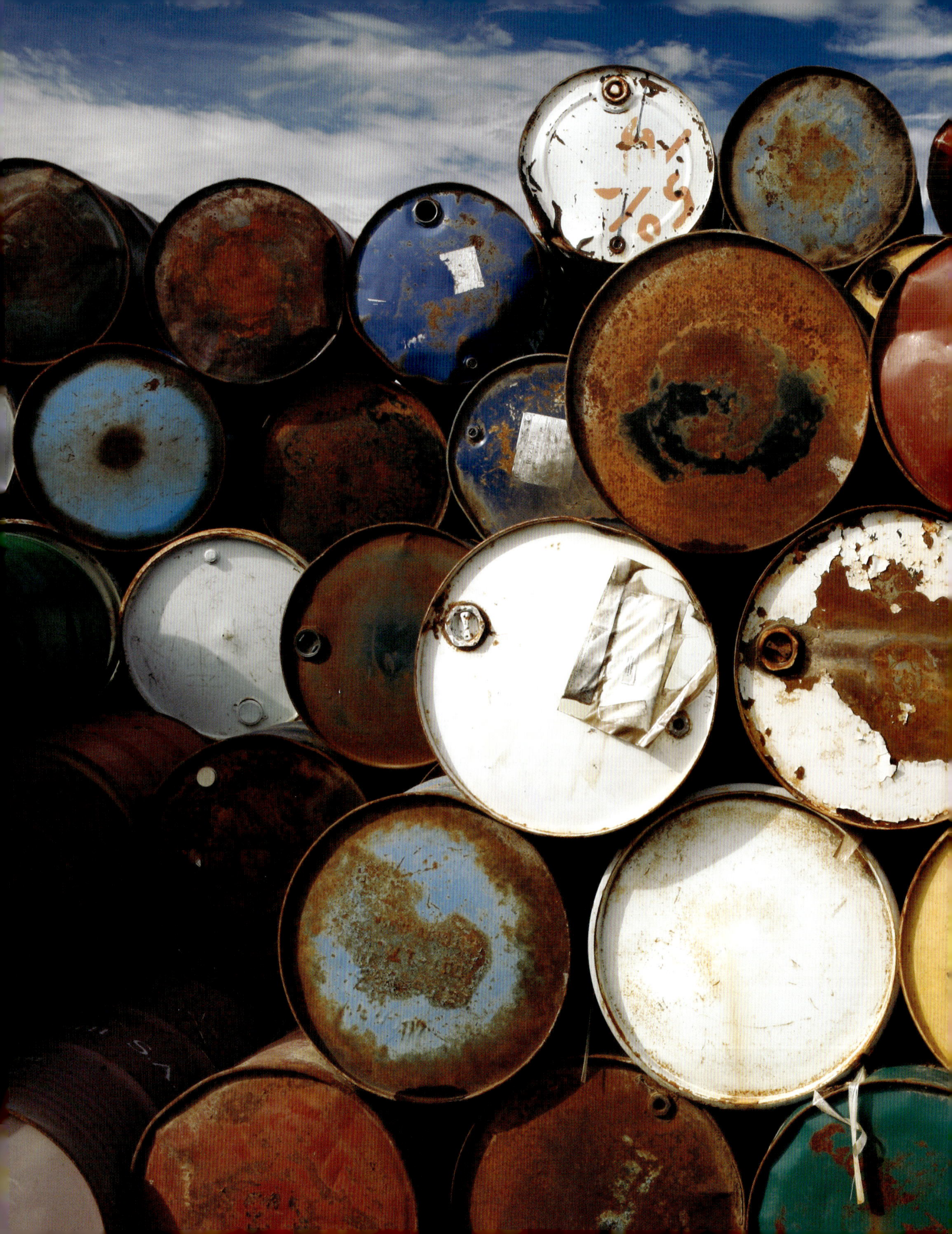

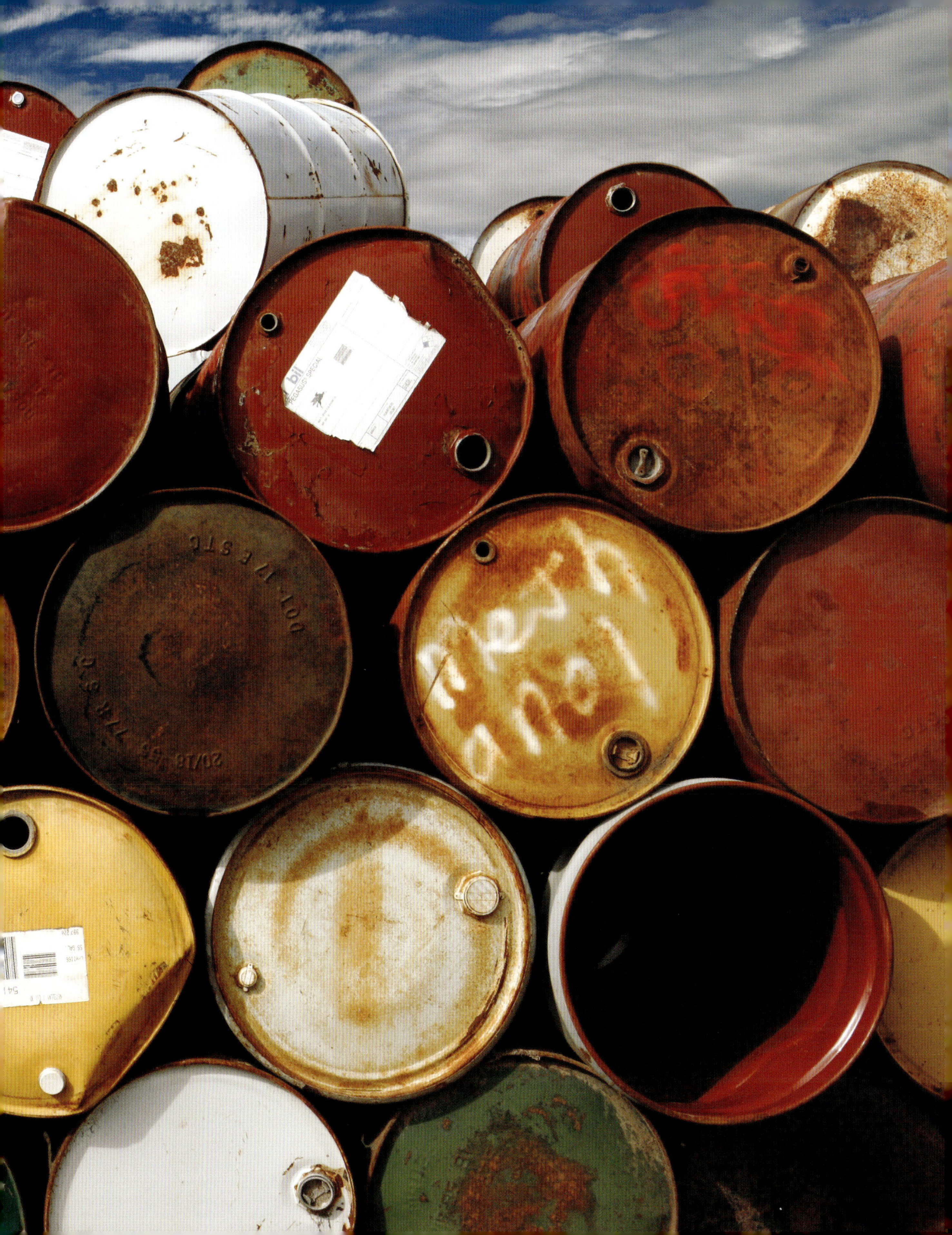
bil
PEGASUS SPECIAL

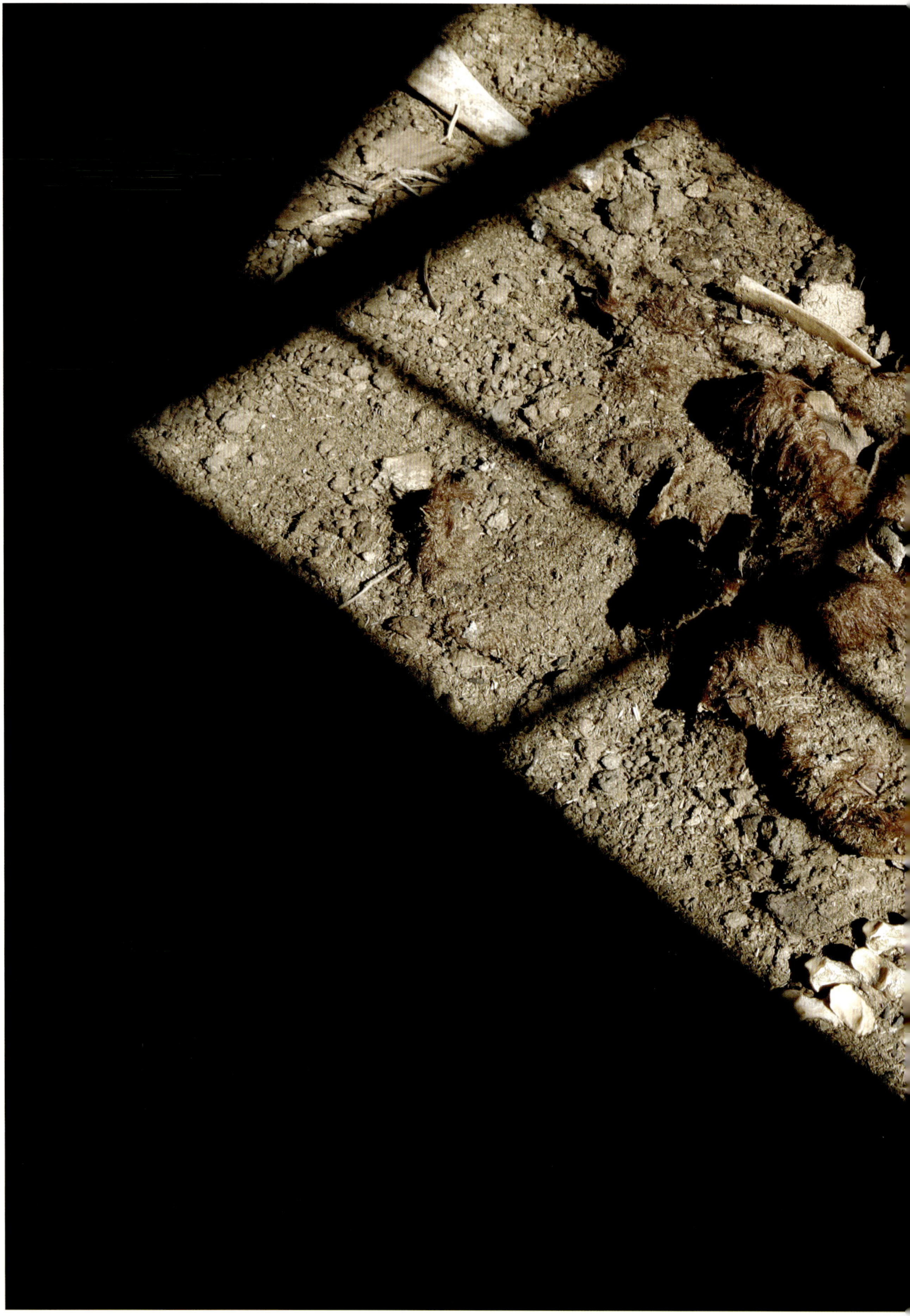

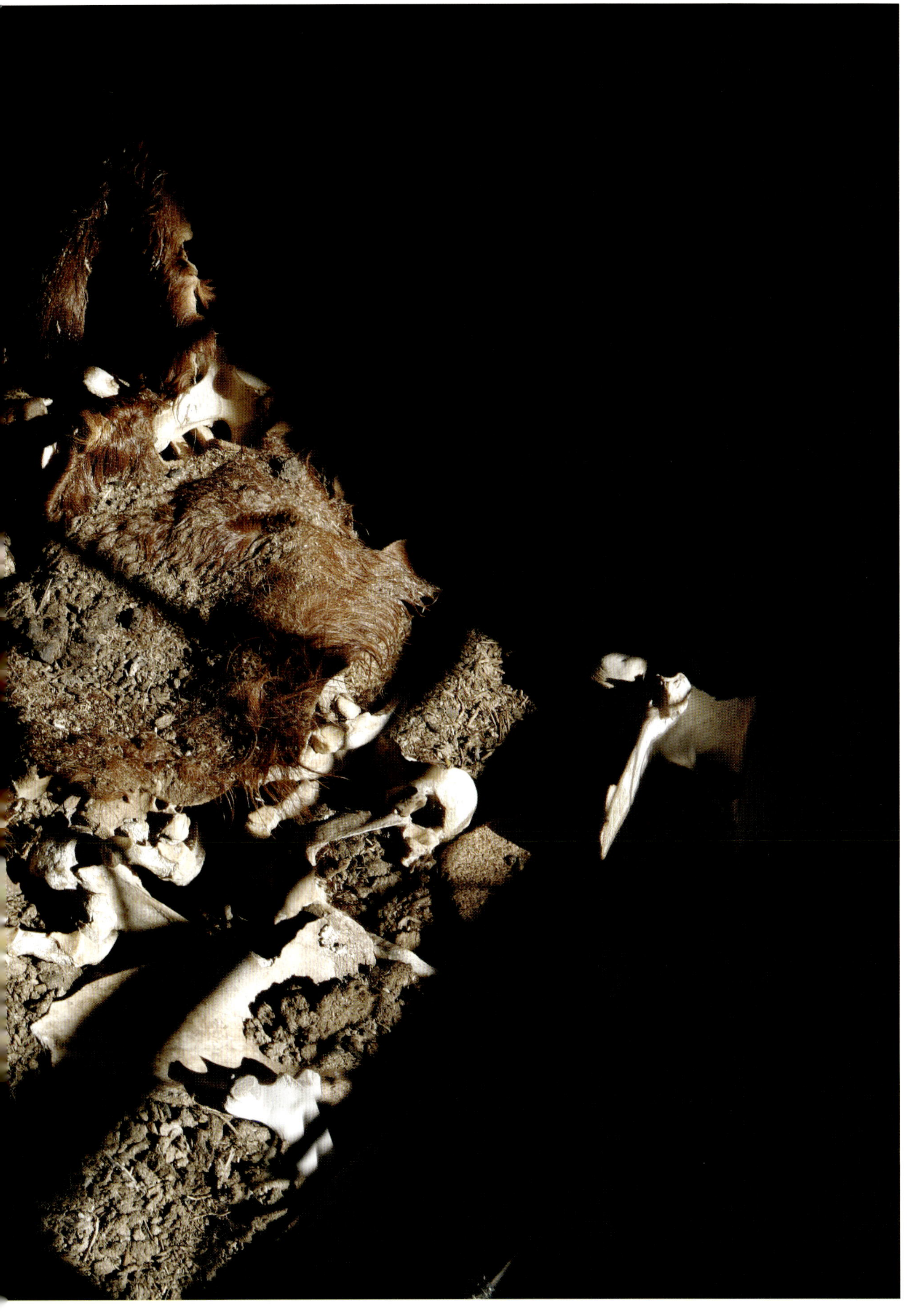

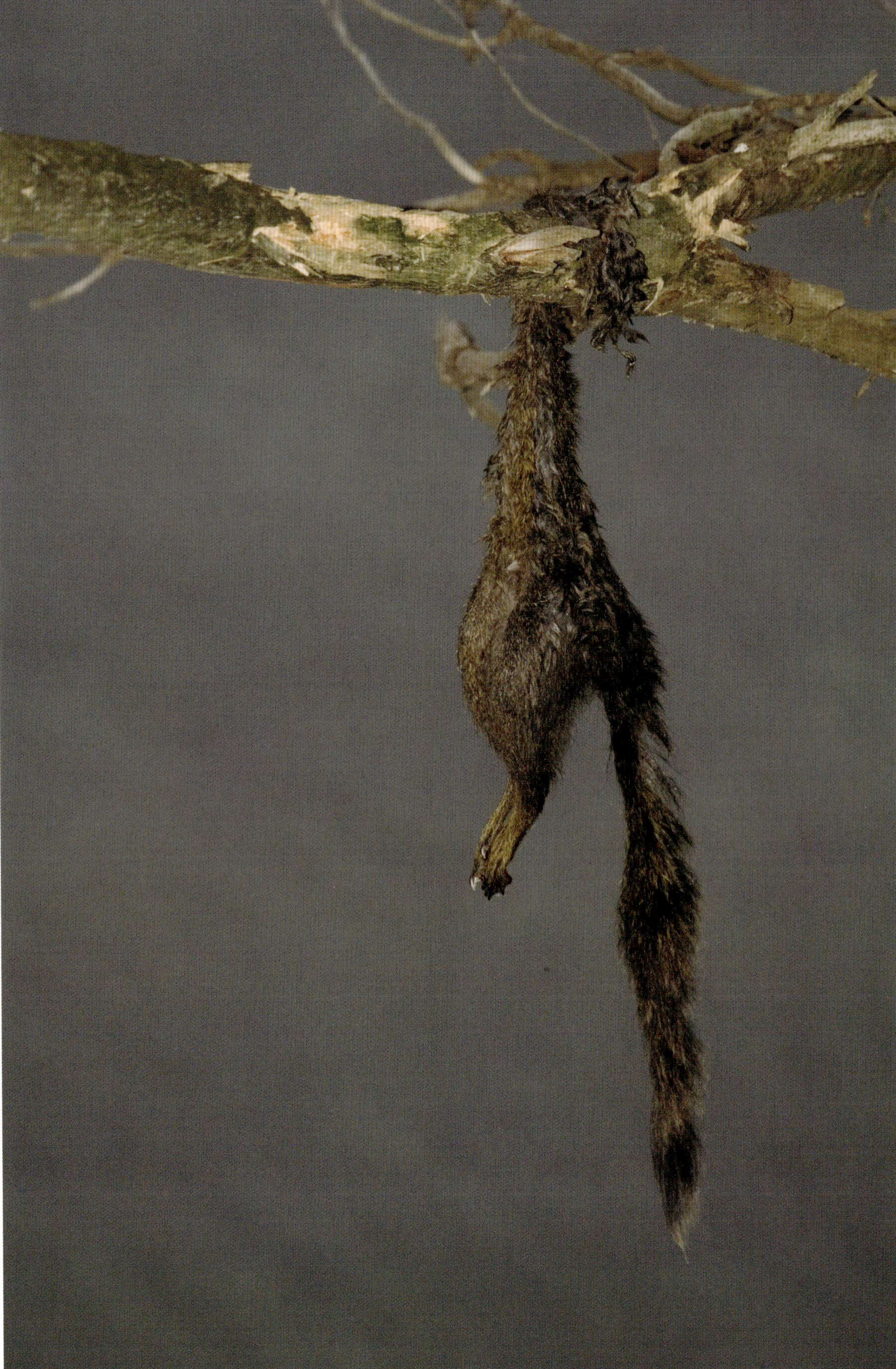

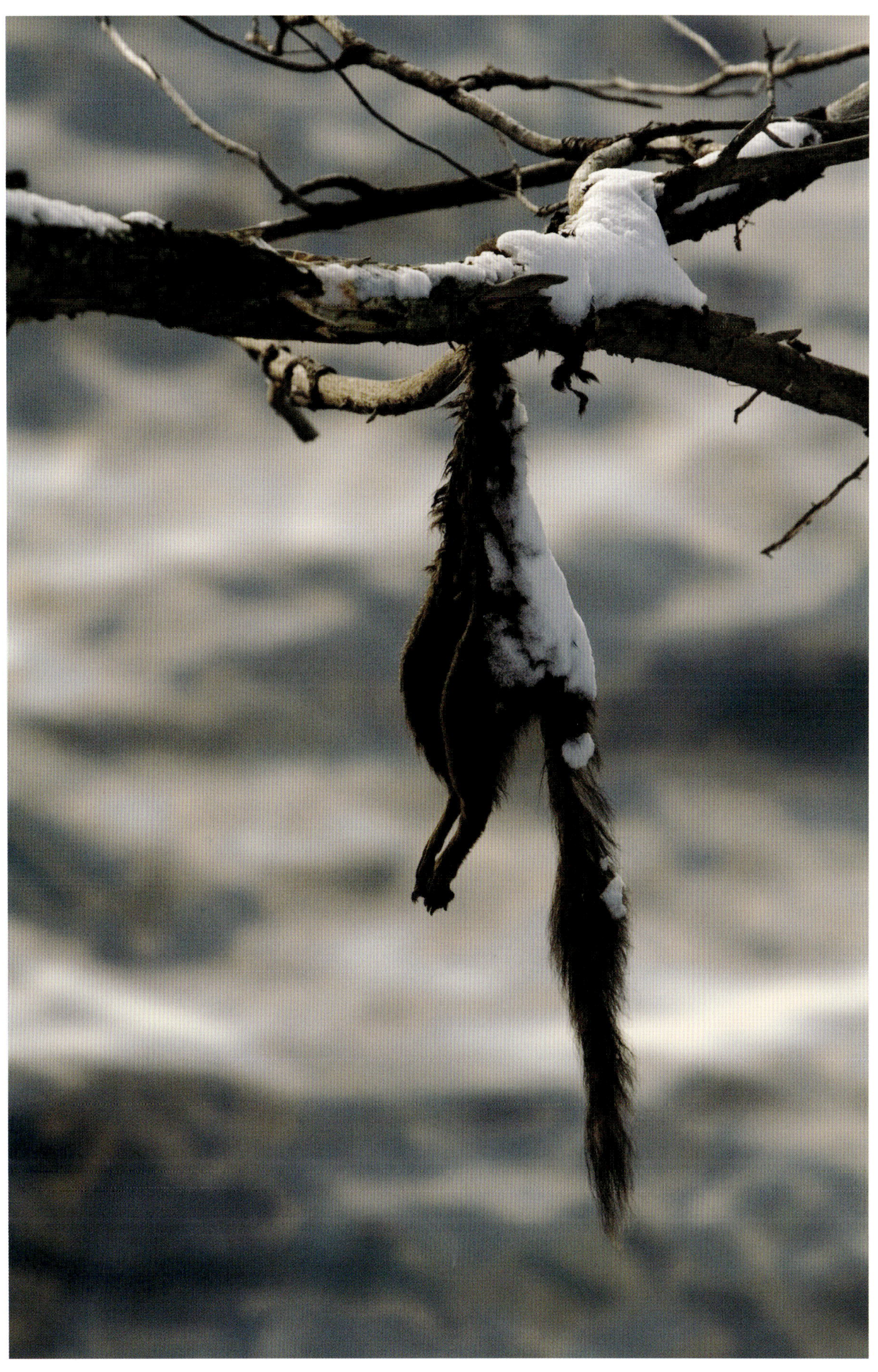

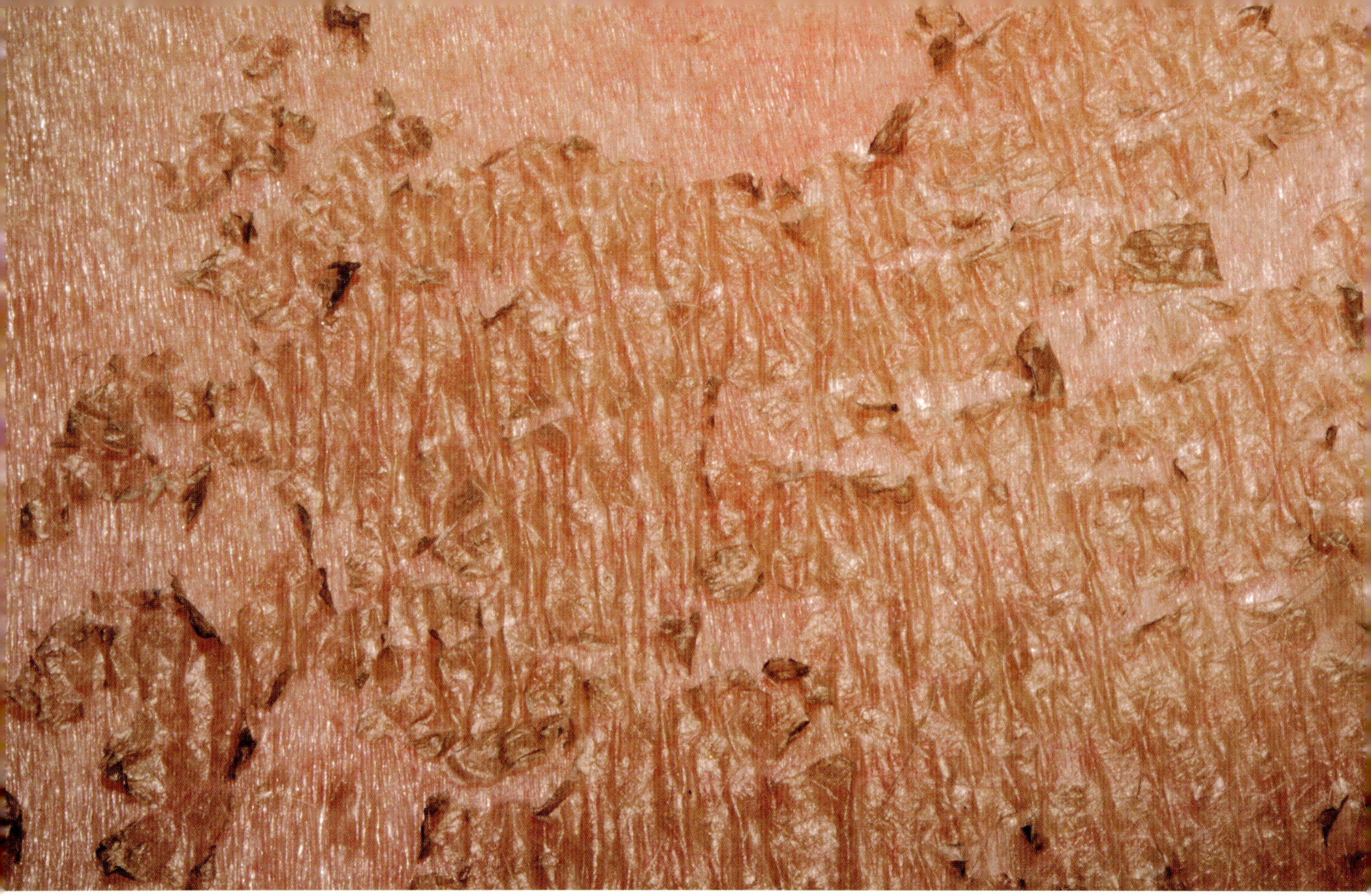

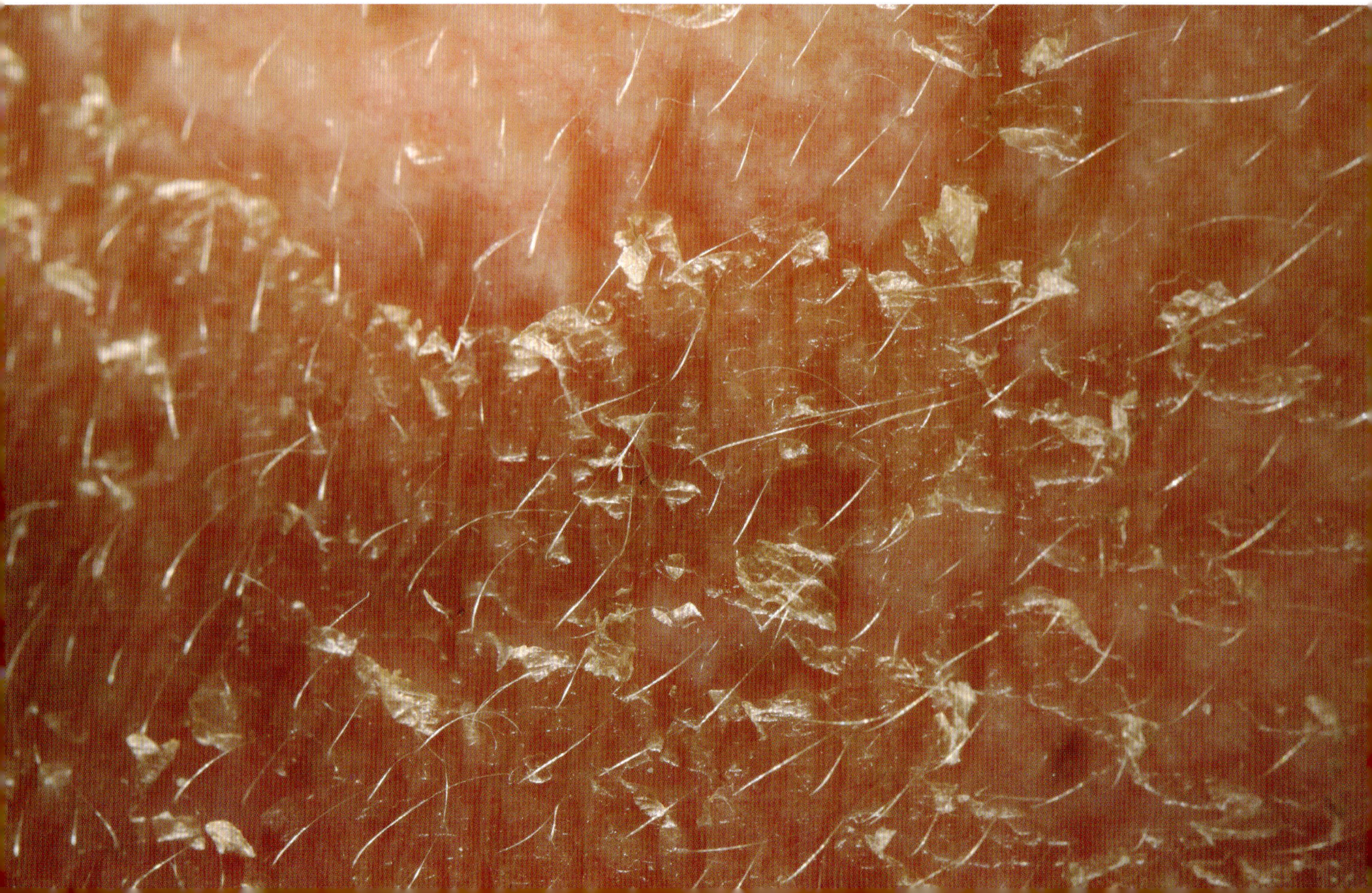

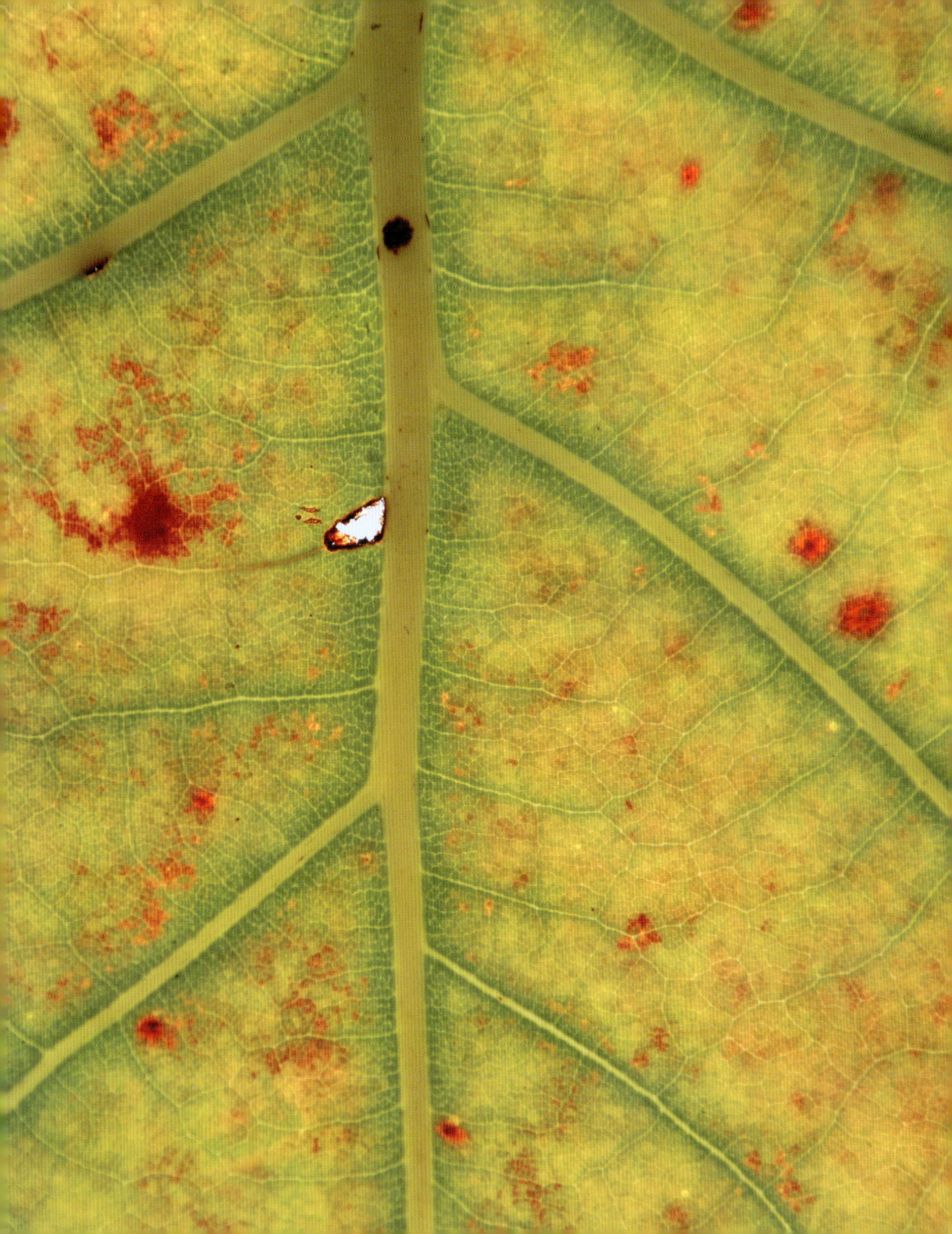

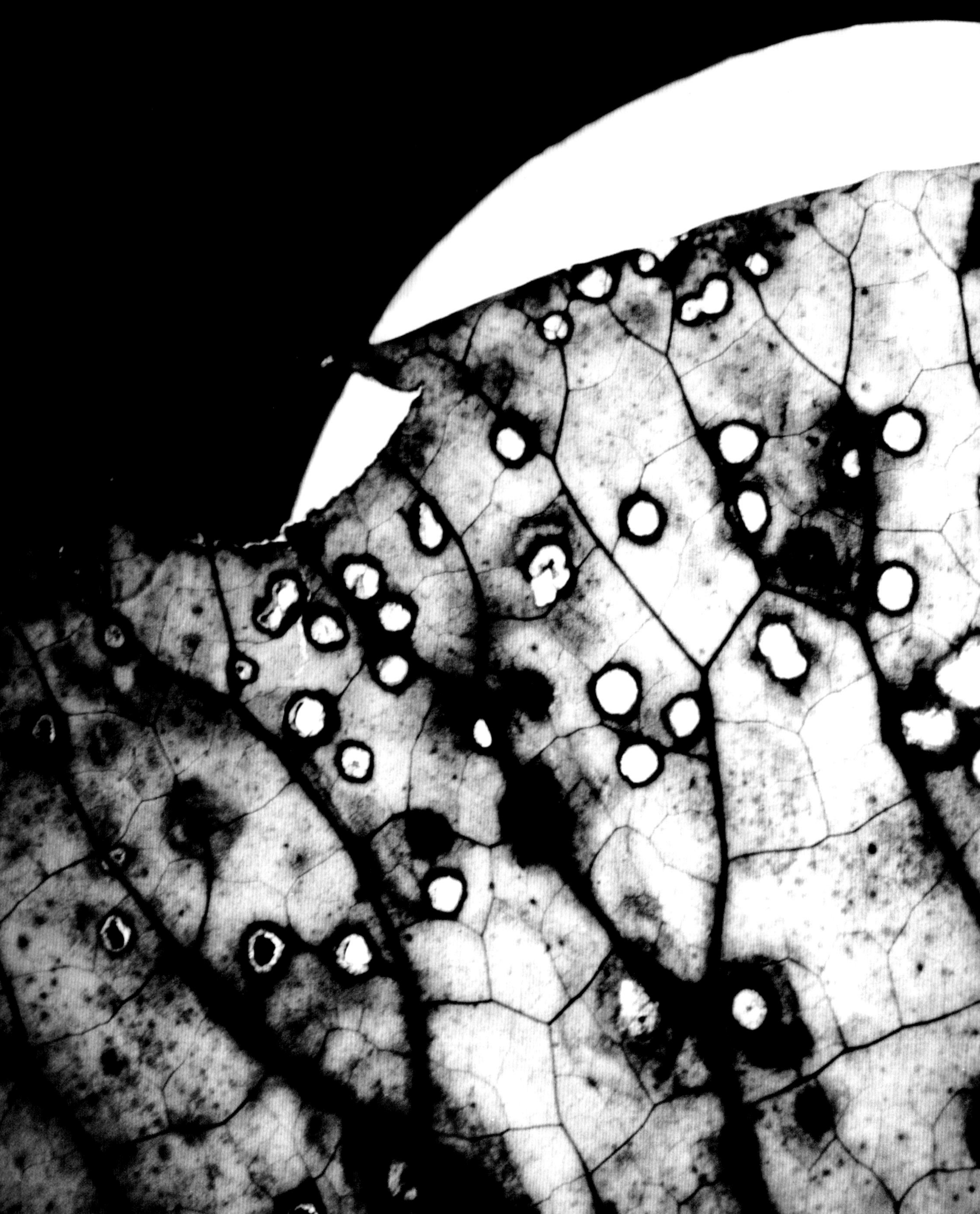

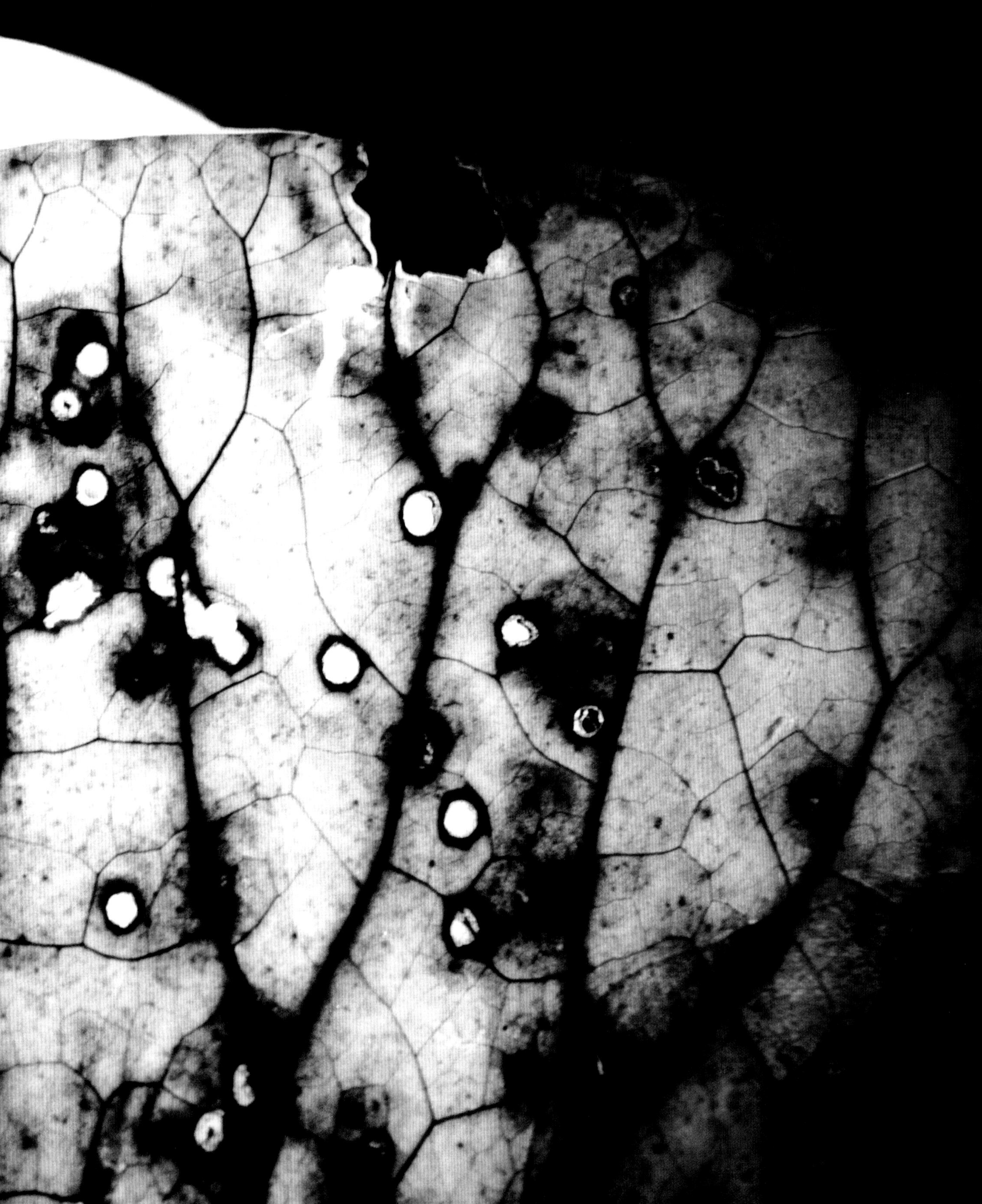

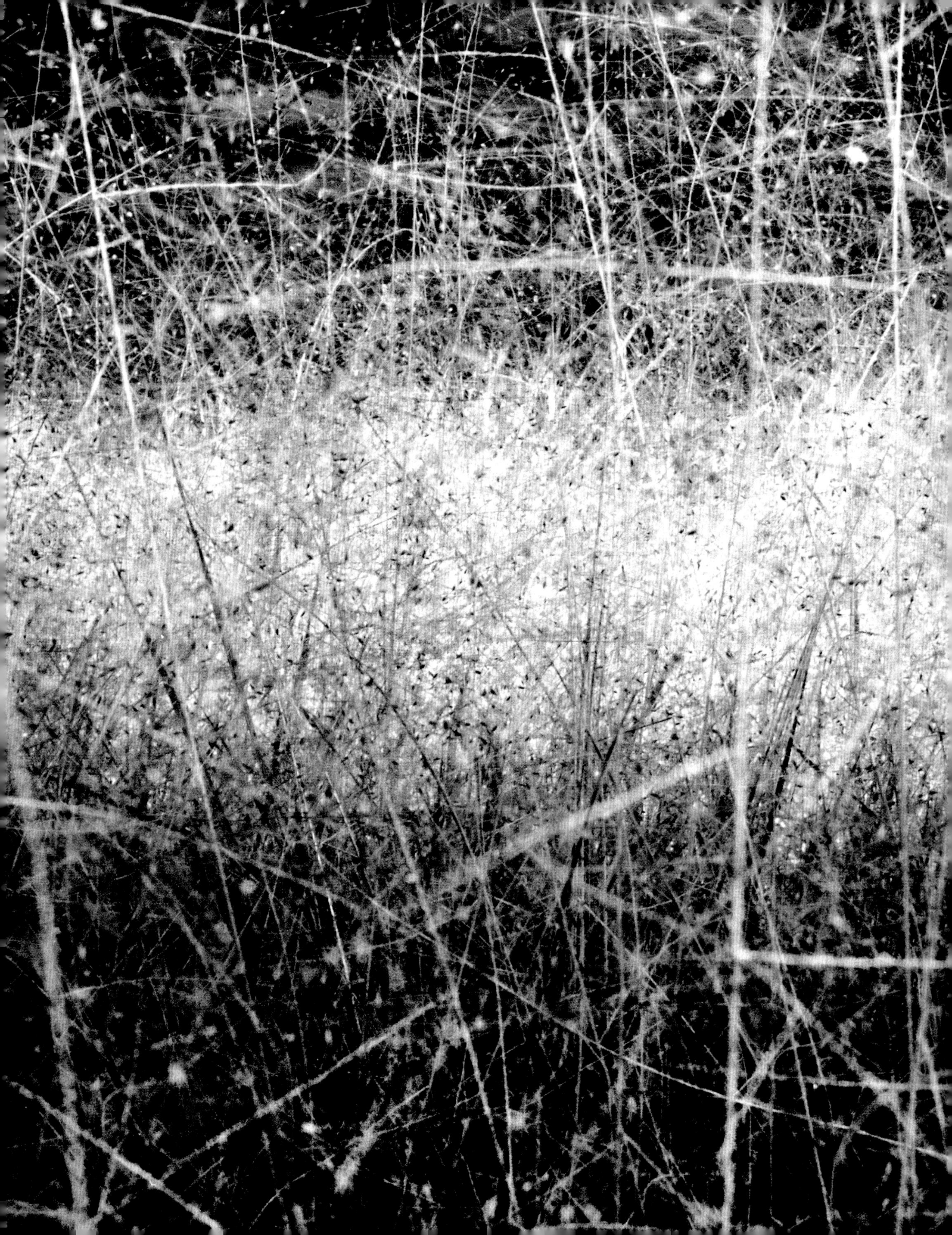

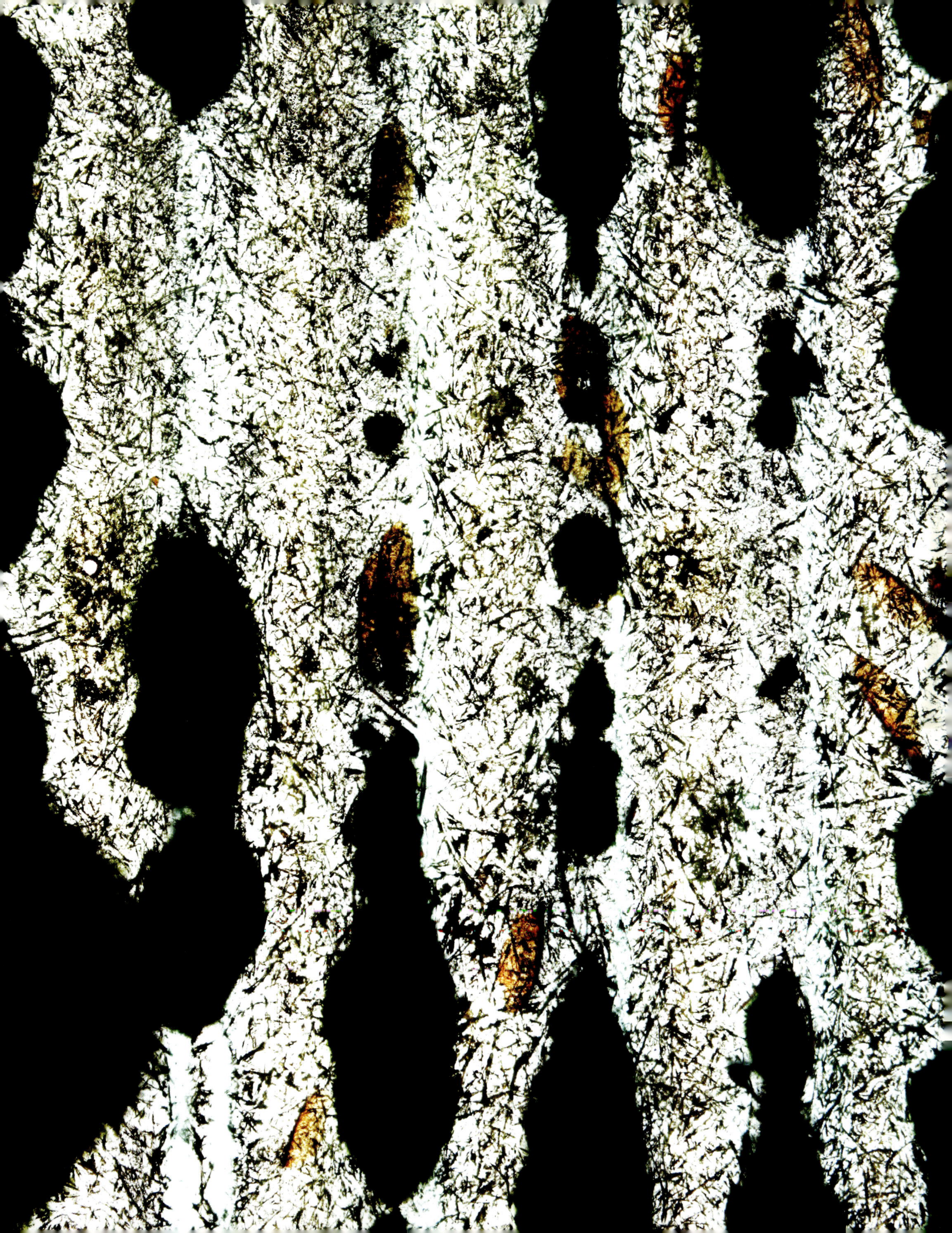

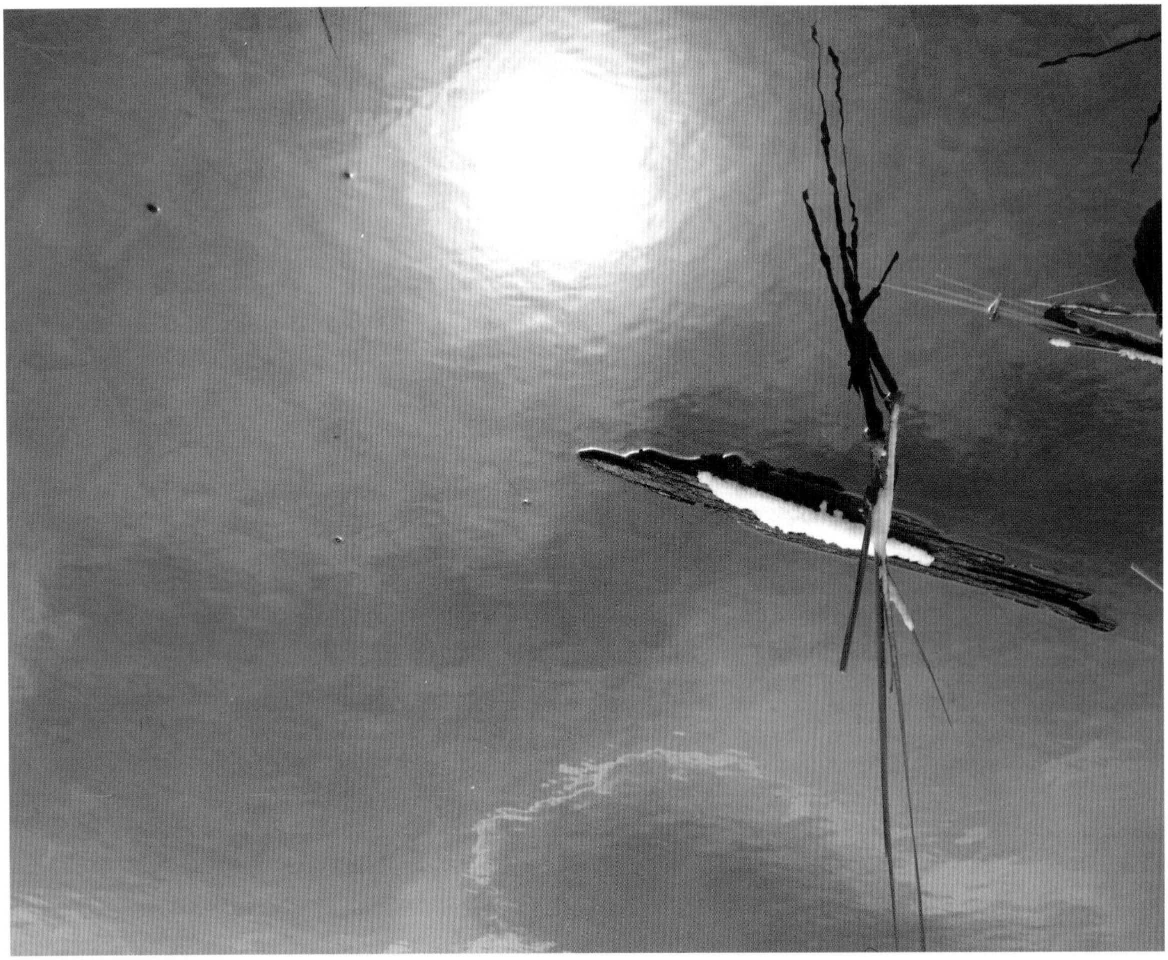

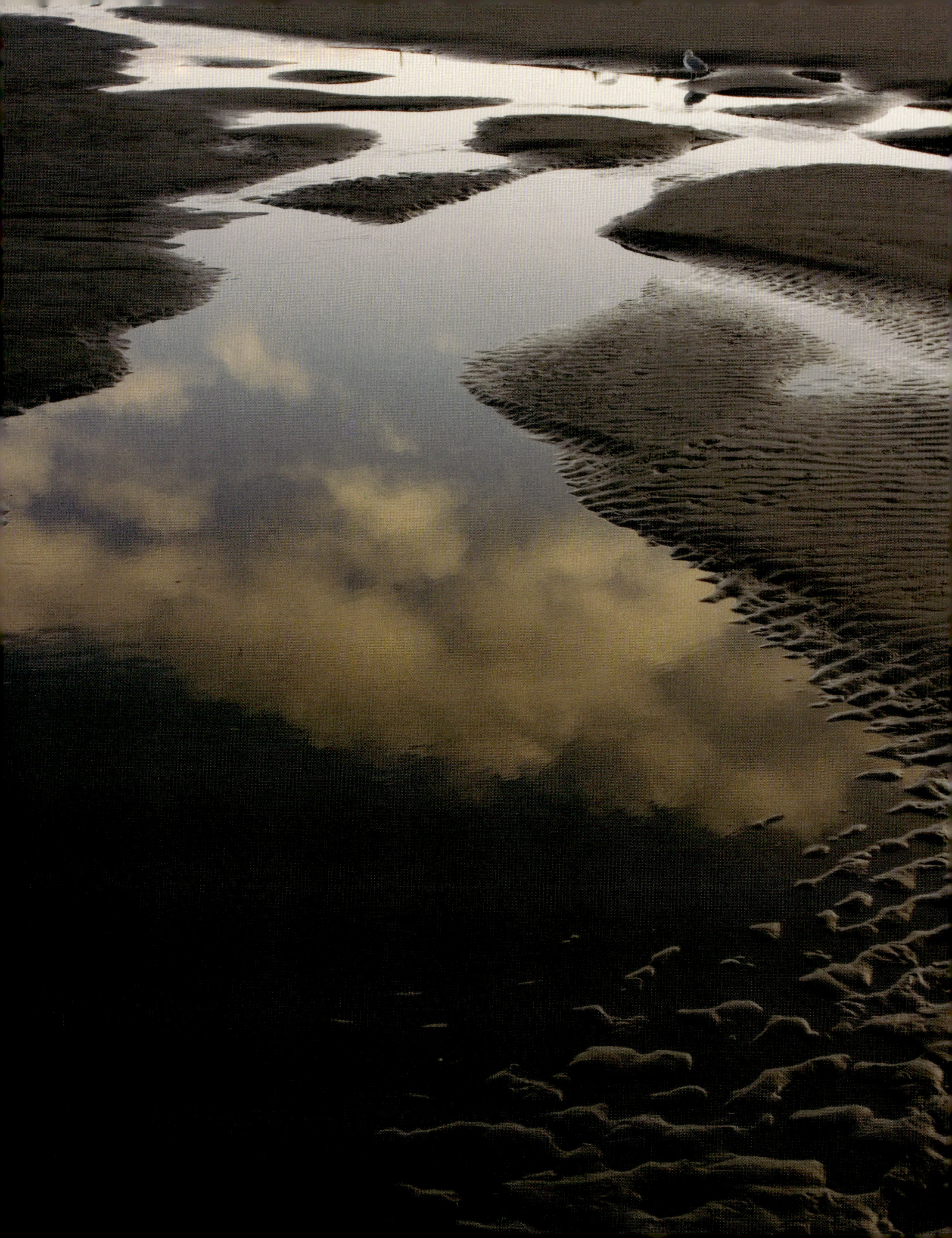

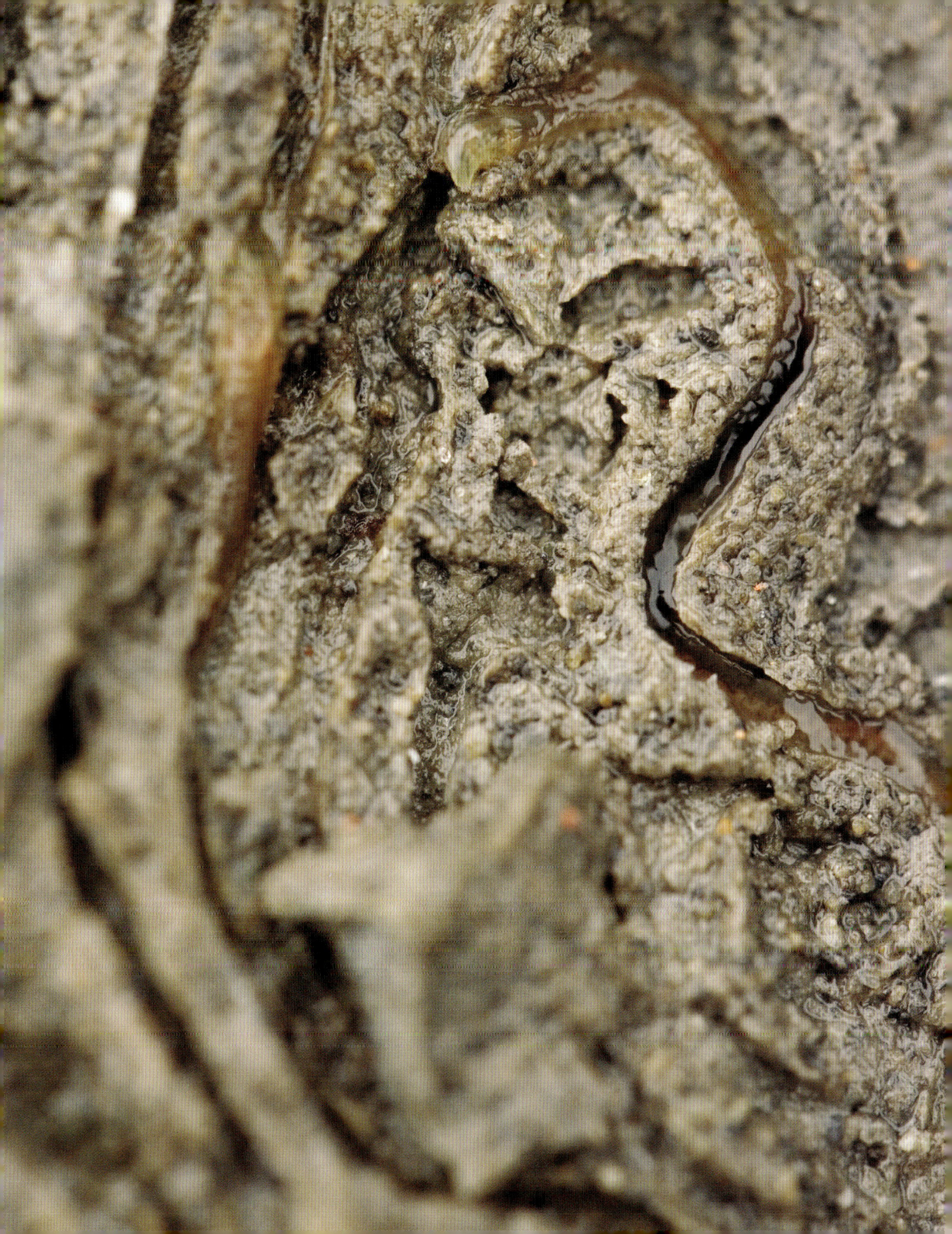

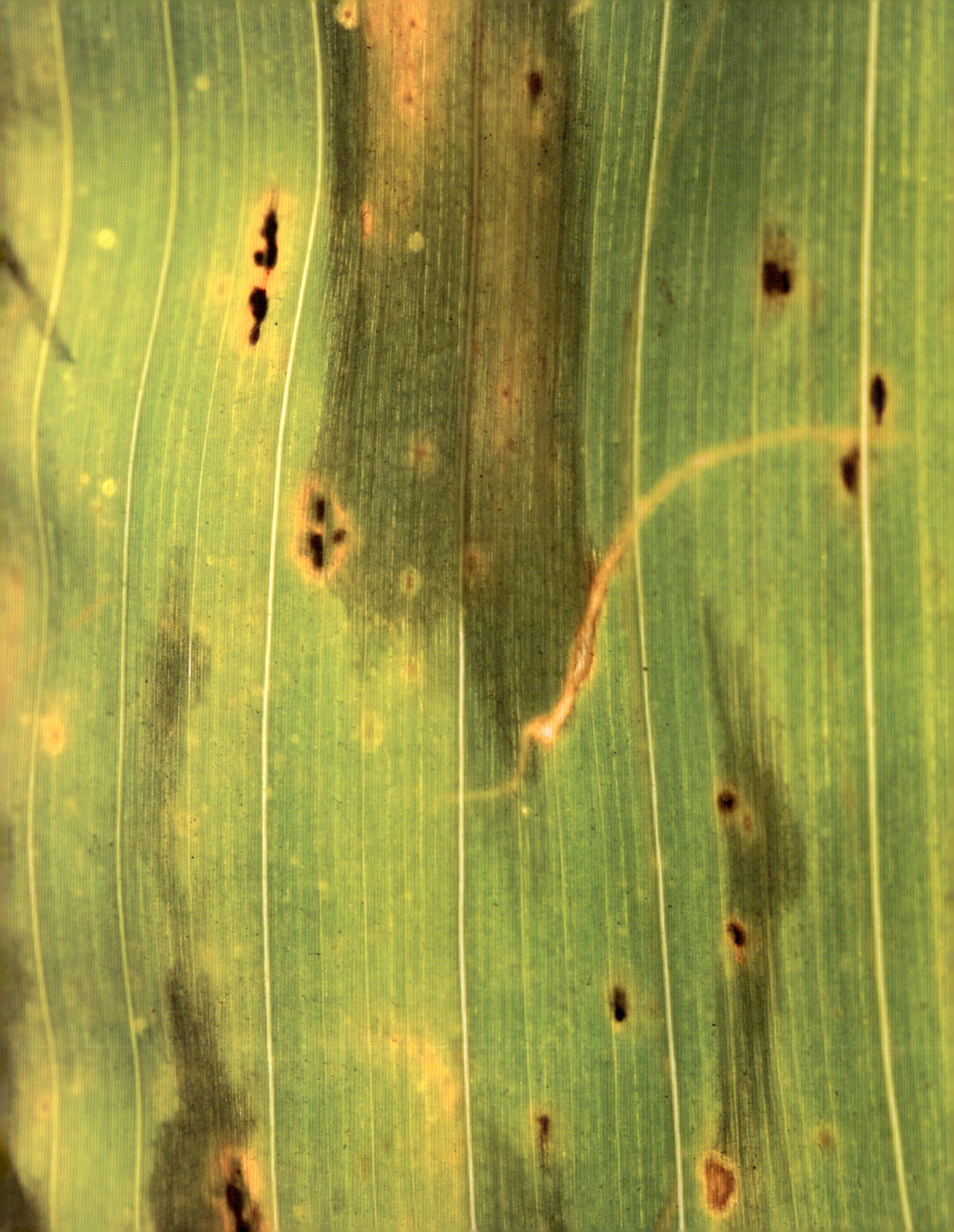

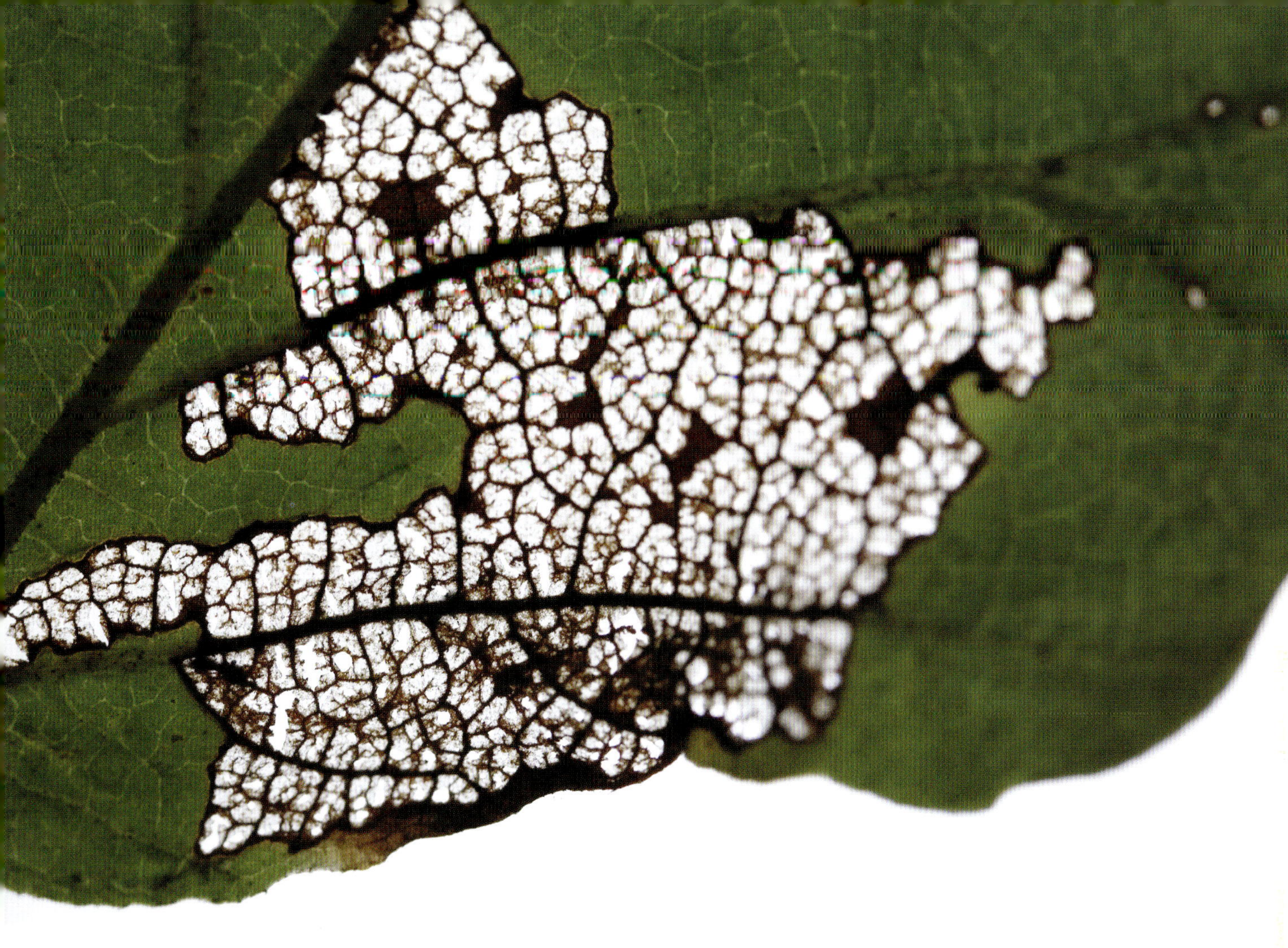

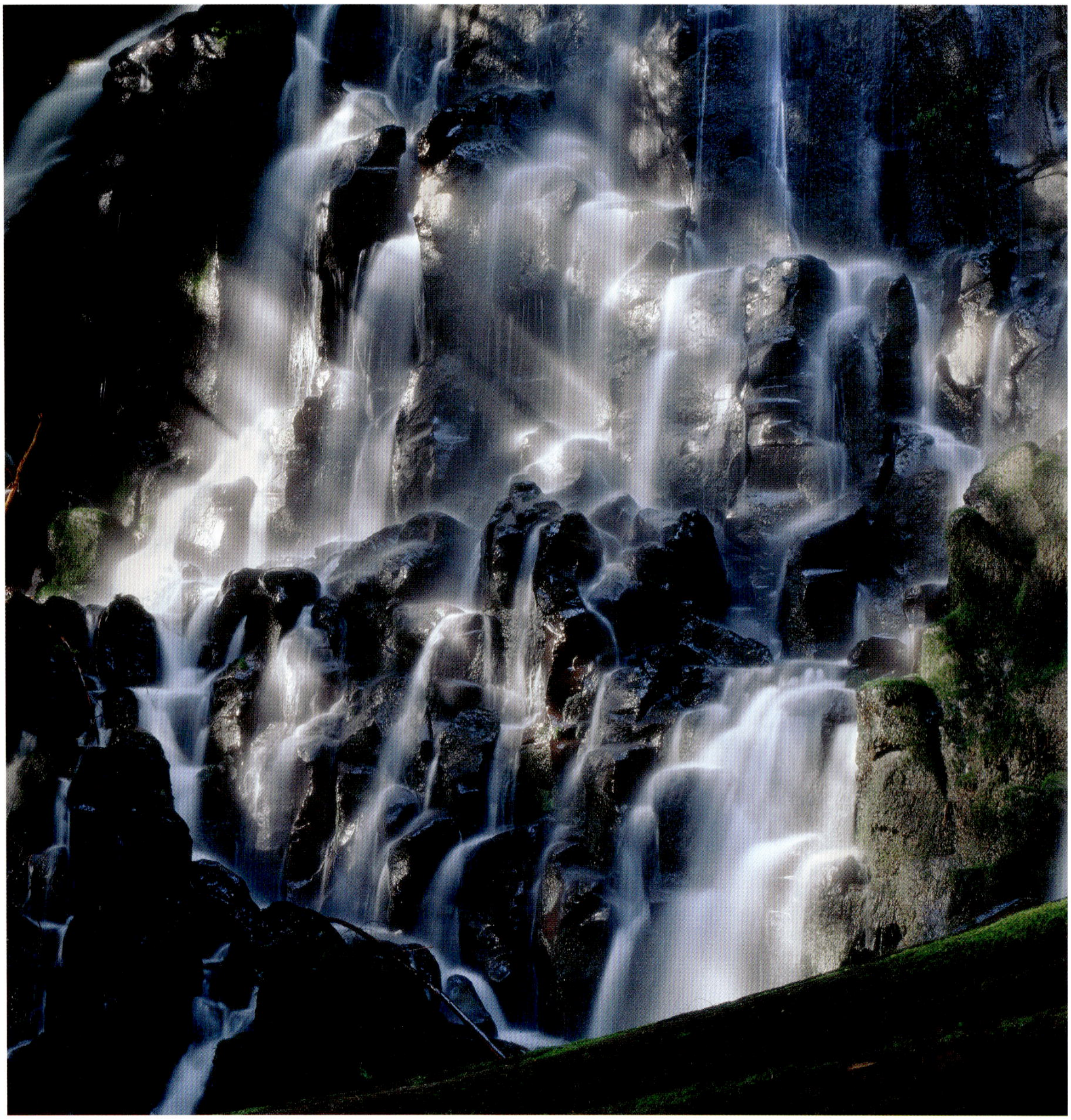

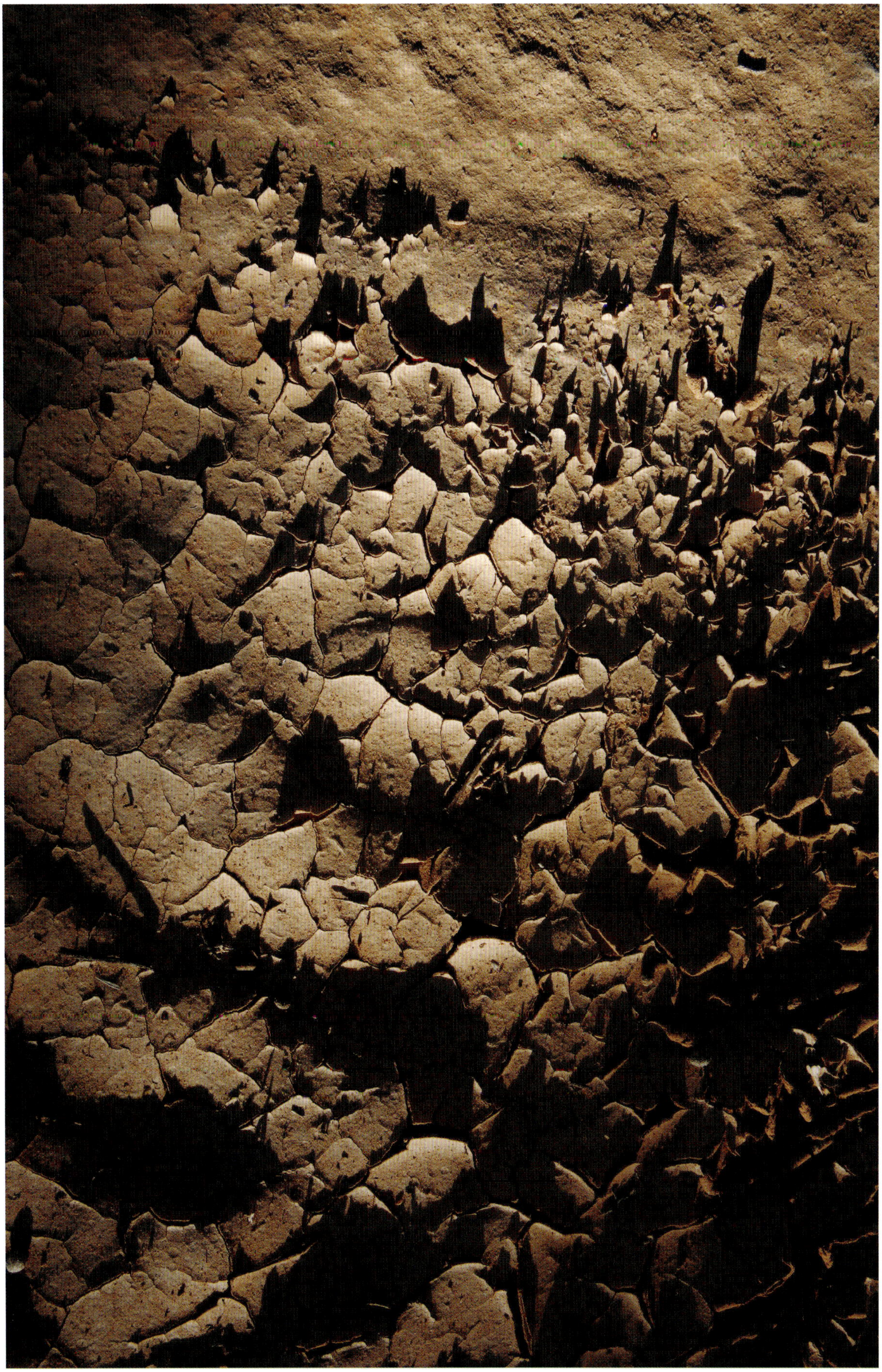

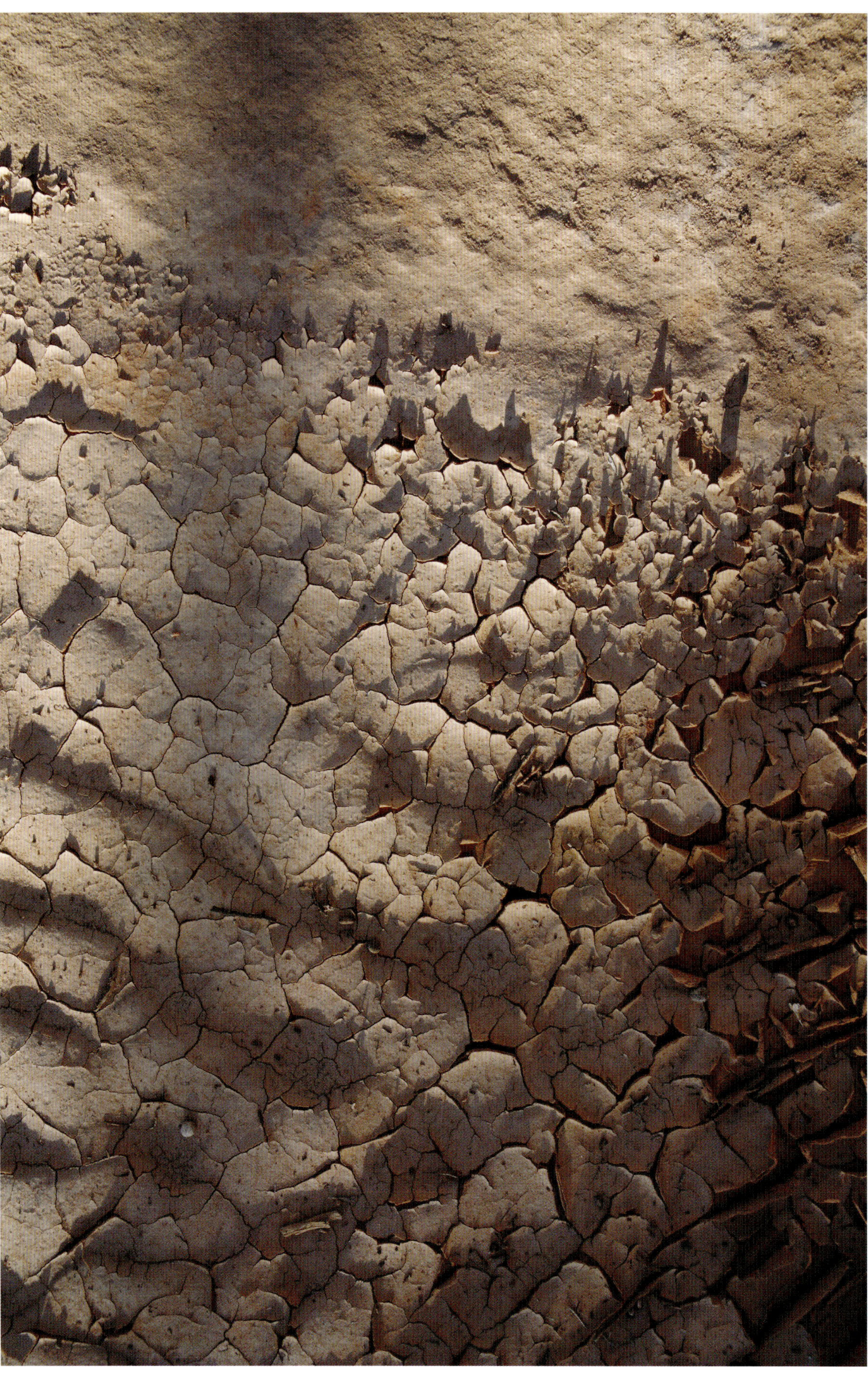

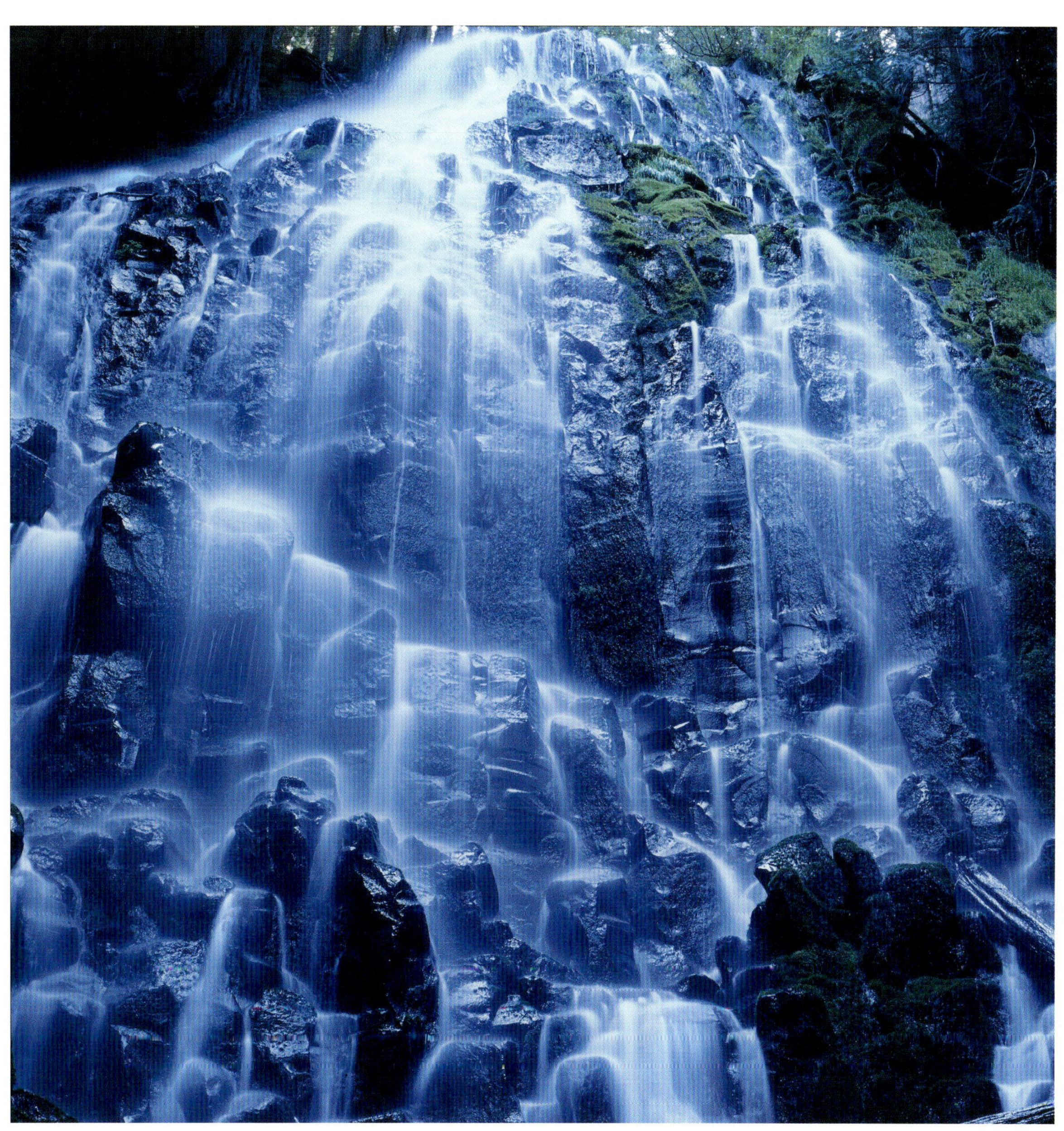

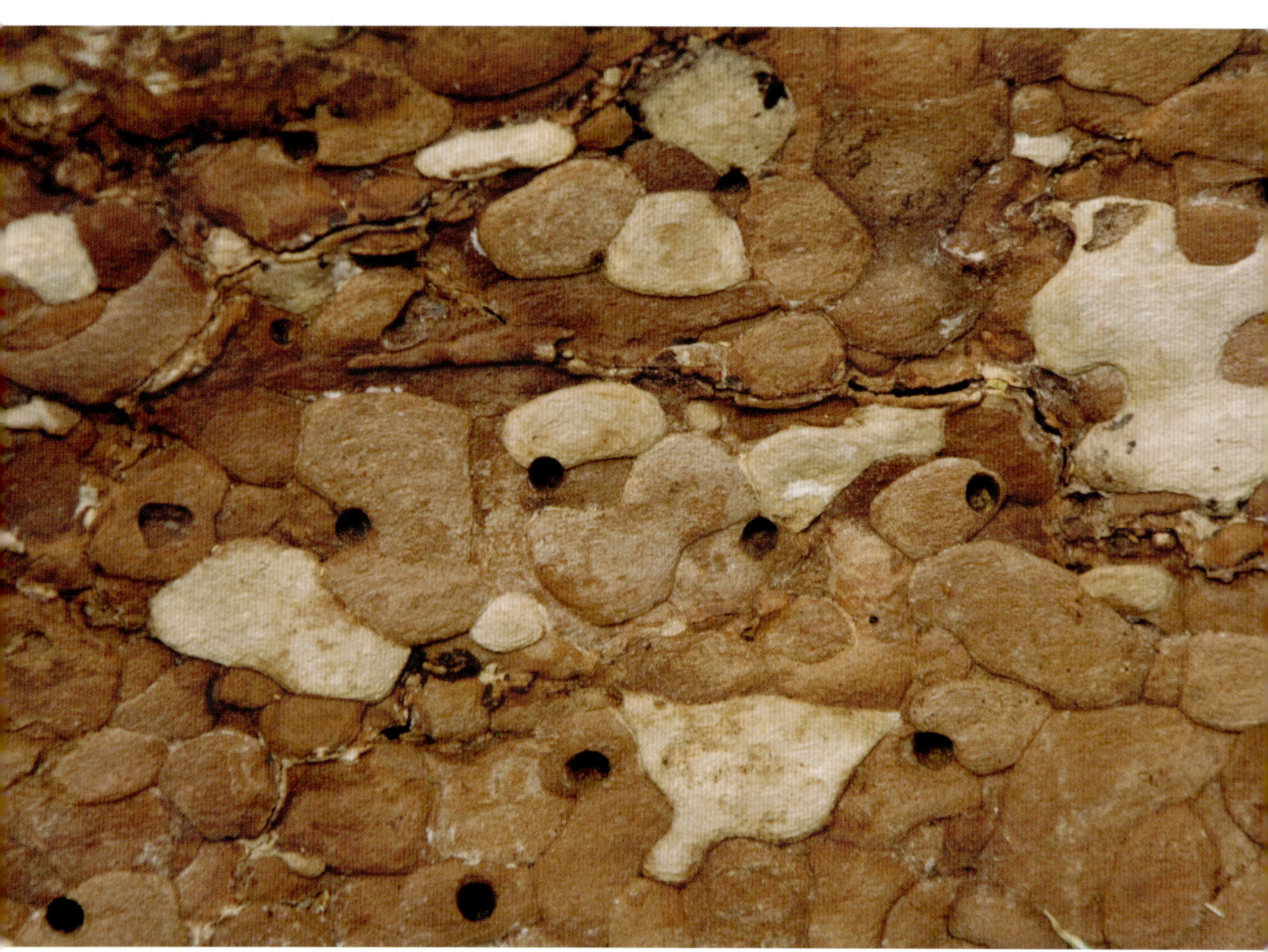

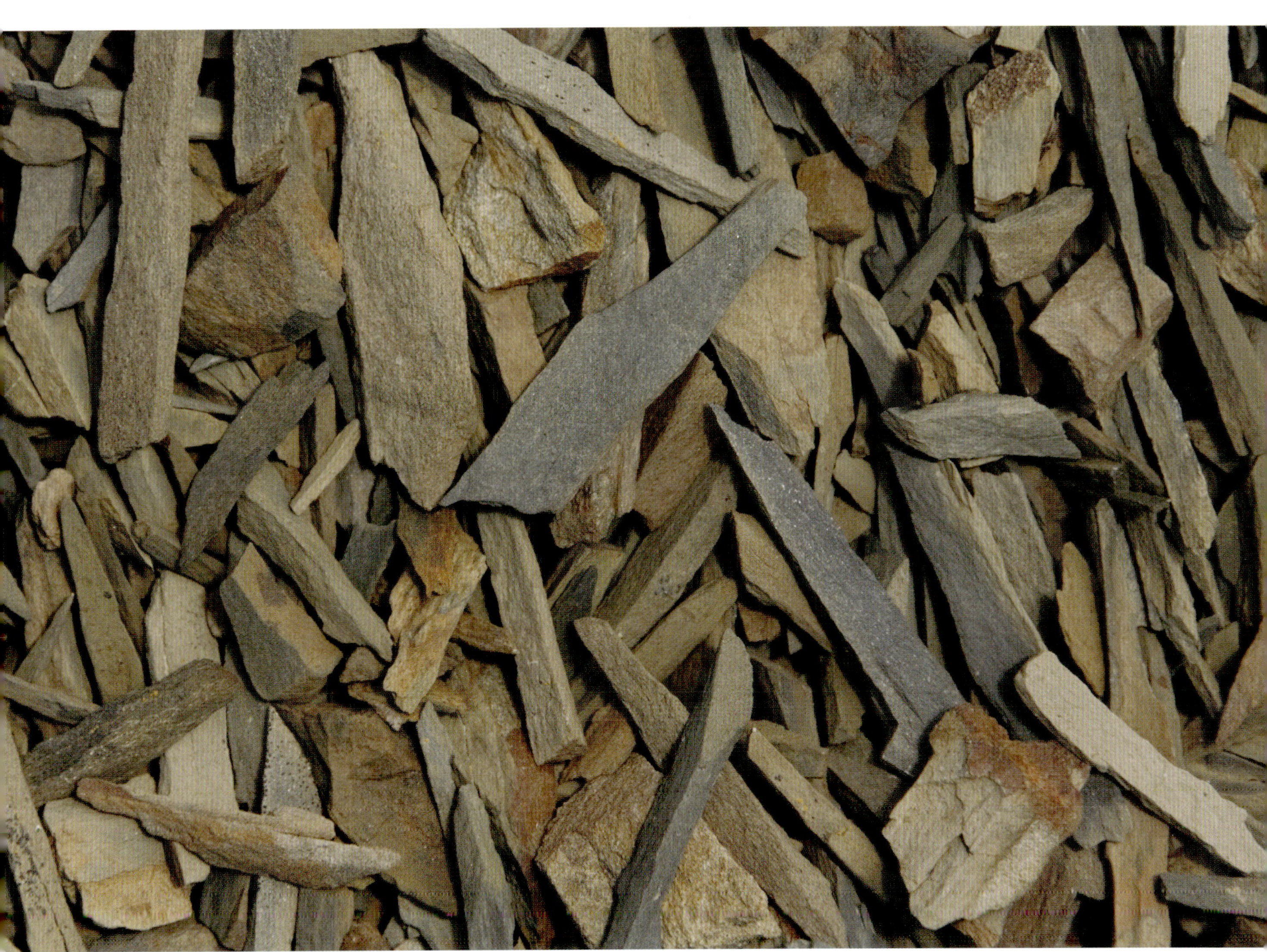

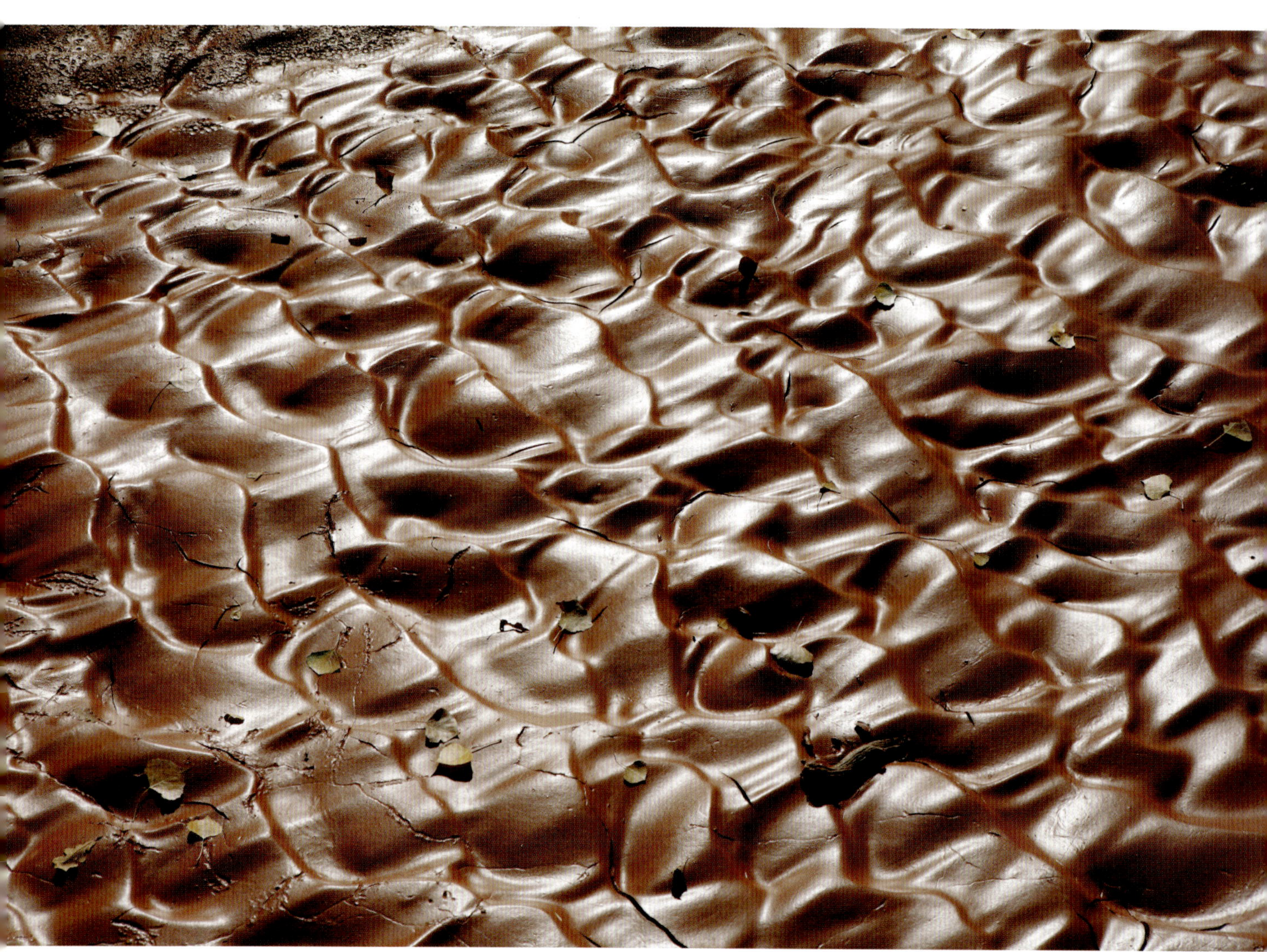

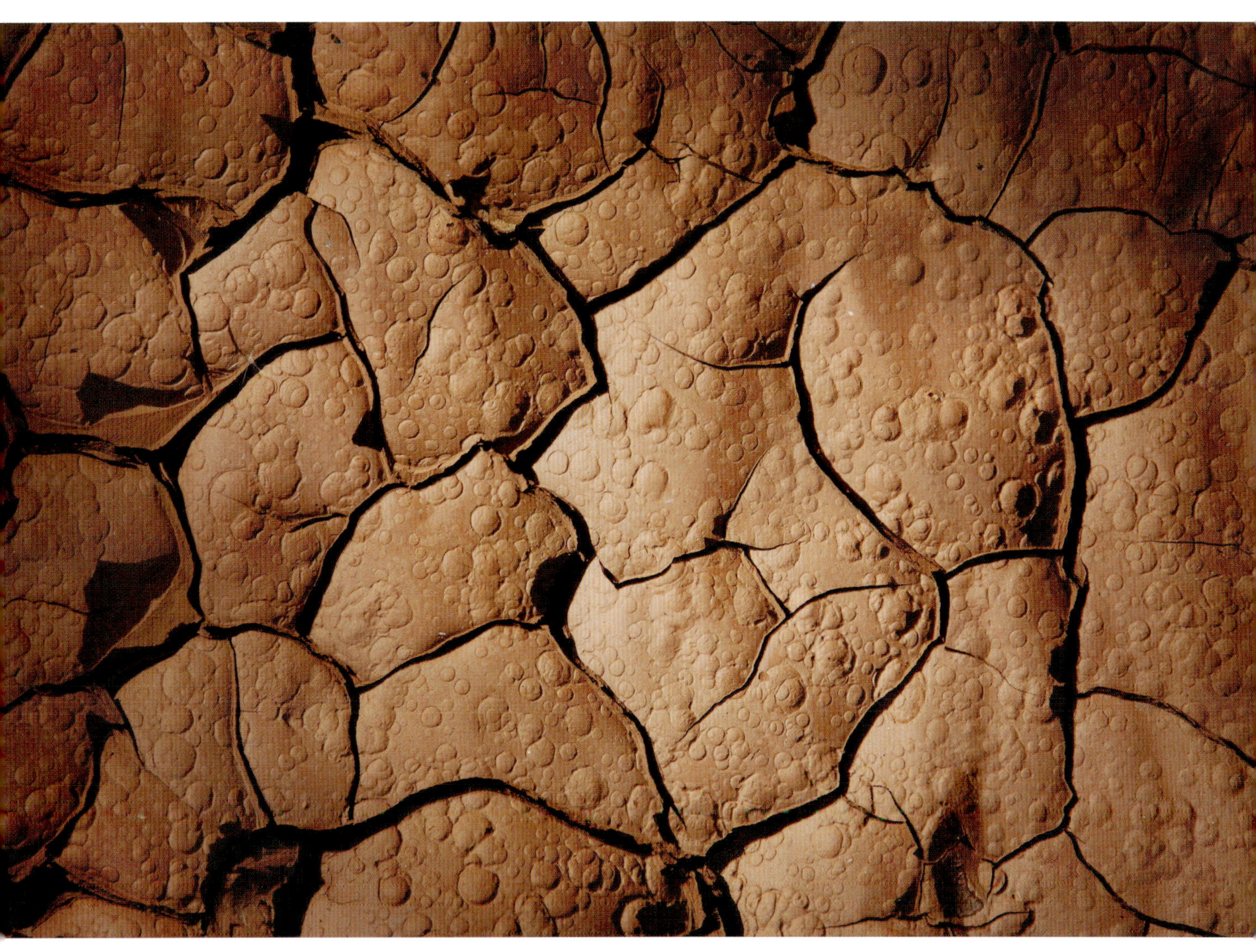

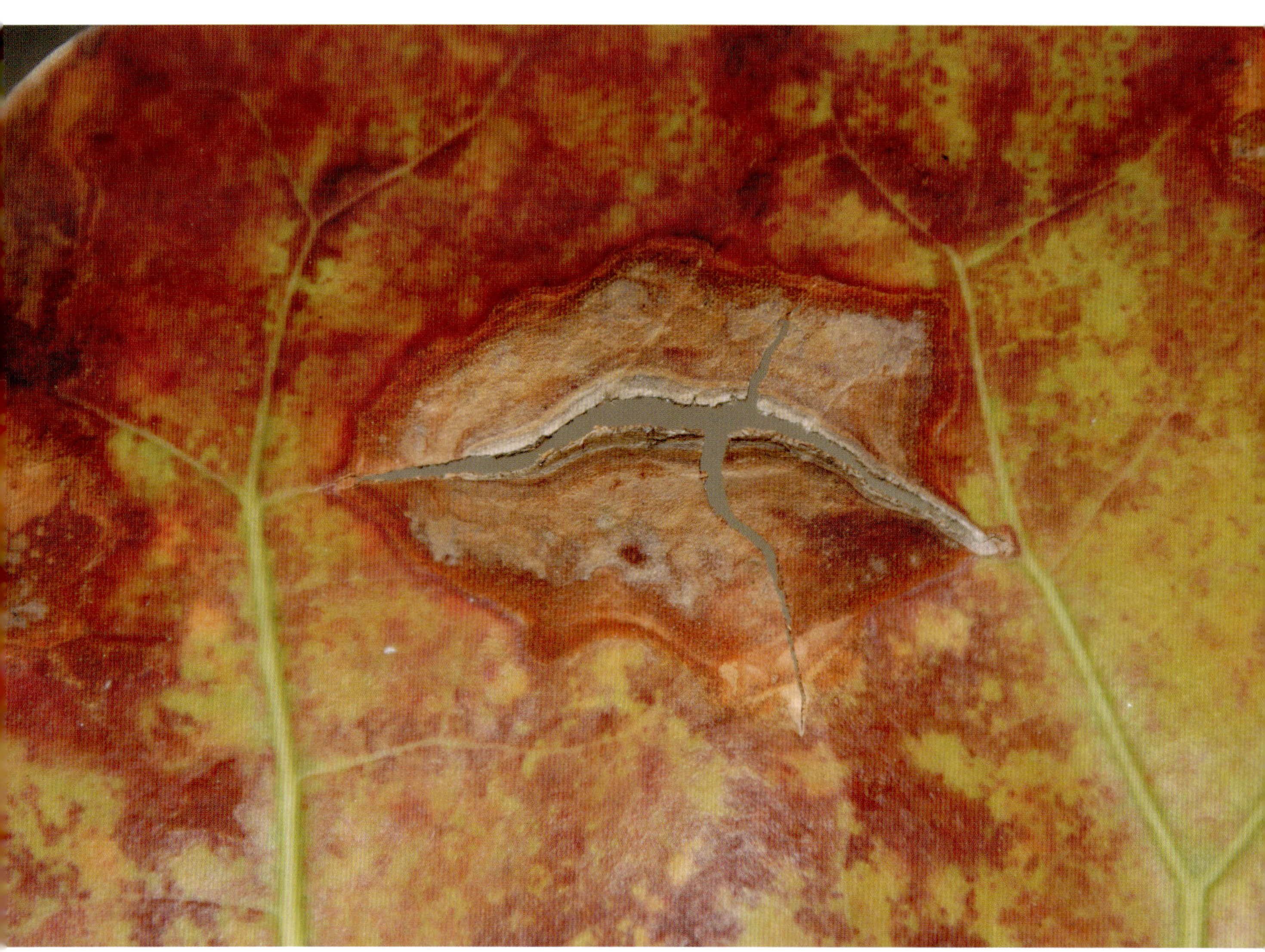

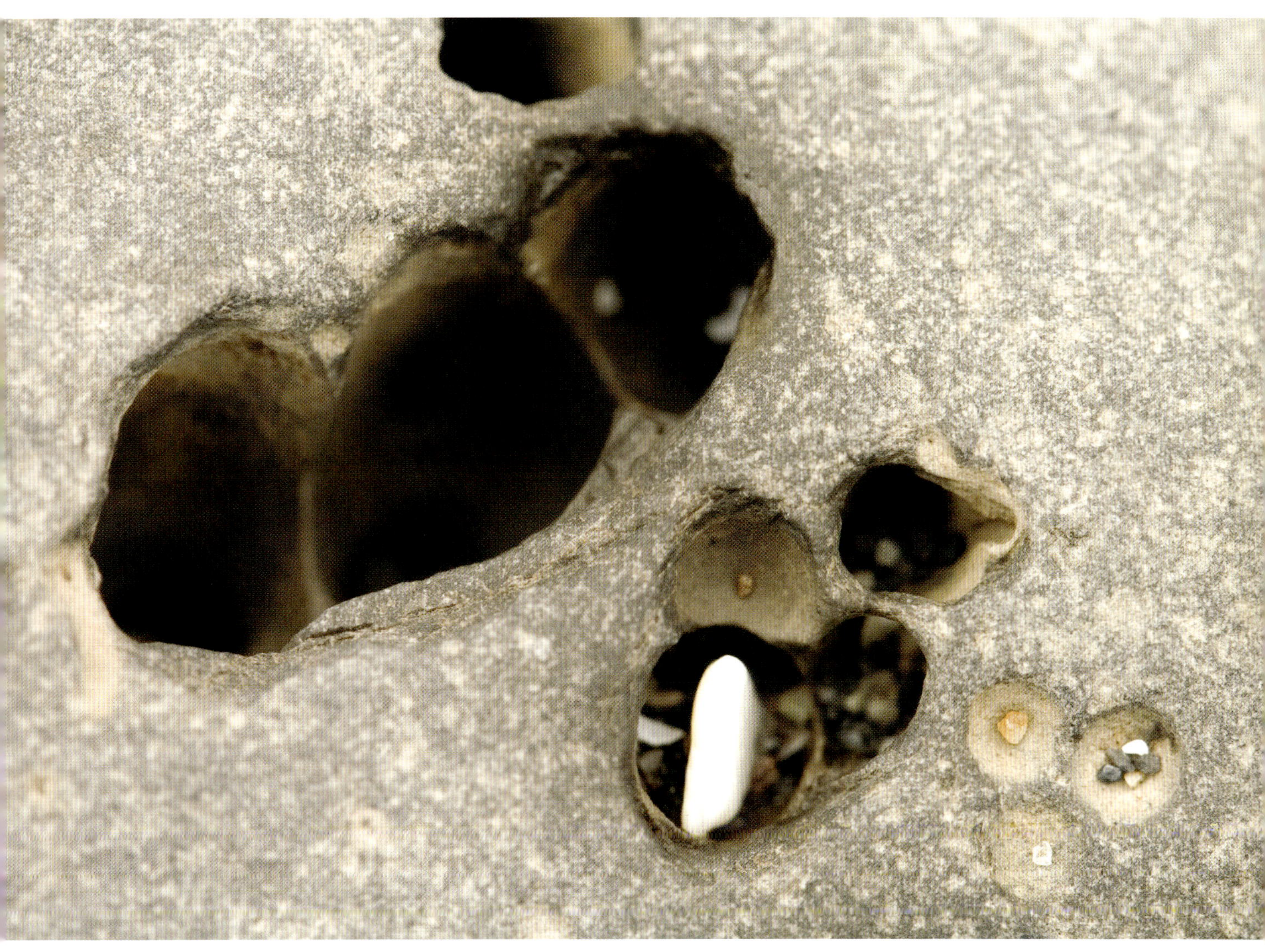

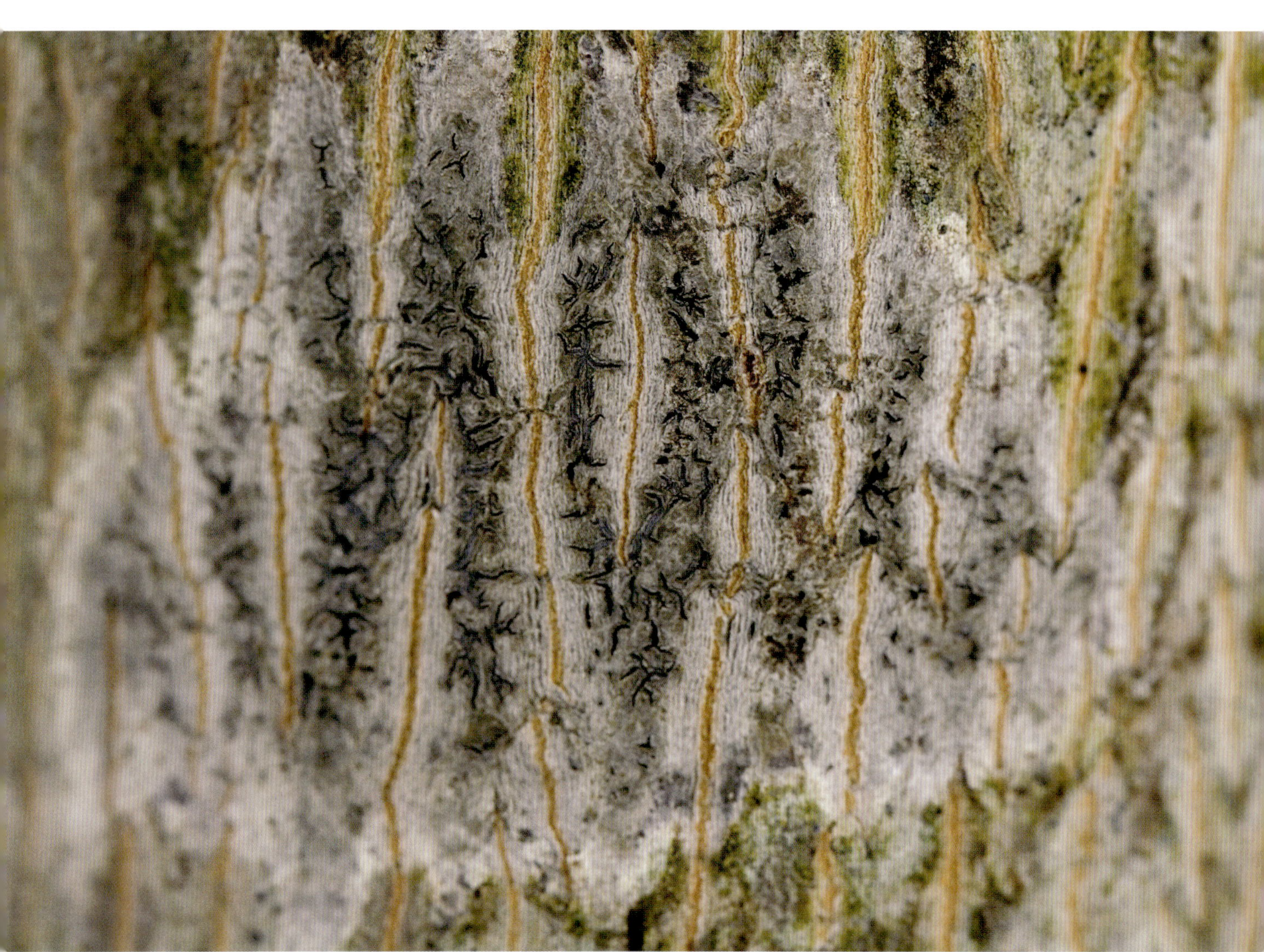

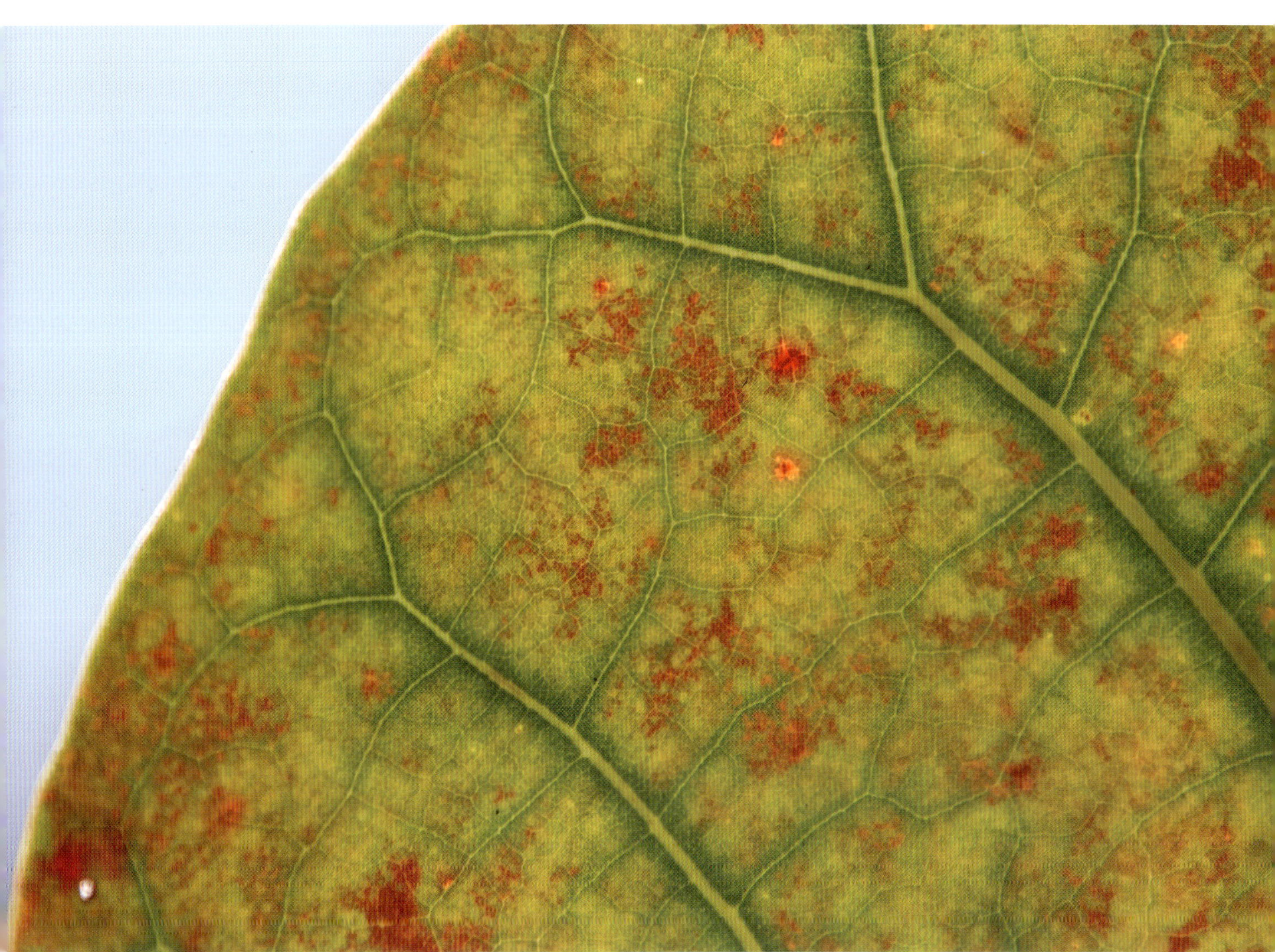

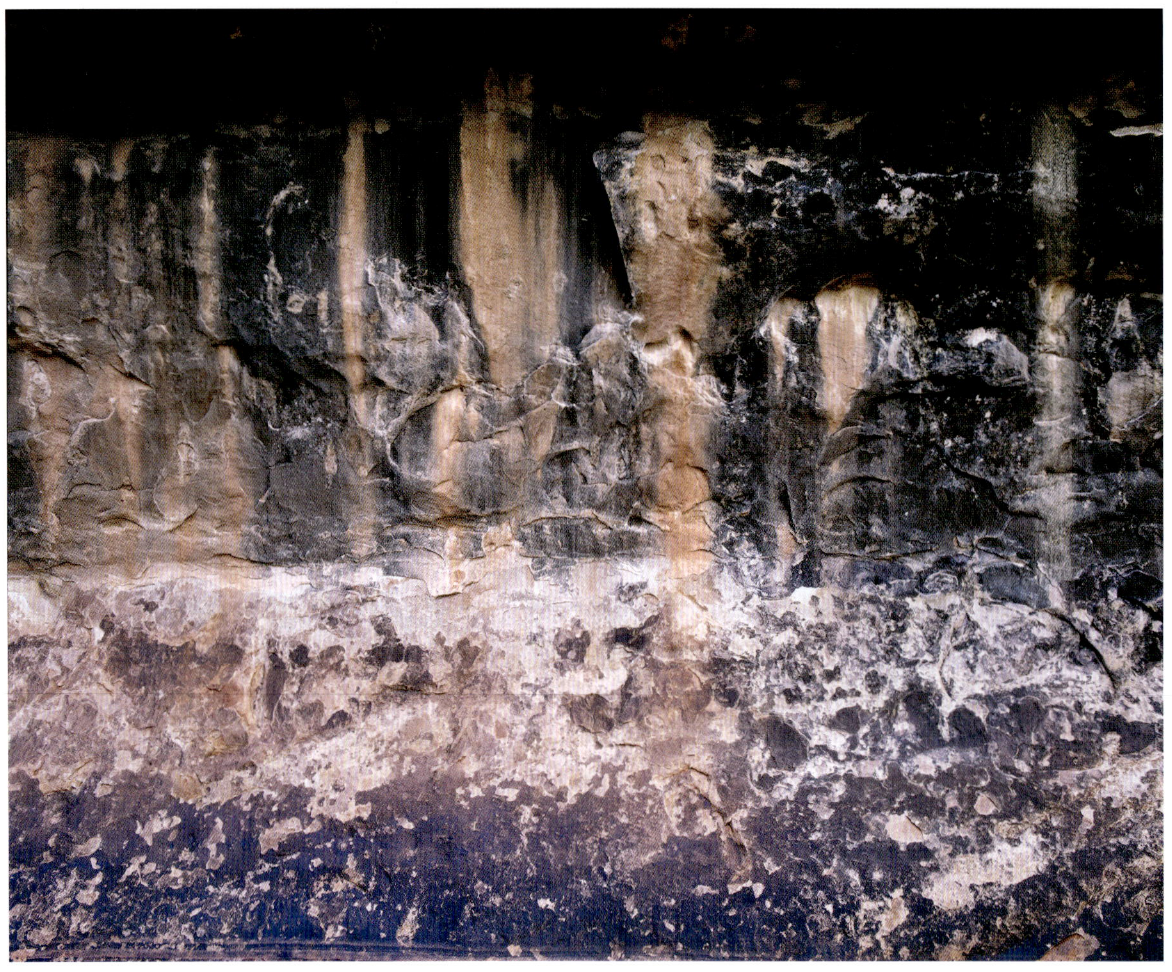

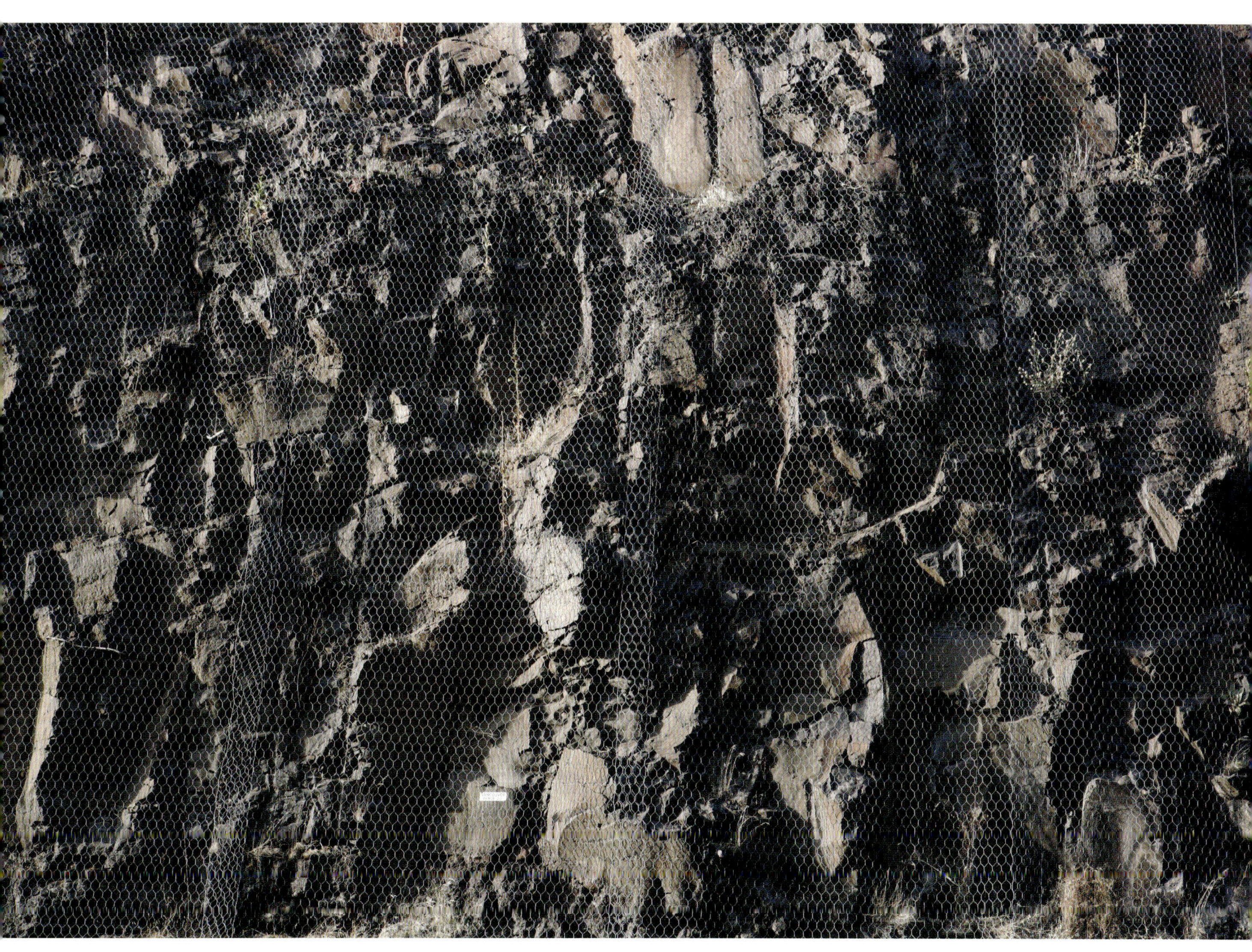
VANCOUVER

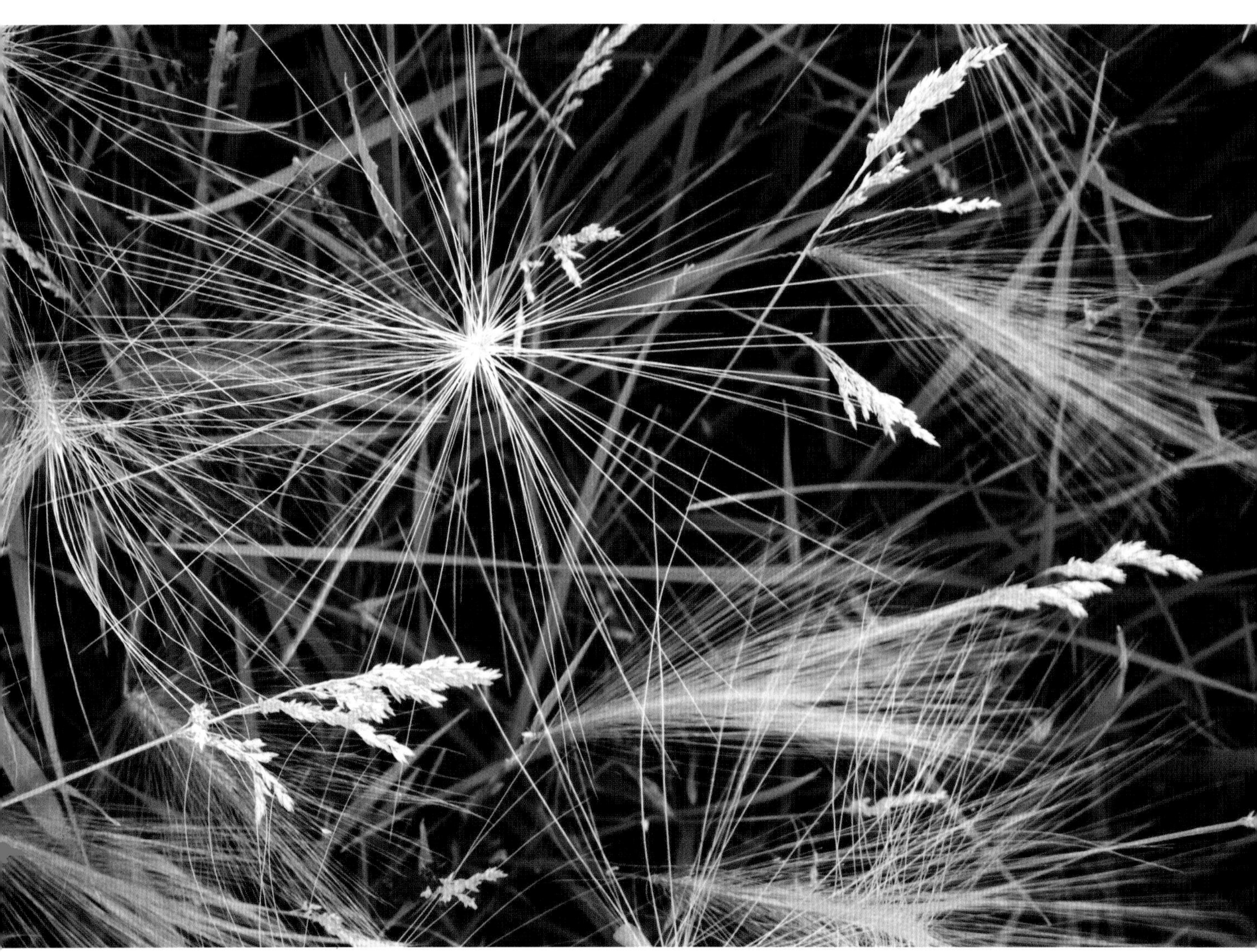

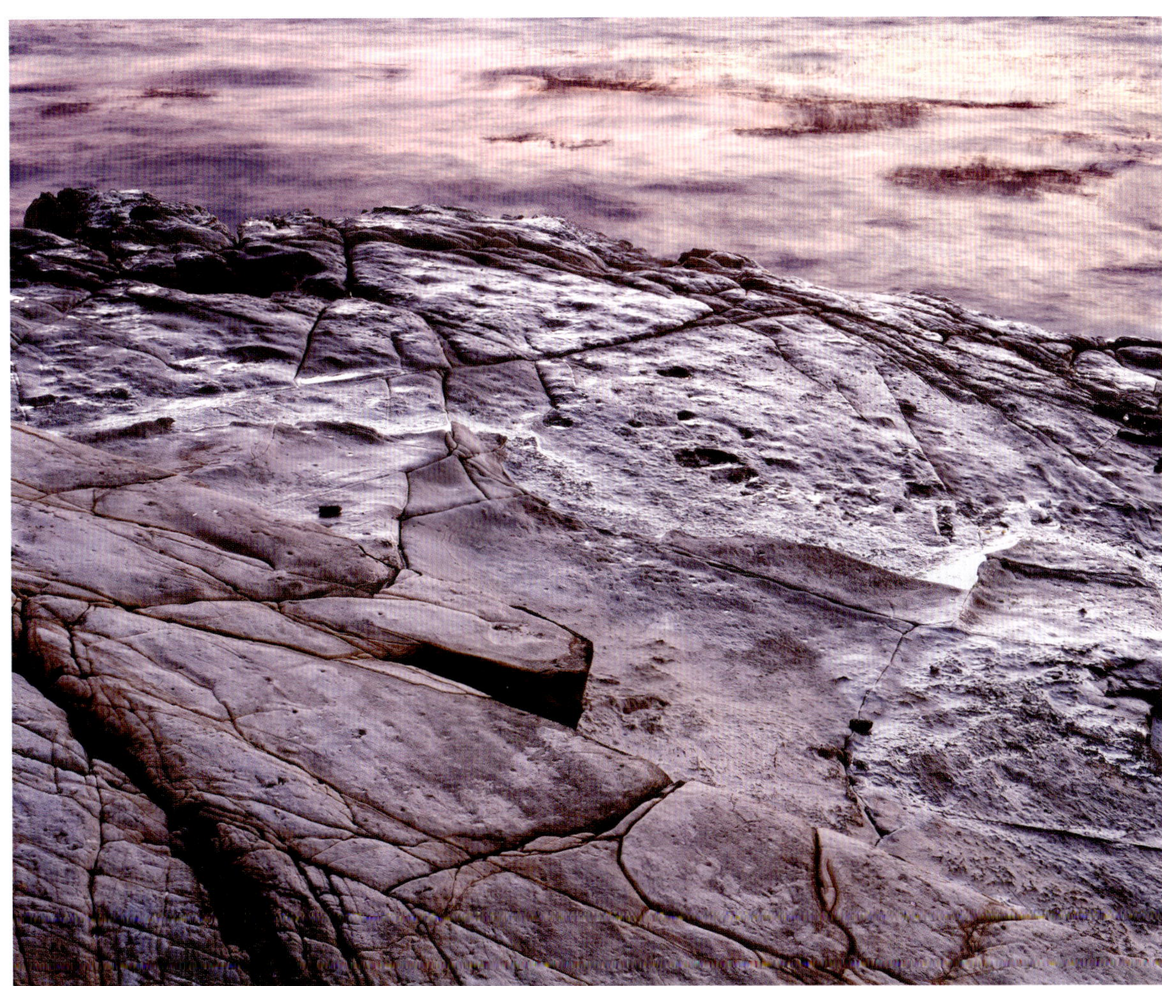

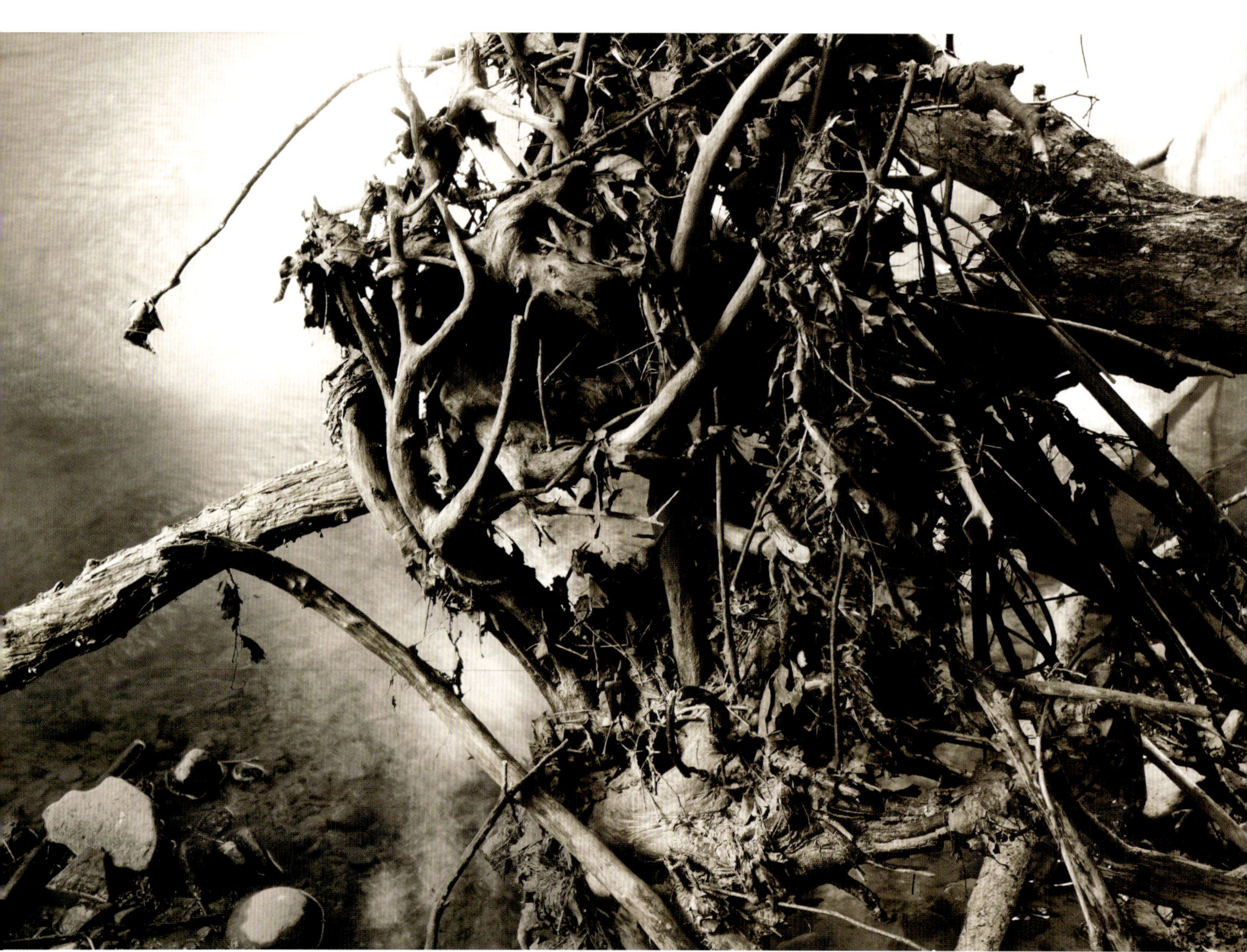

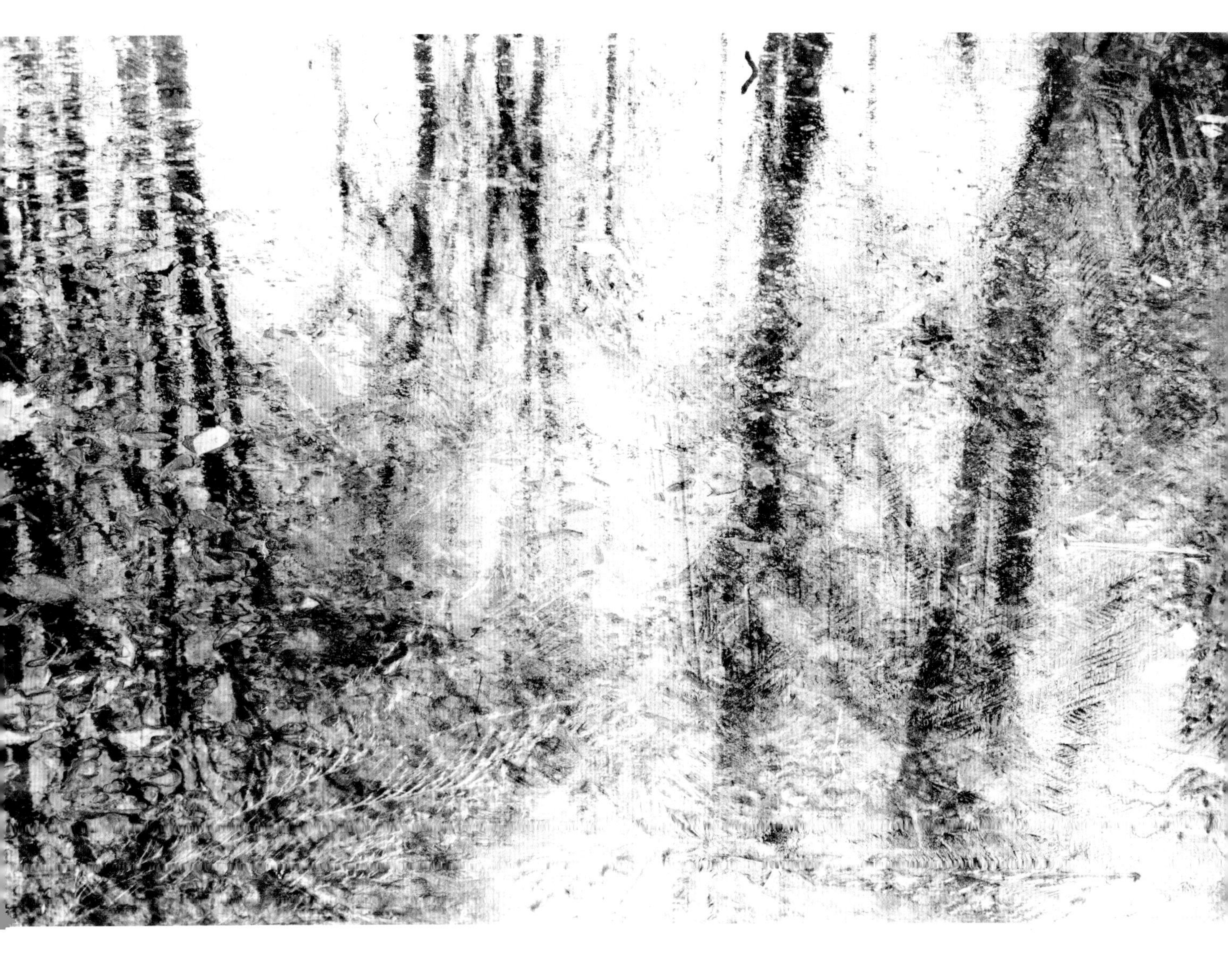

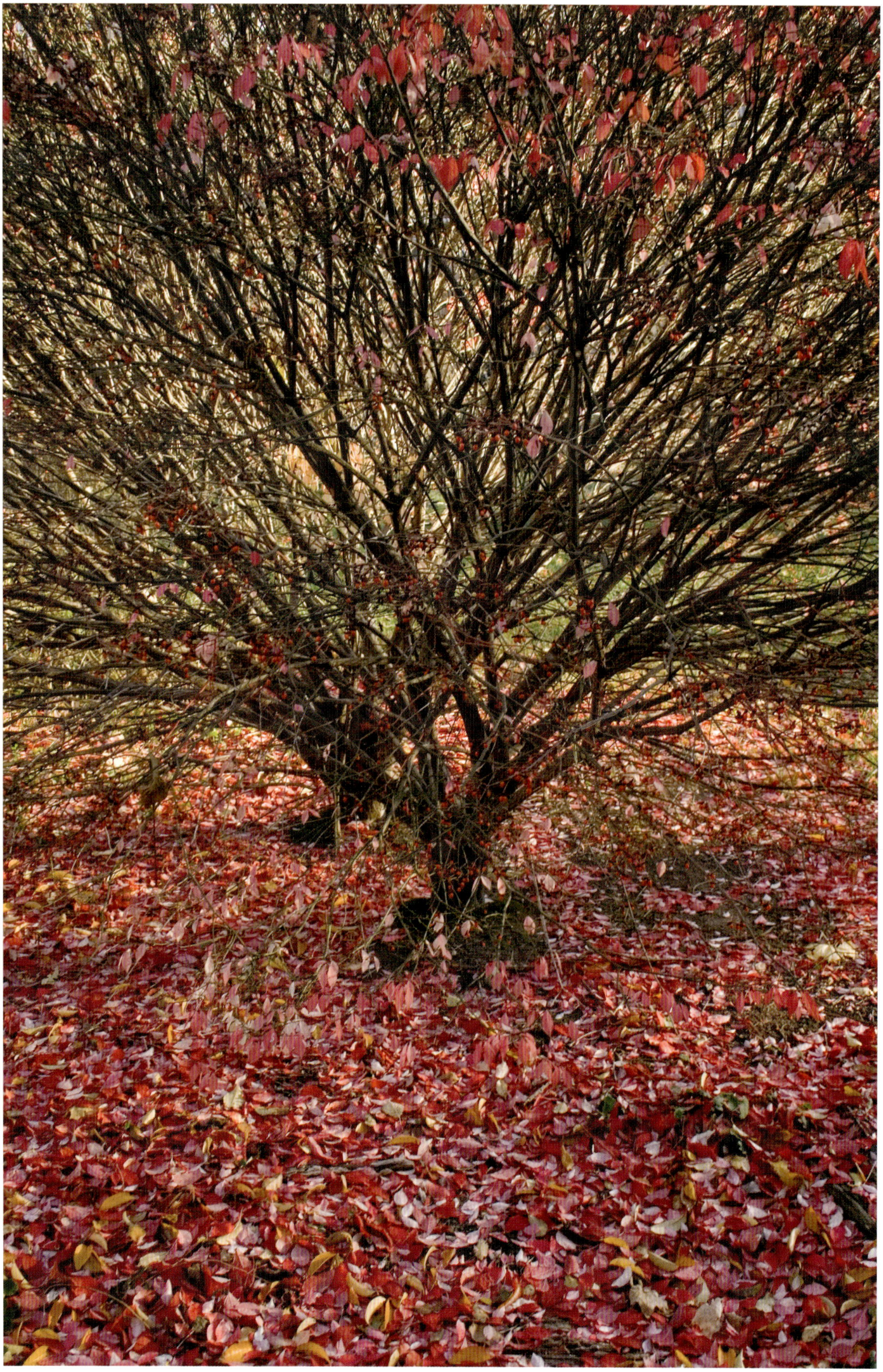

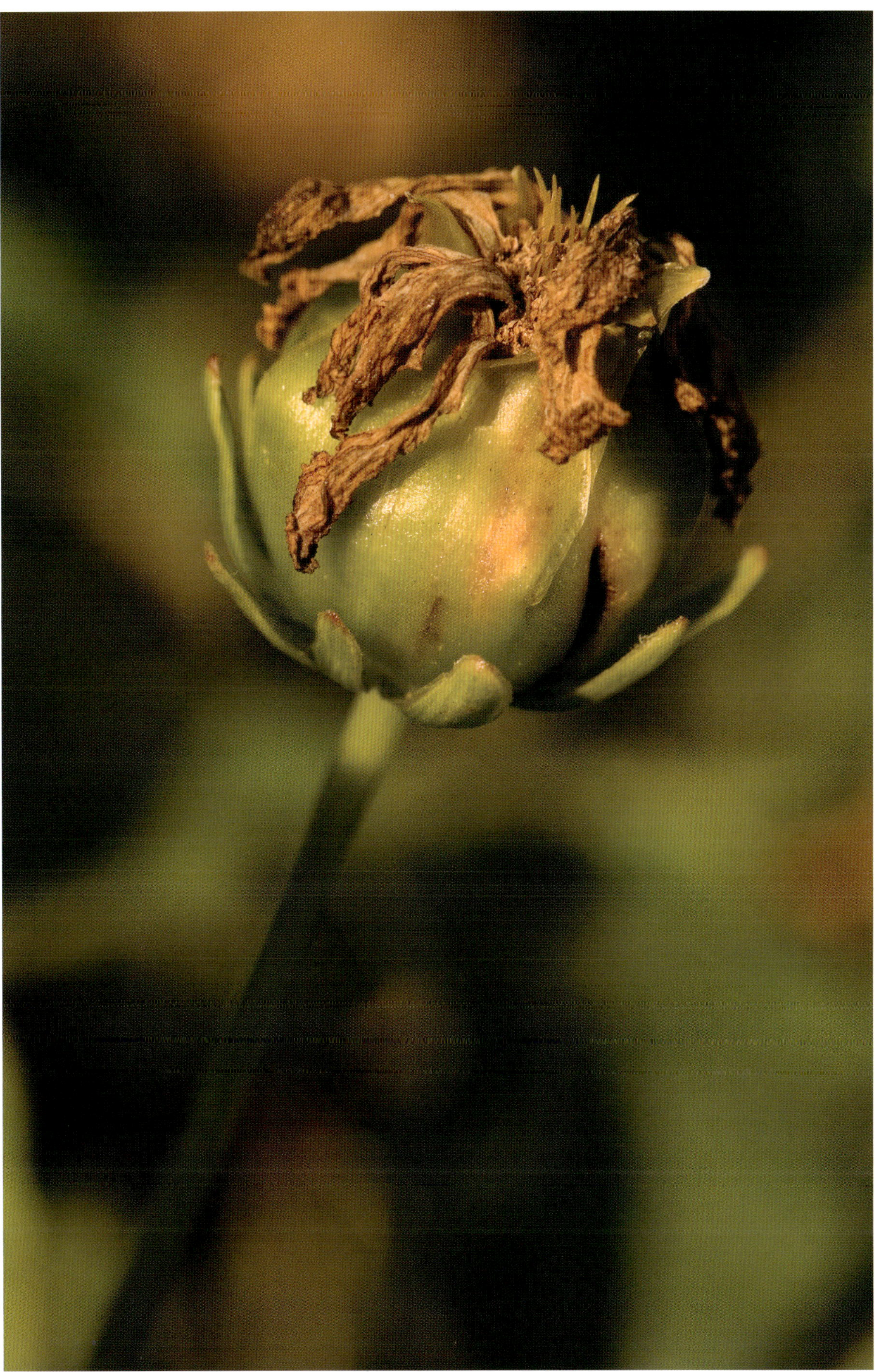

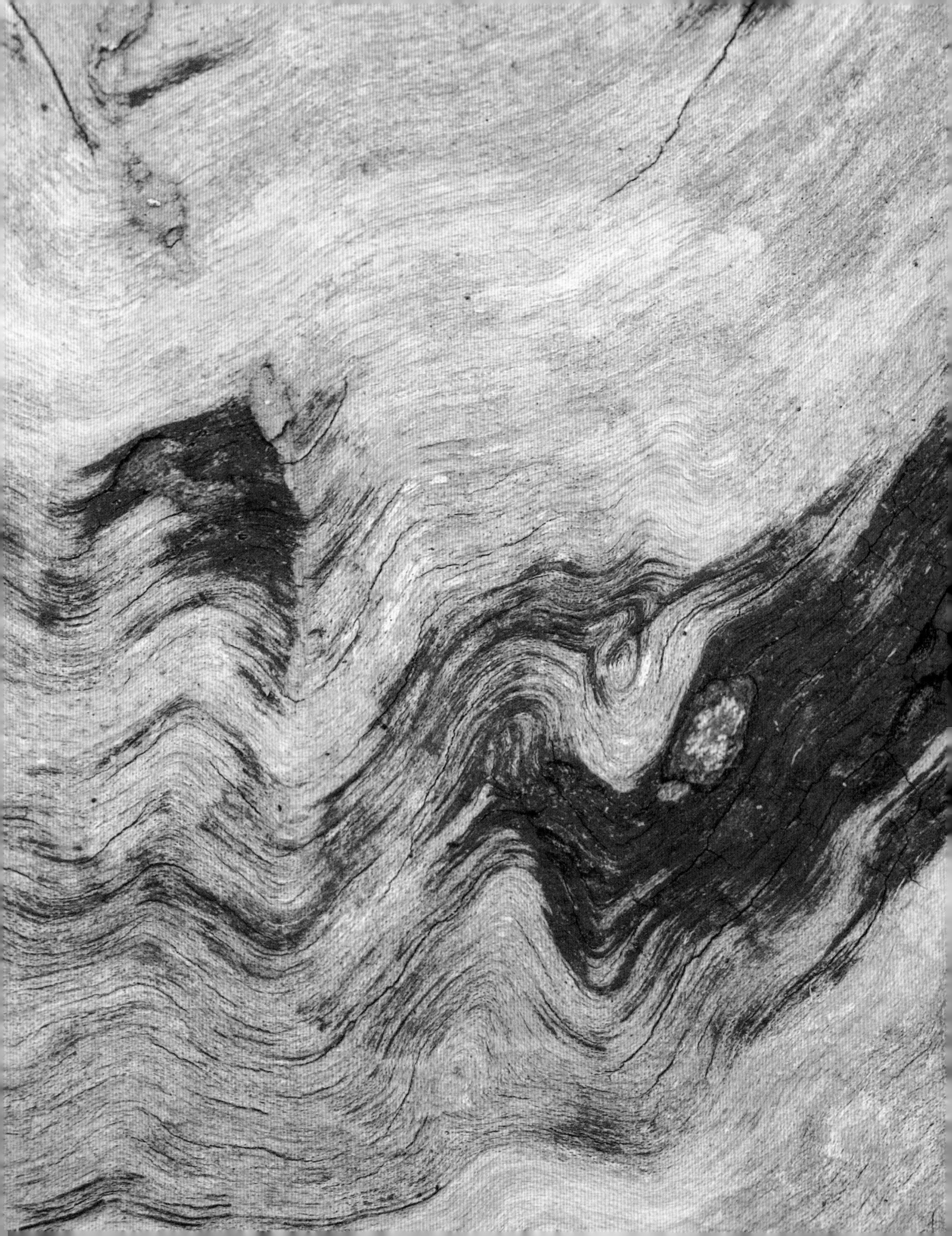

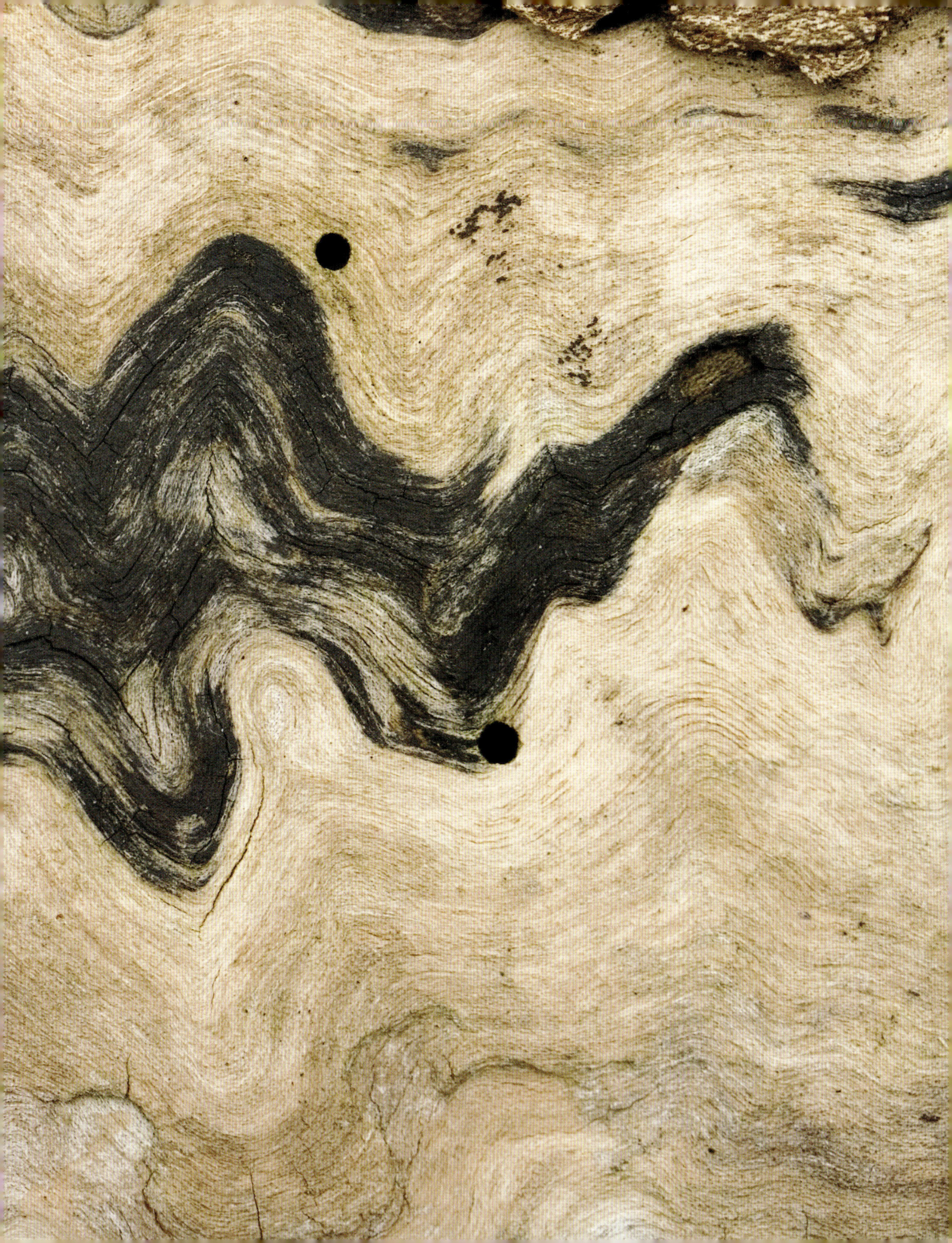

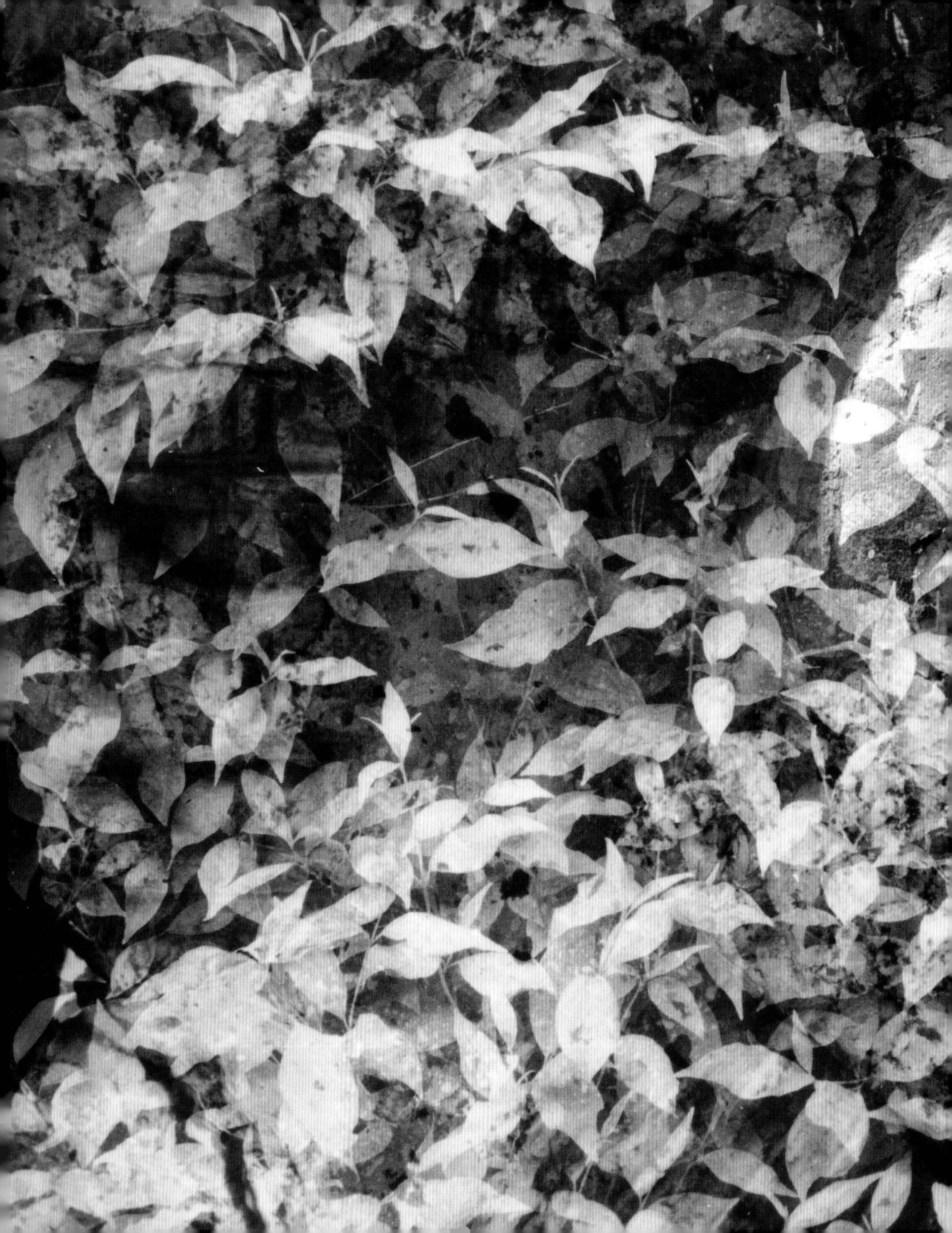

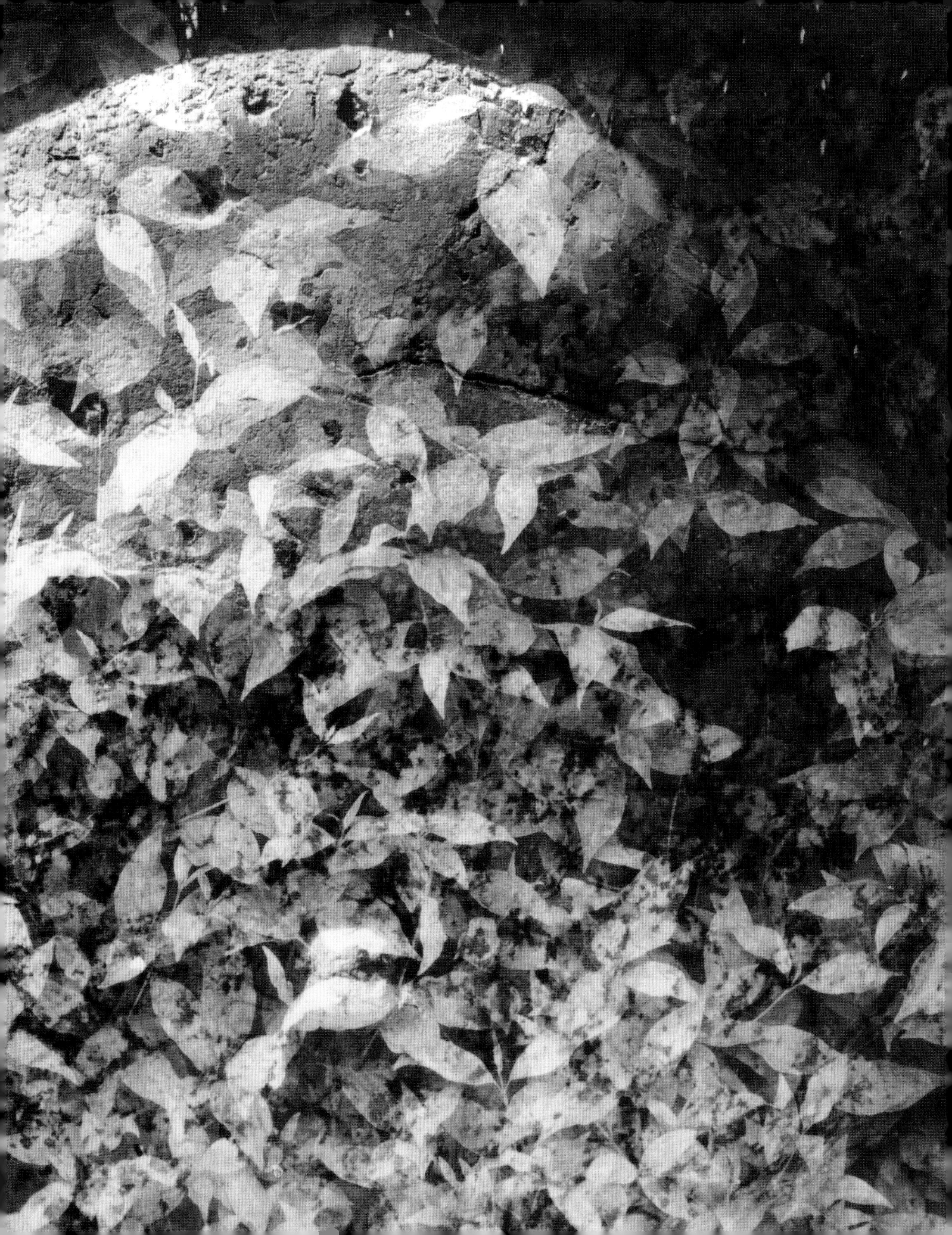

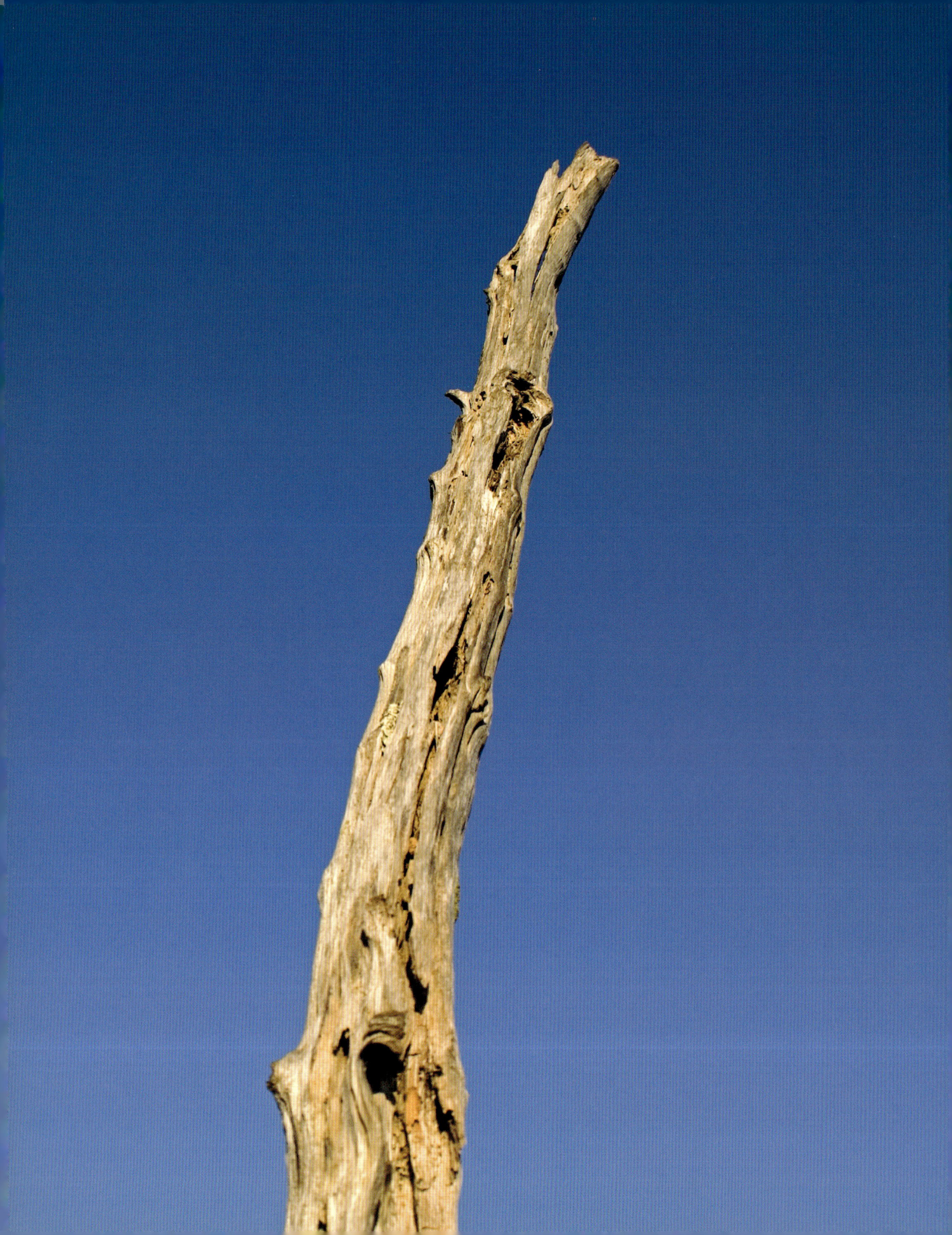

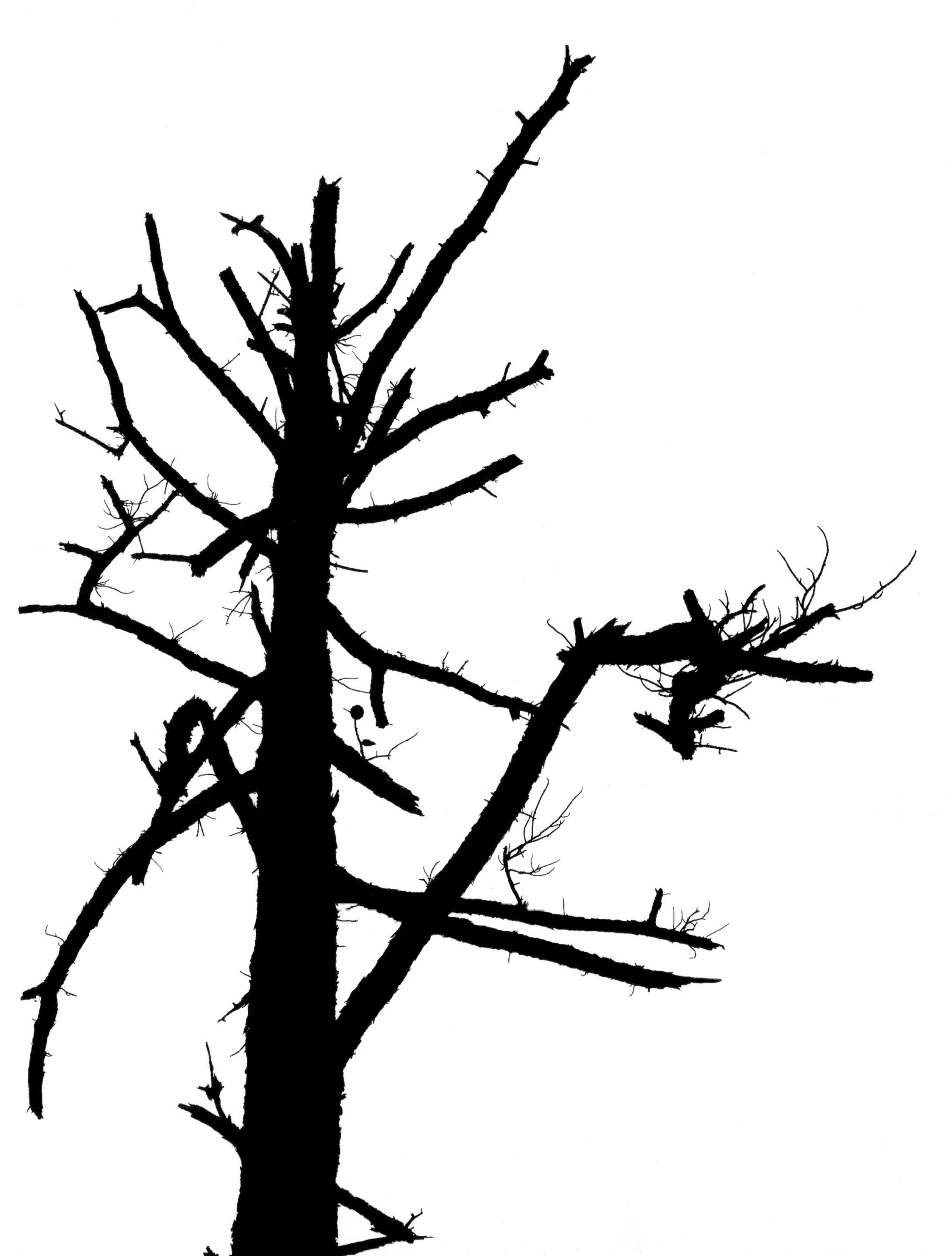

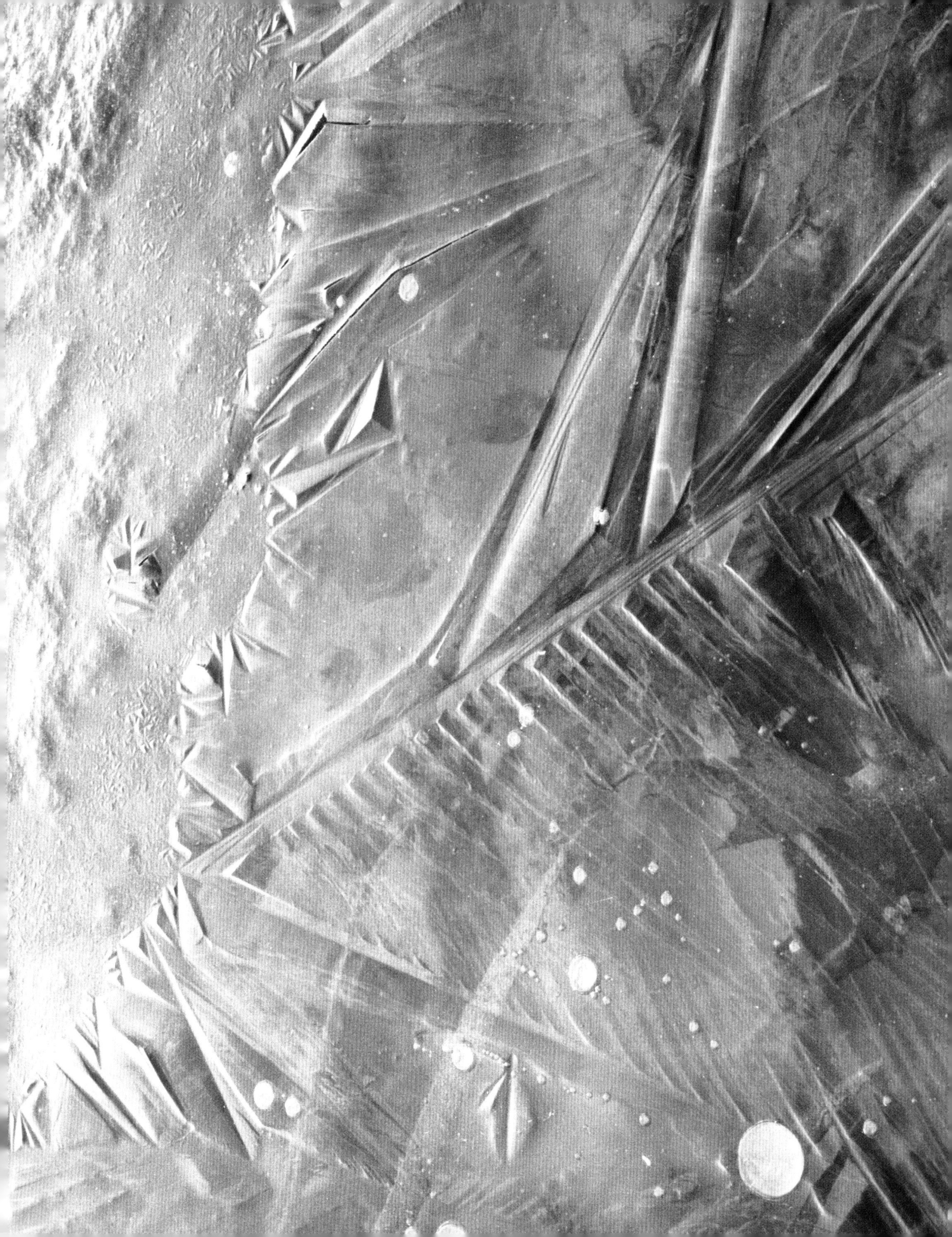

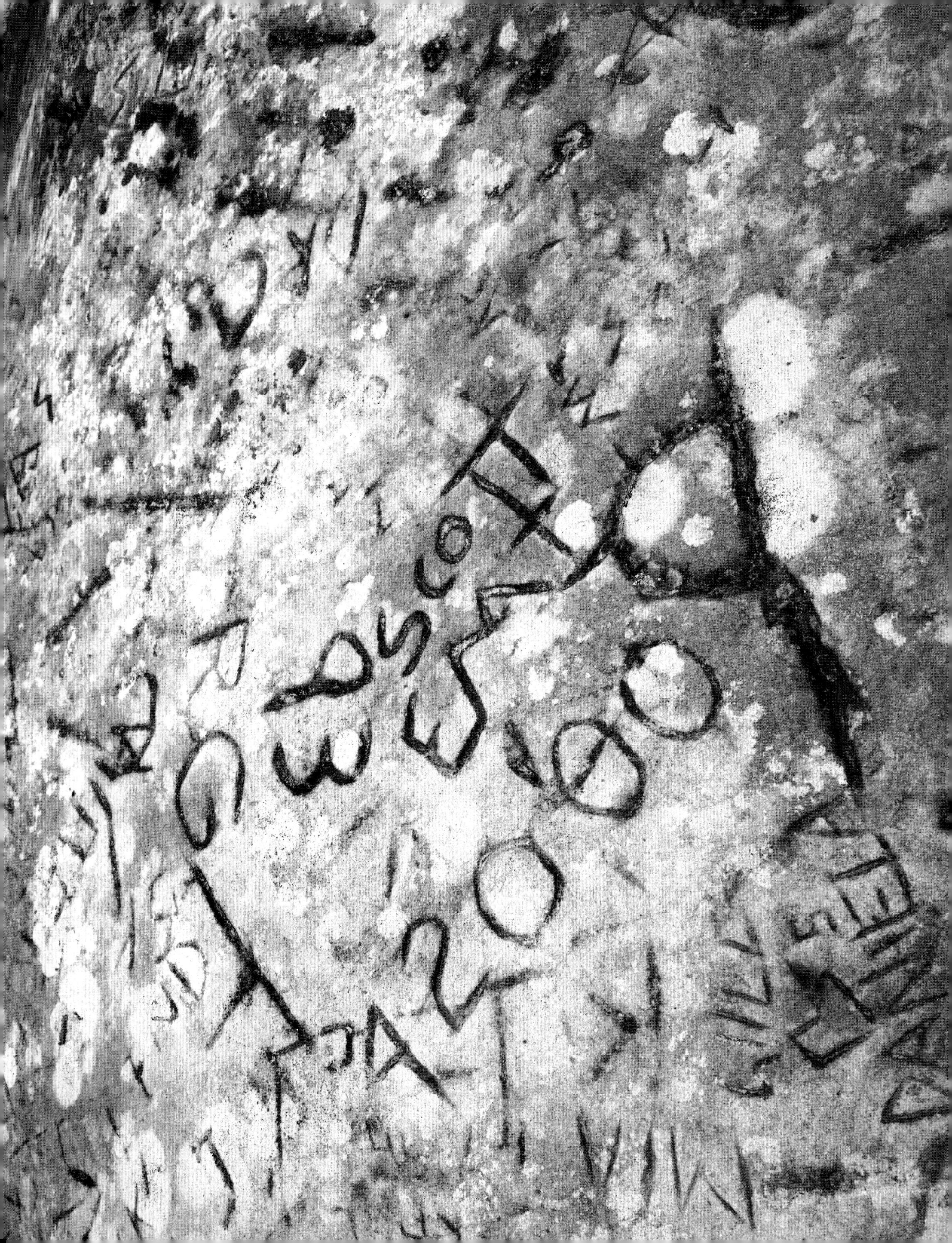

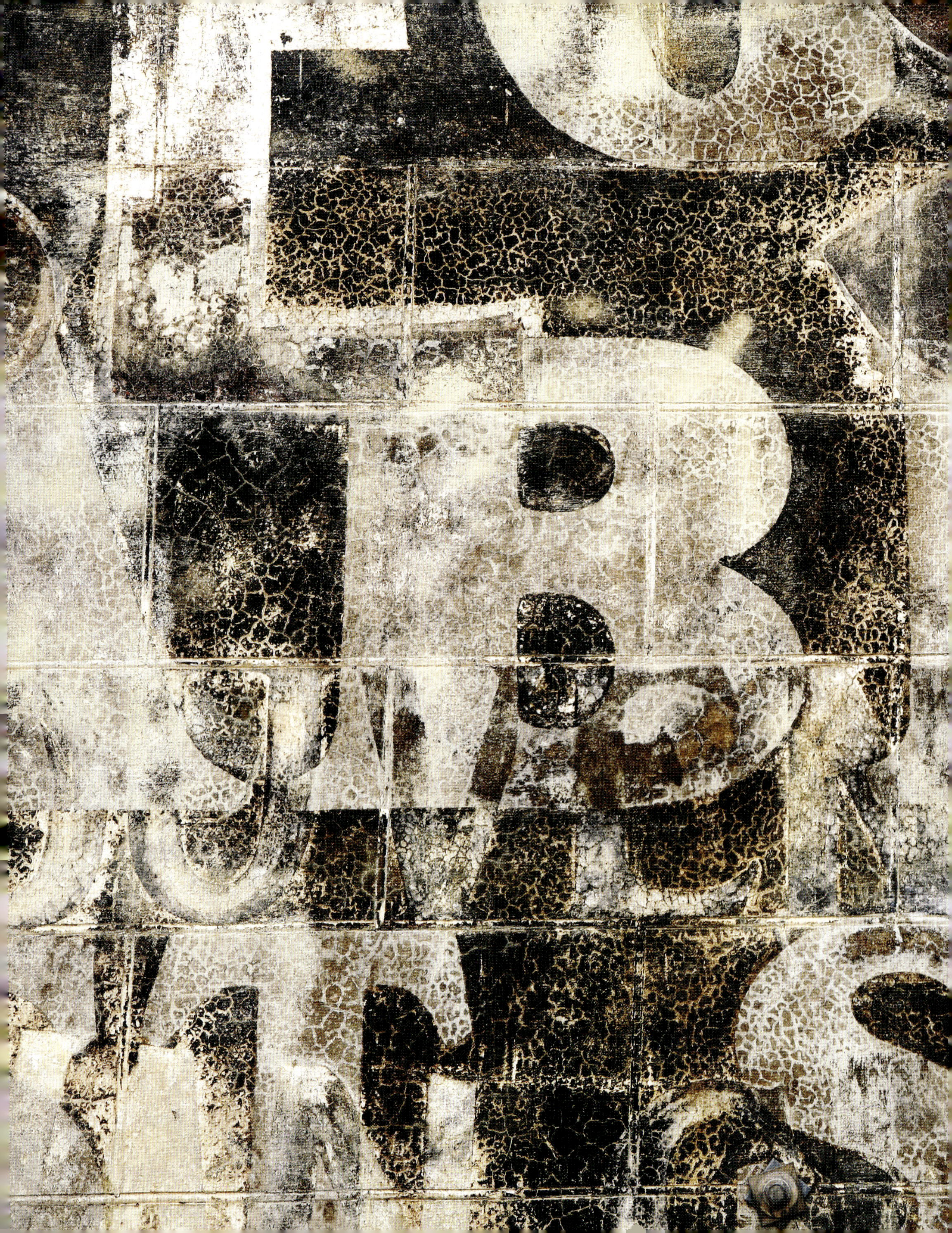

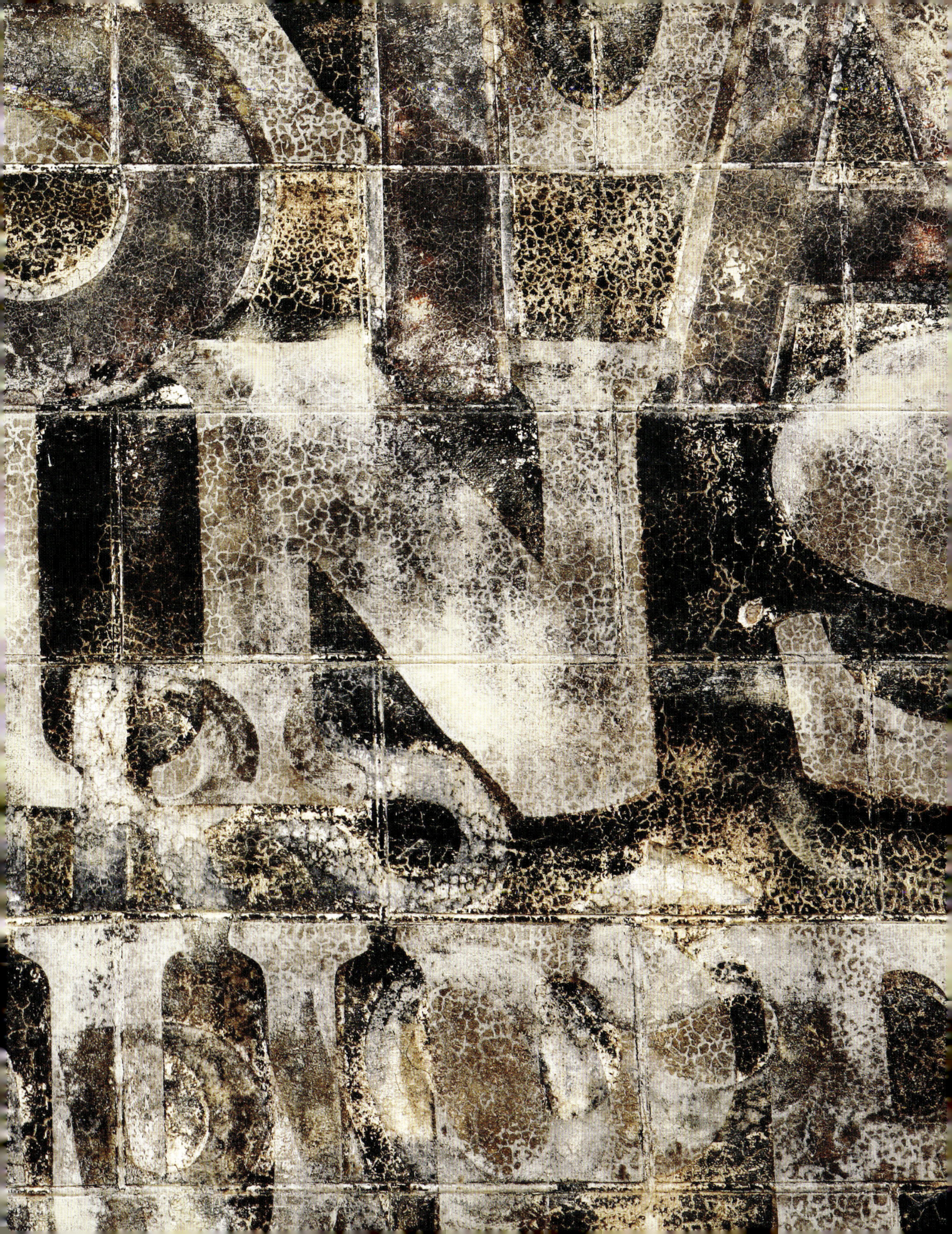

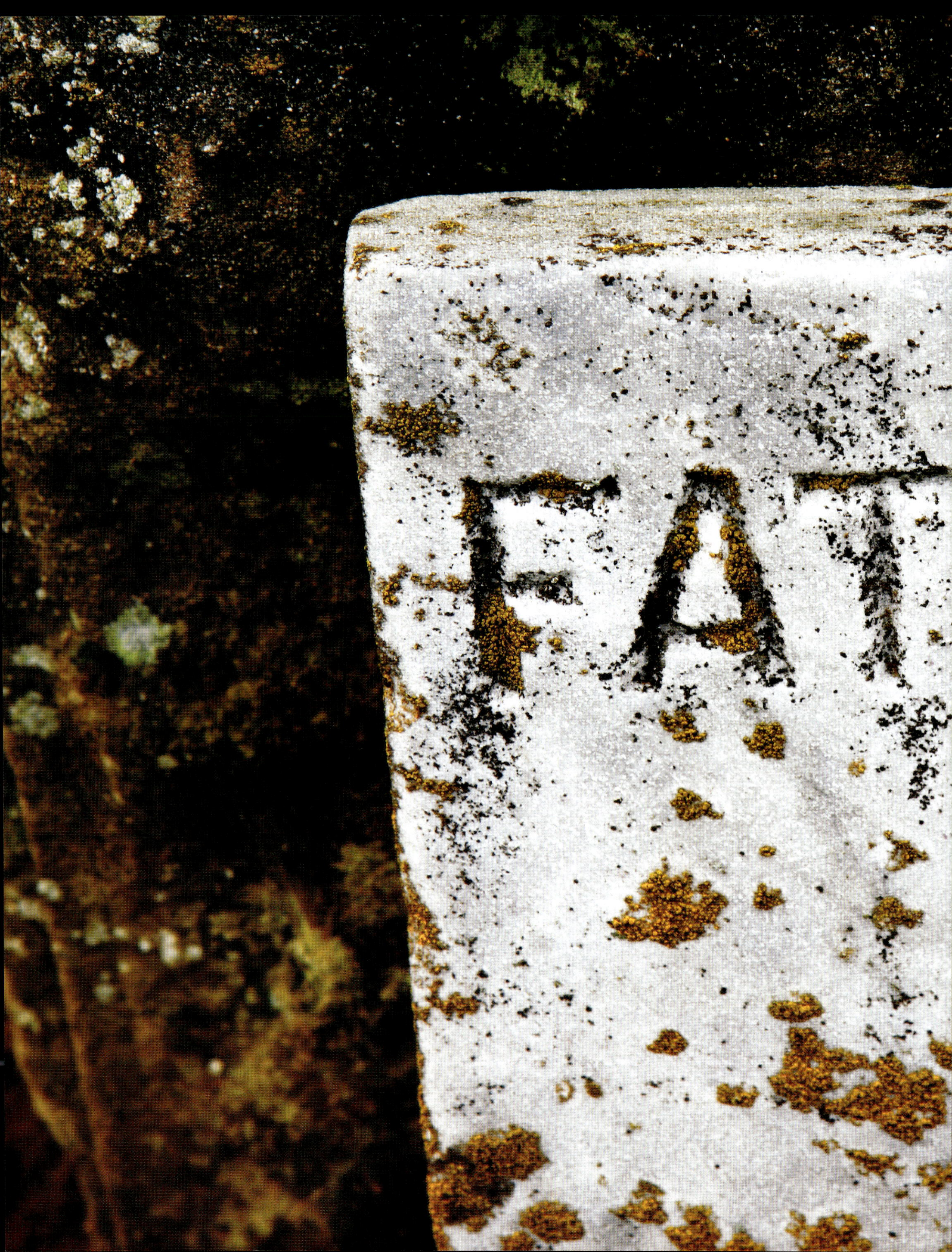
FAT

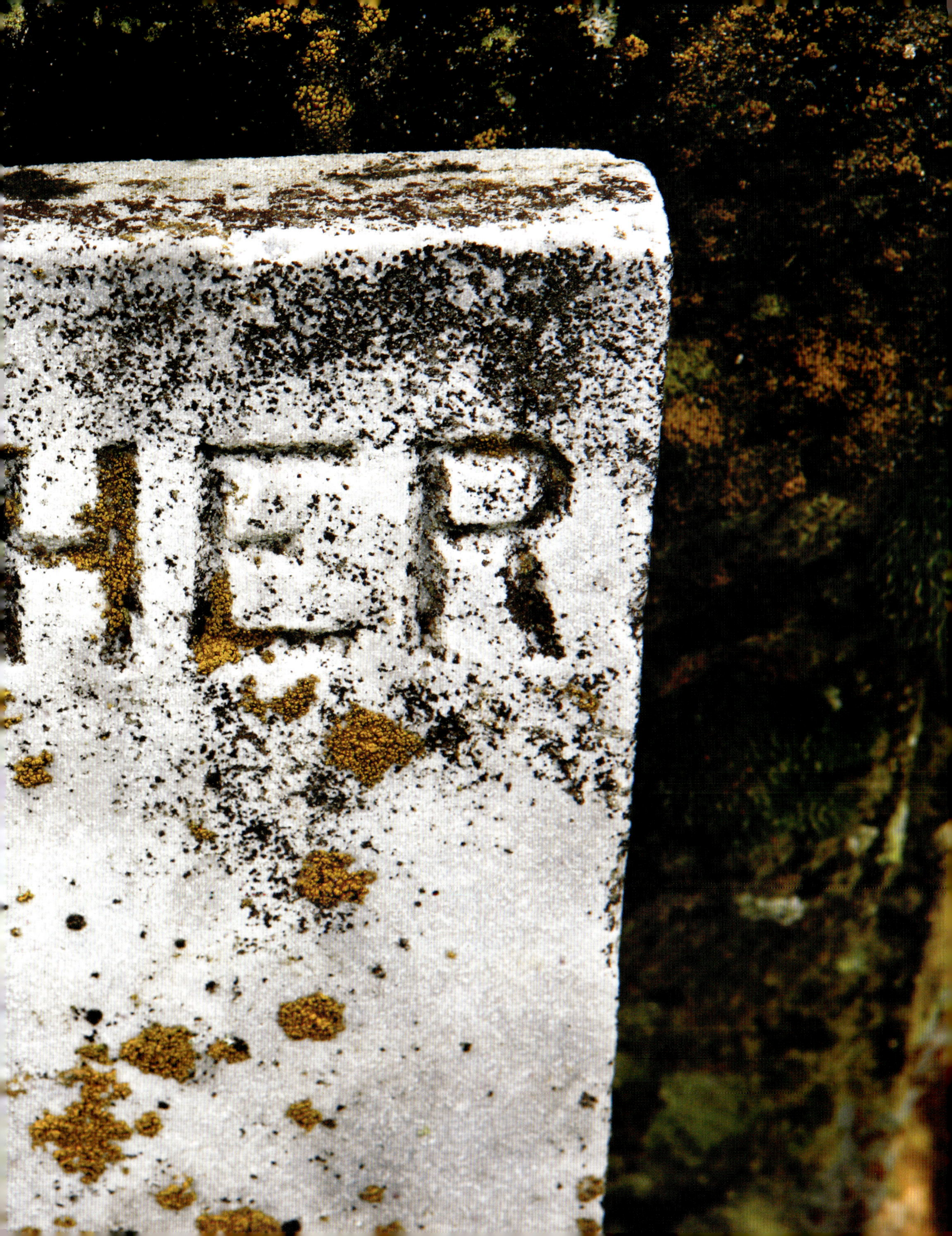
HER

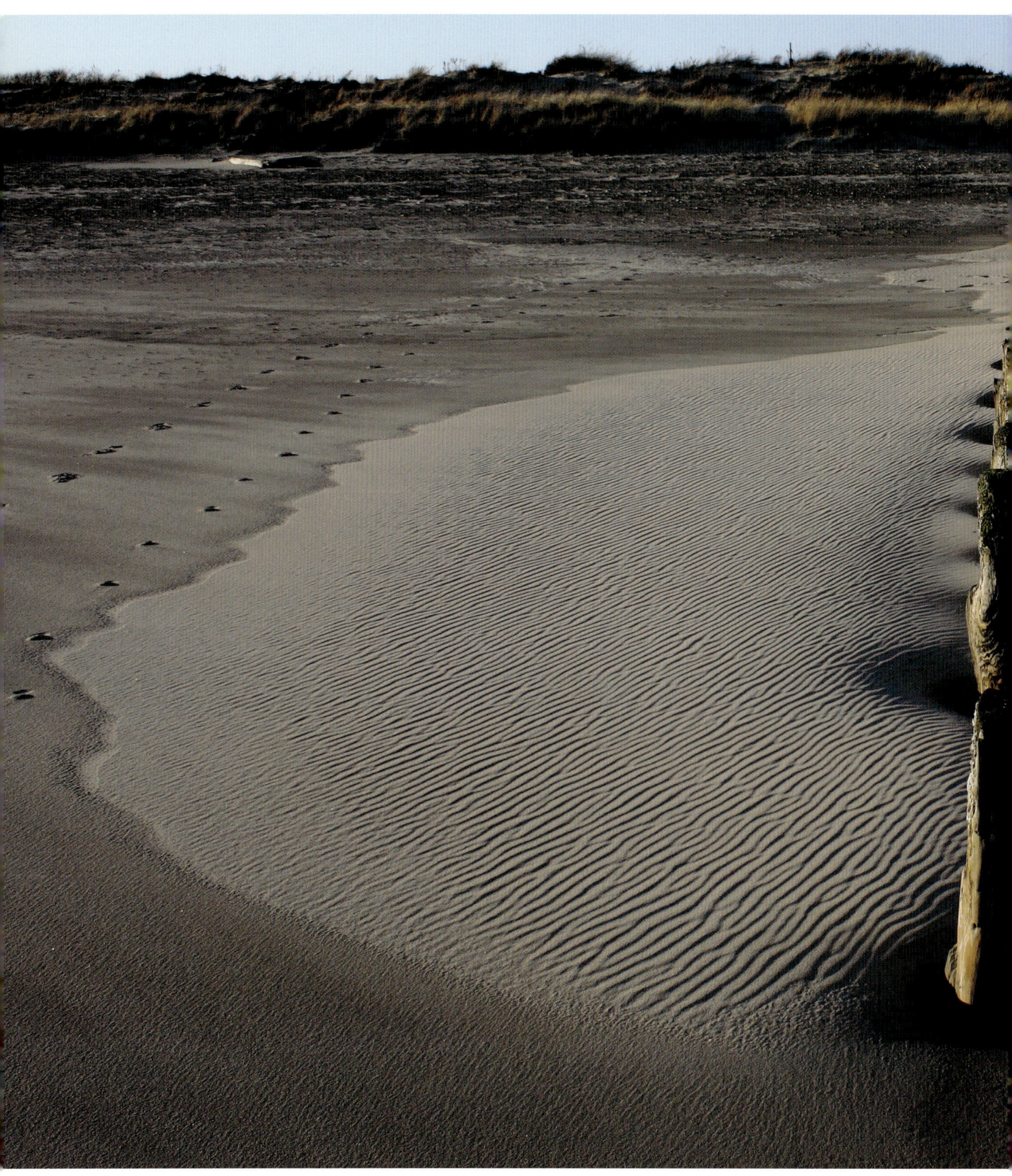

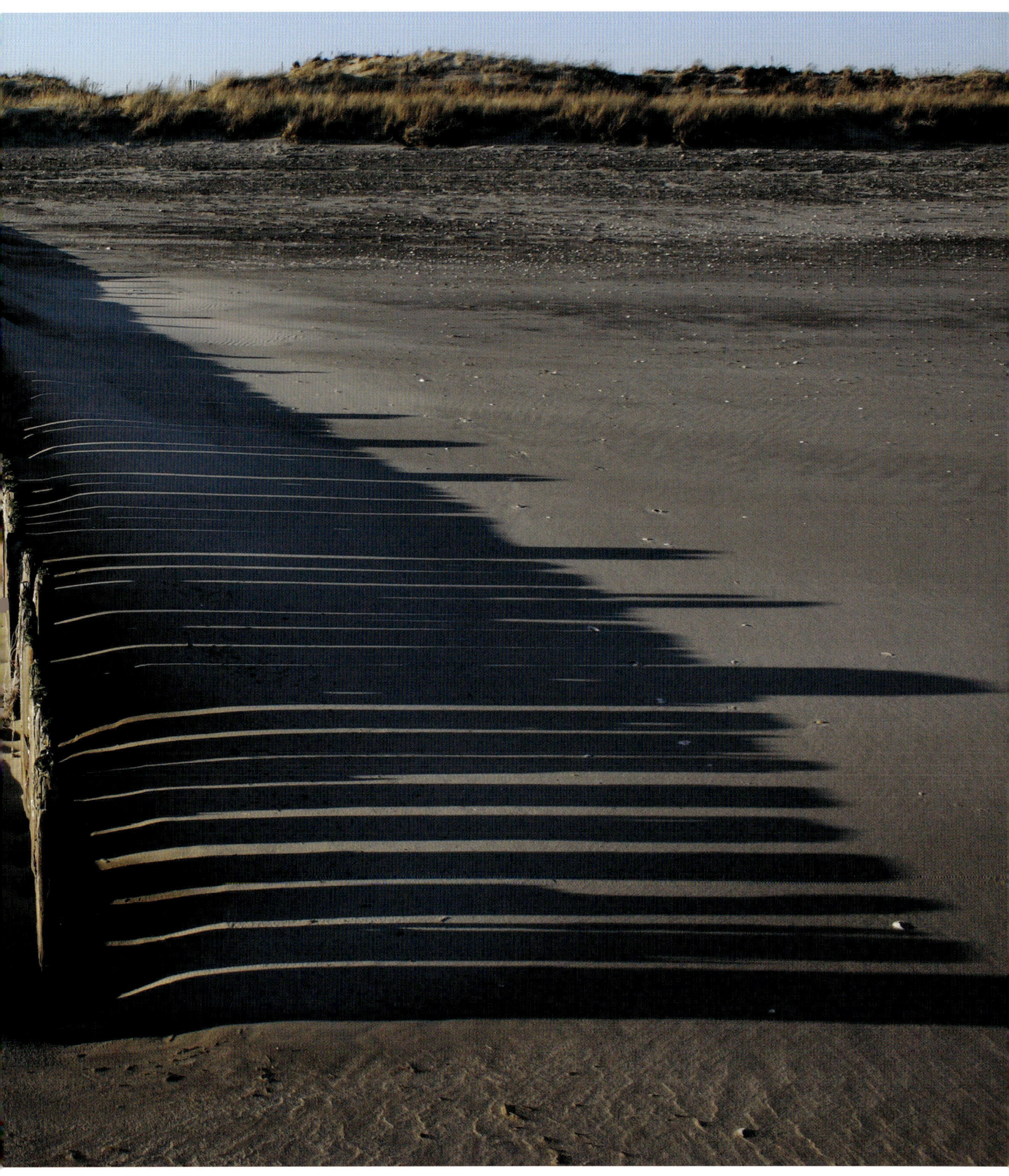

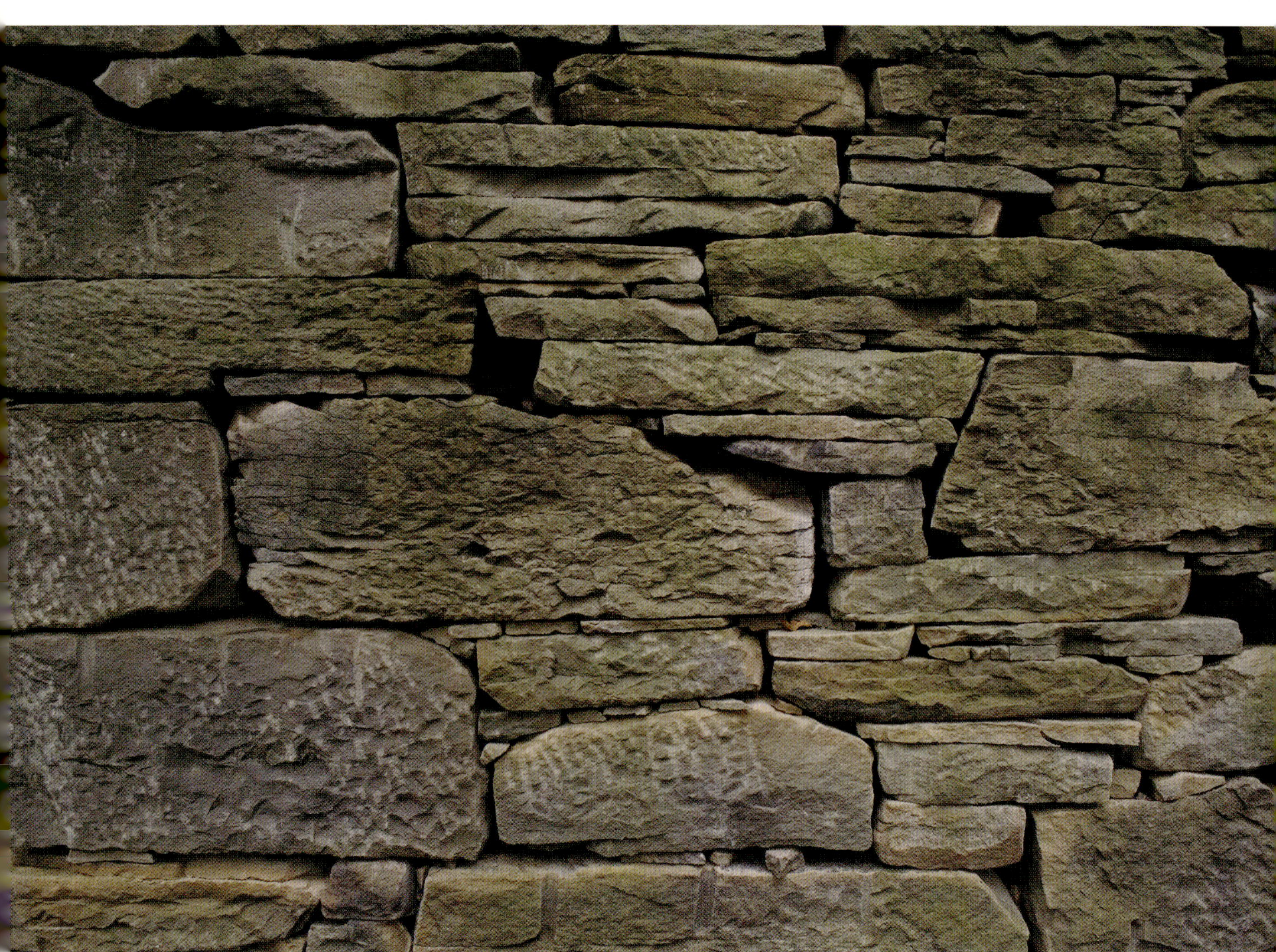

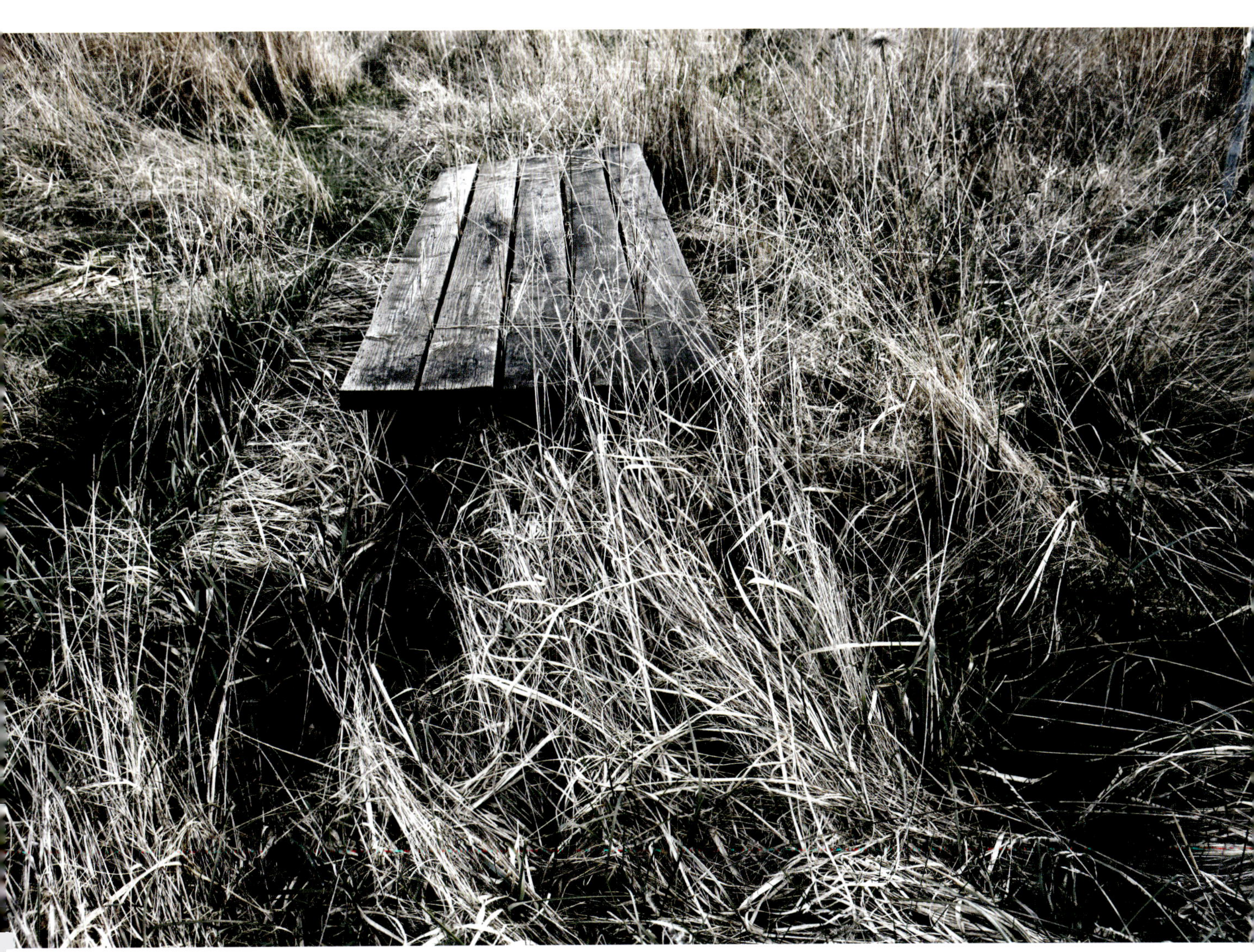

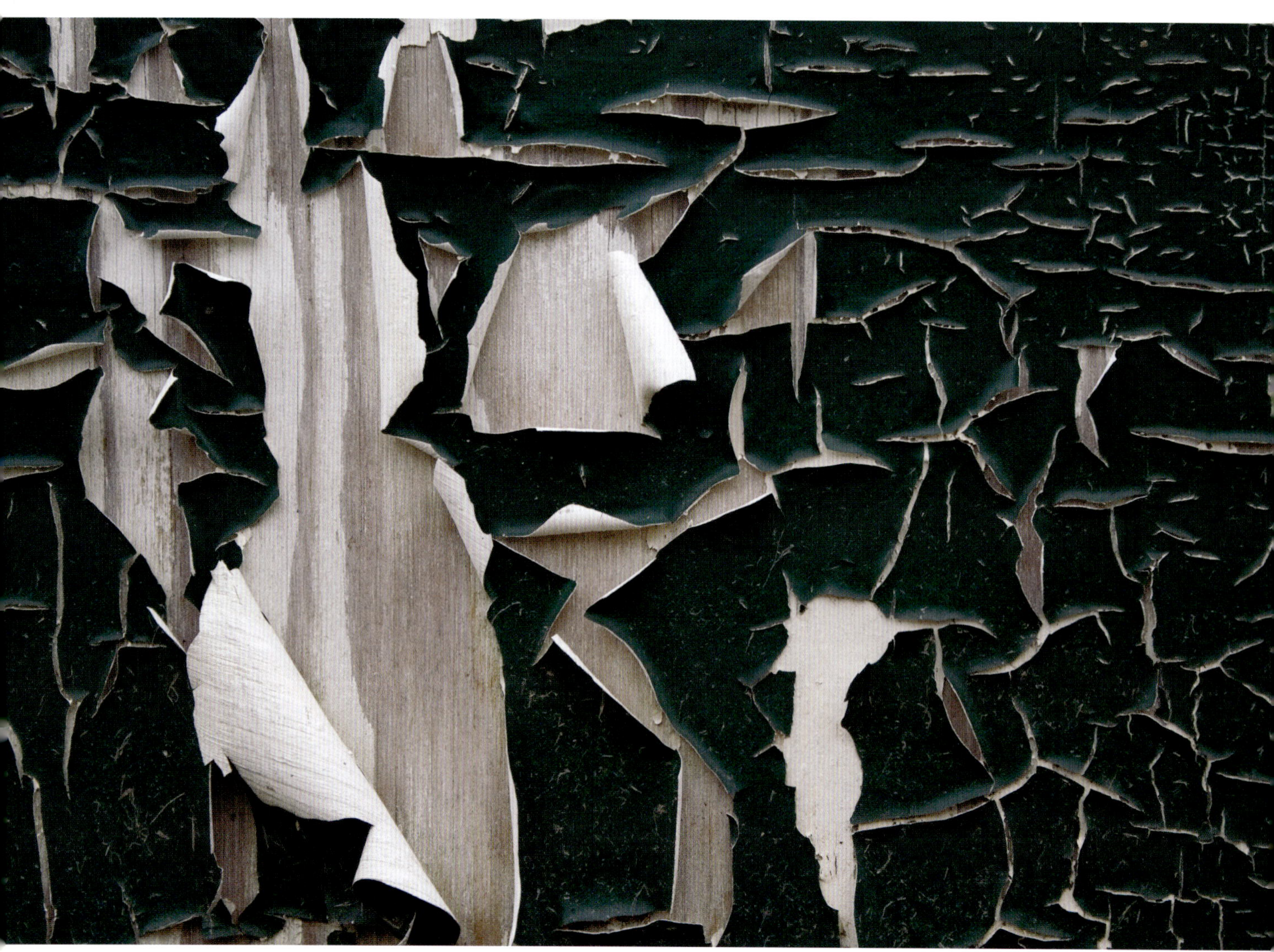

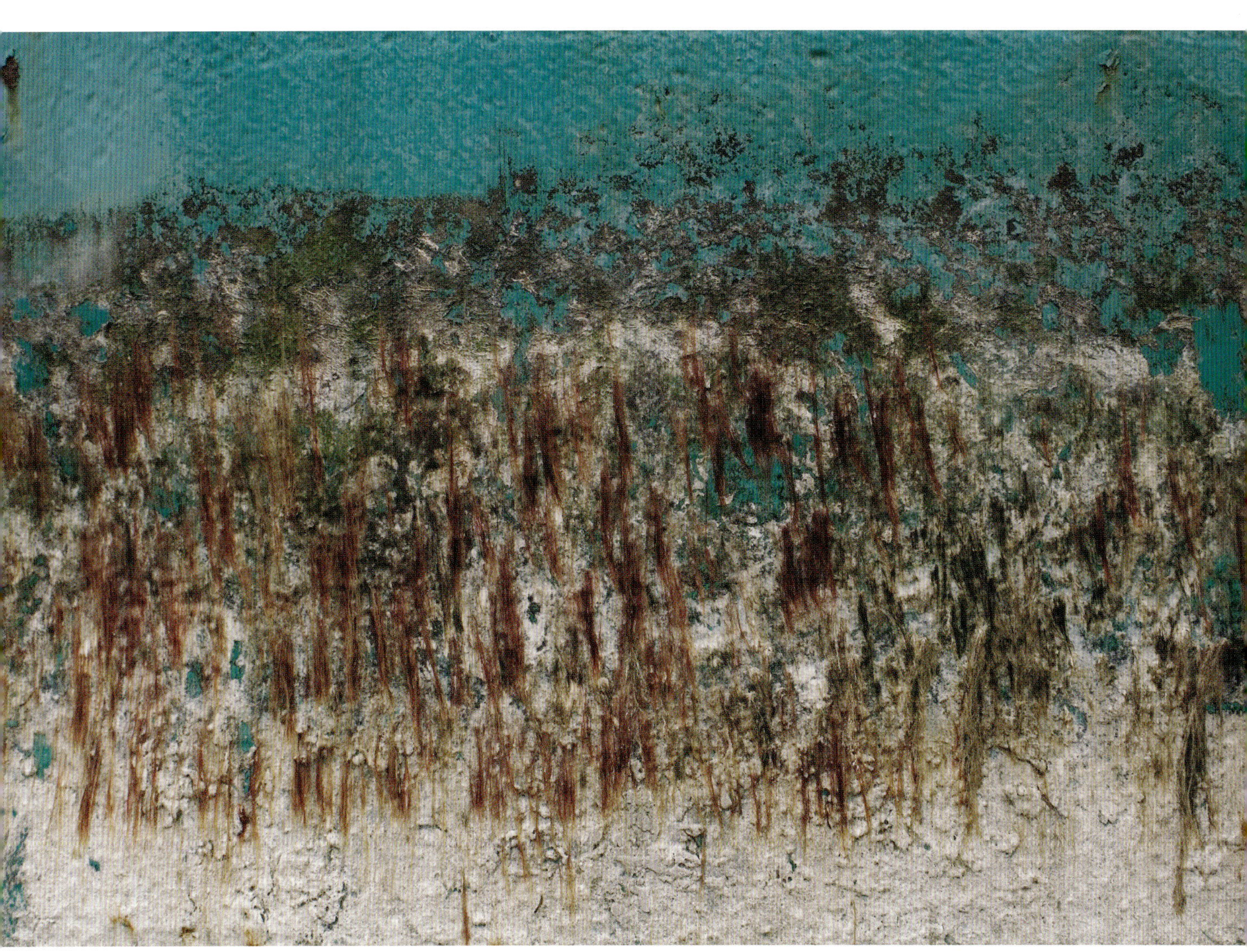

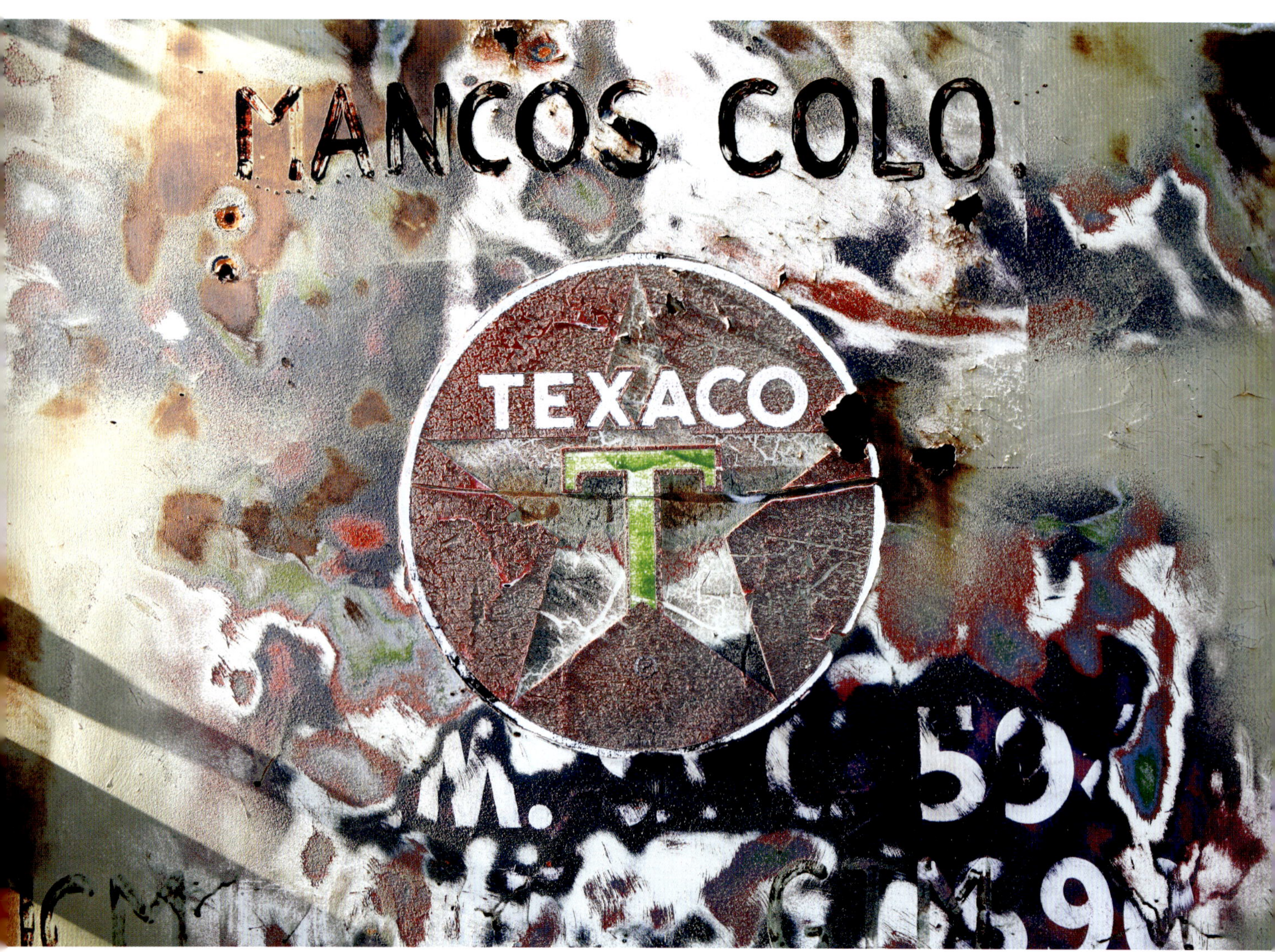
MANCOS COLO
TEXACO
T

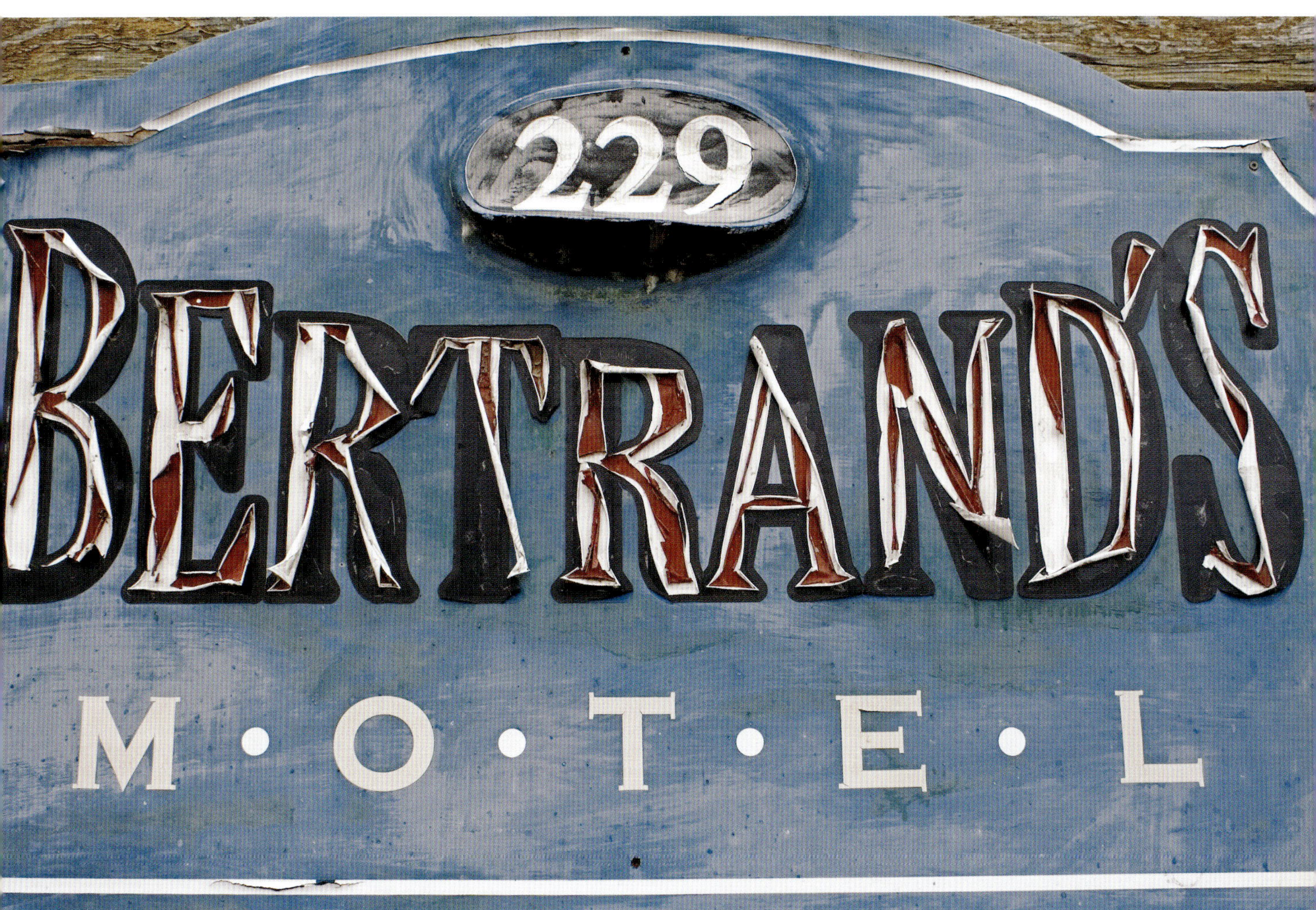
229
BERTRAND'S
M•O•T•E•L

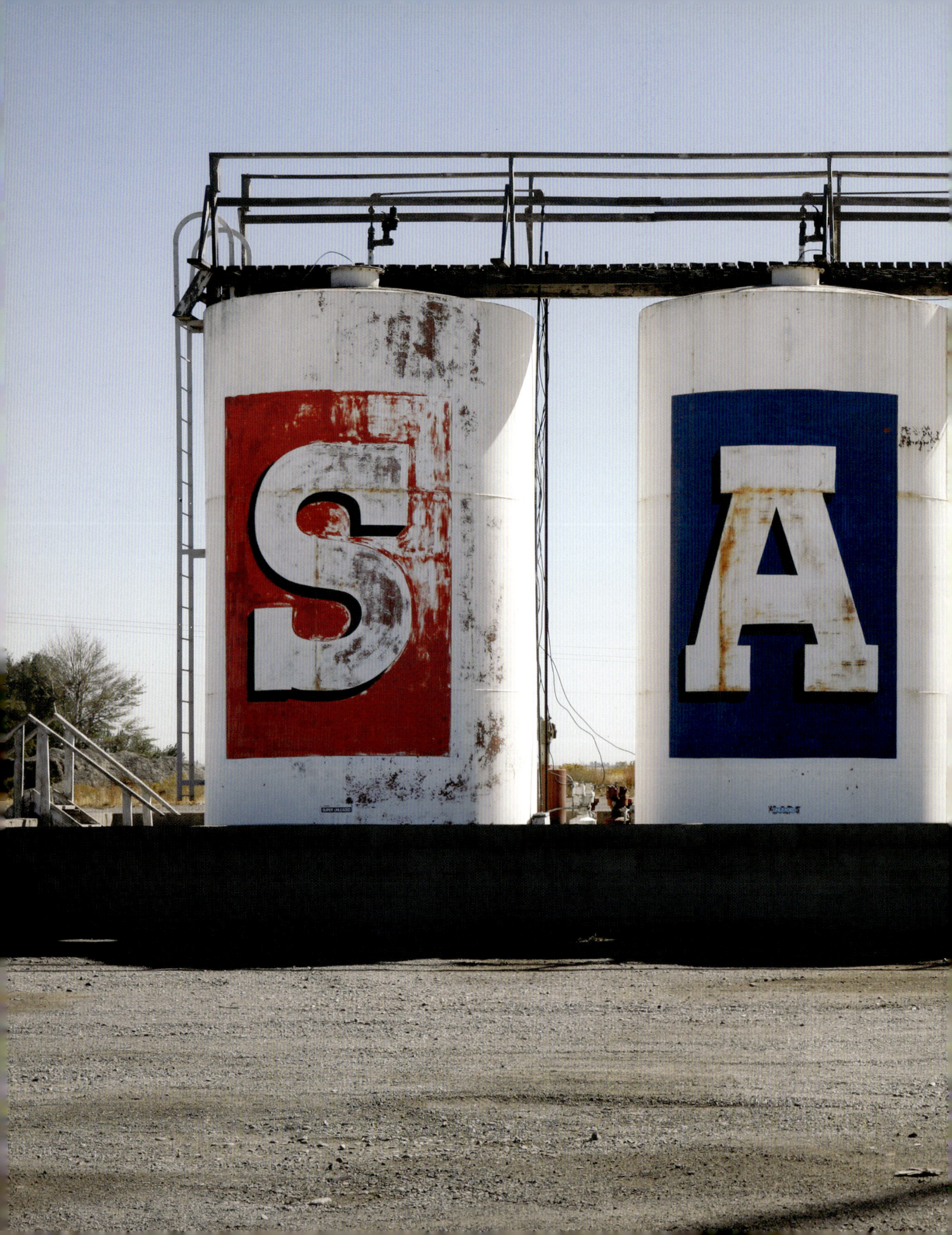
S
A

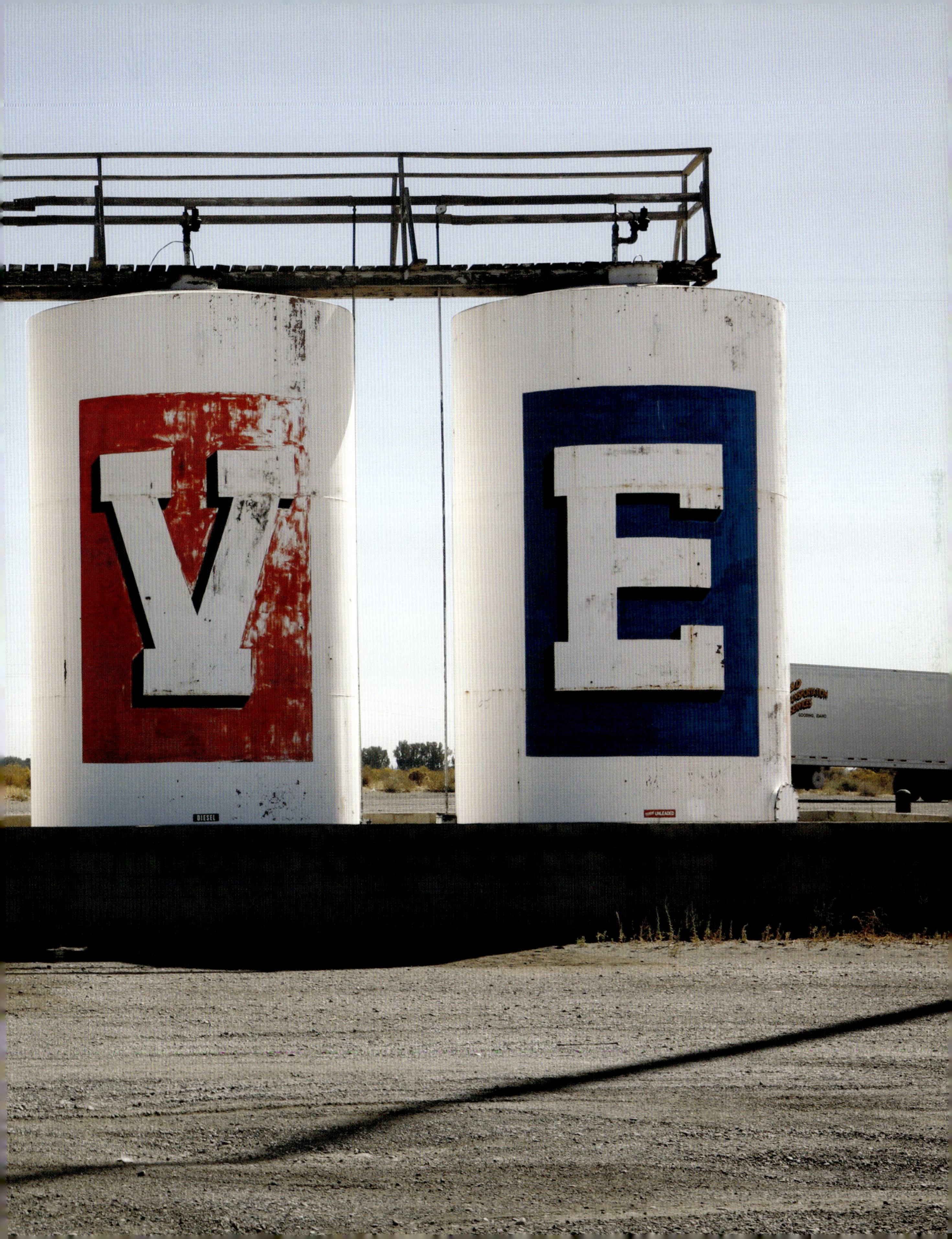
V
E
DIESEL
UNLEADED

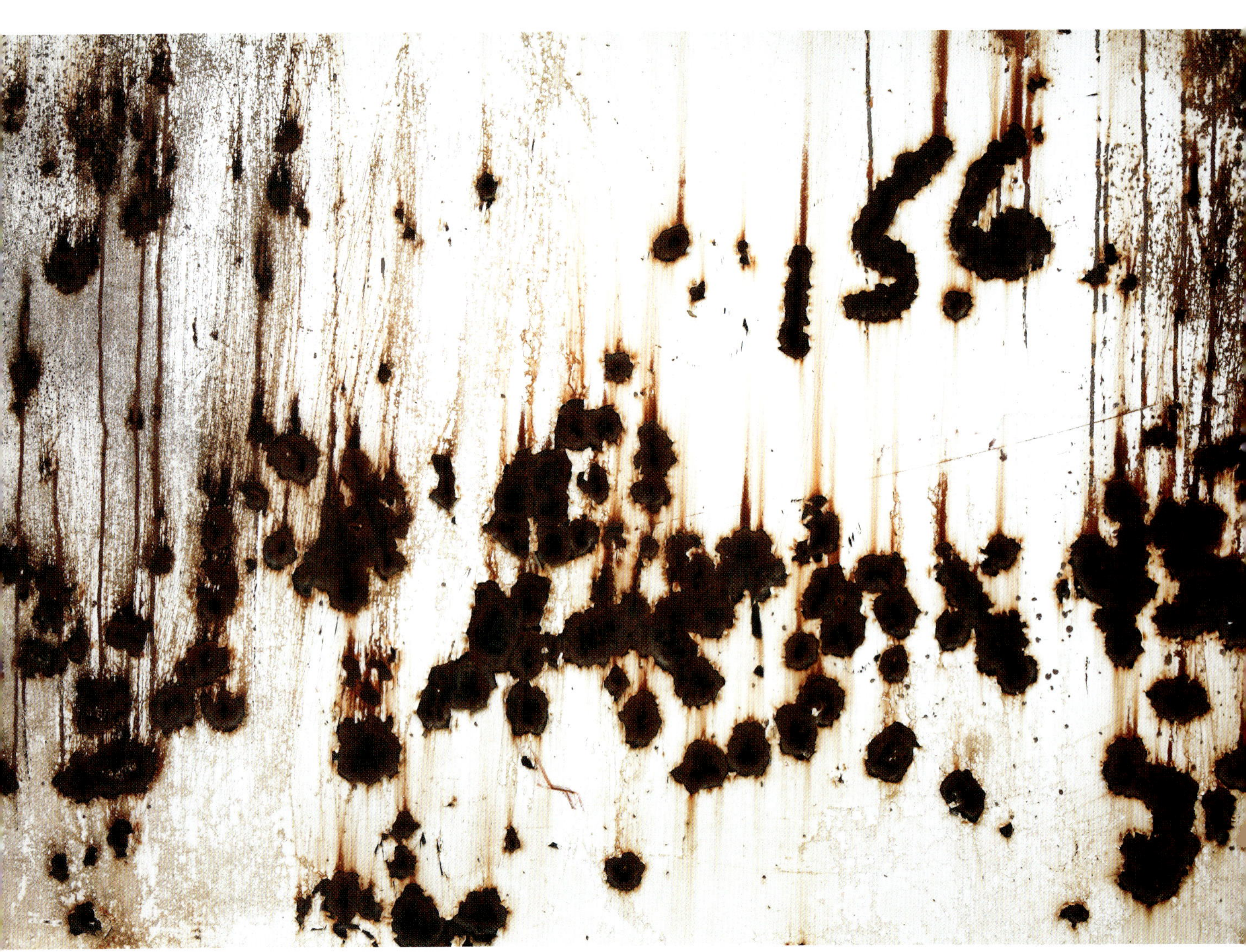
156

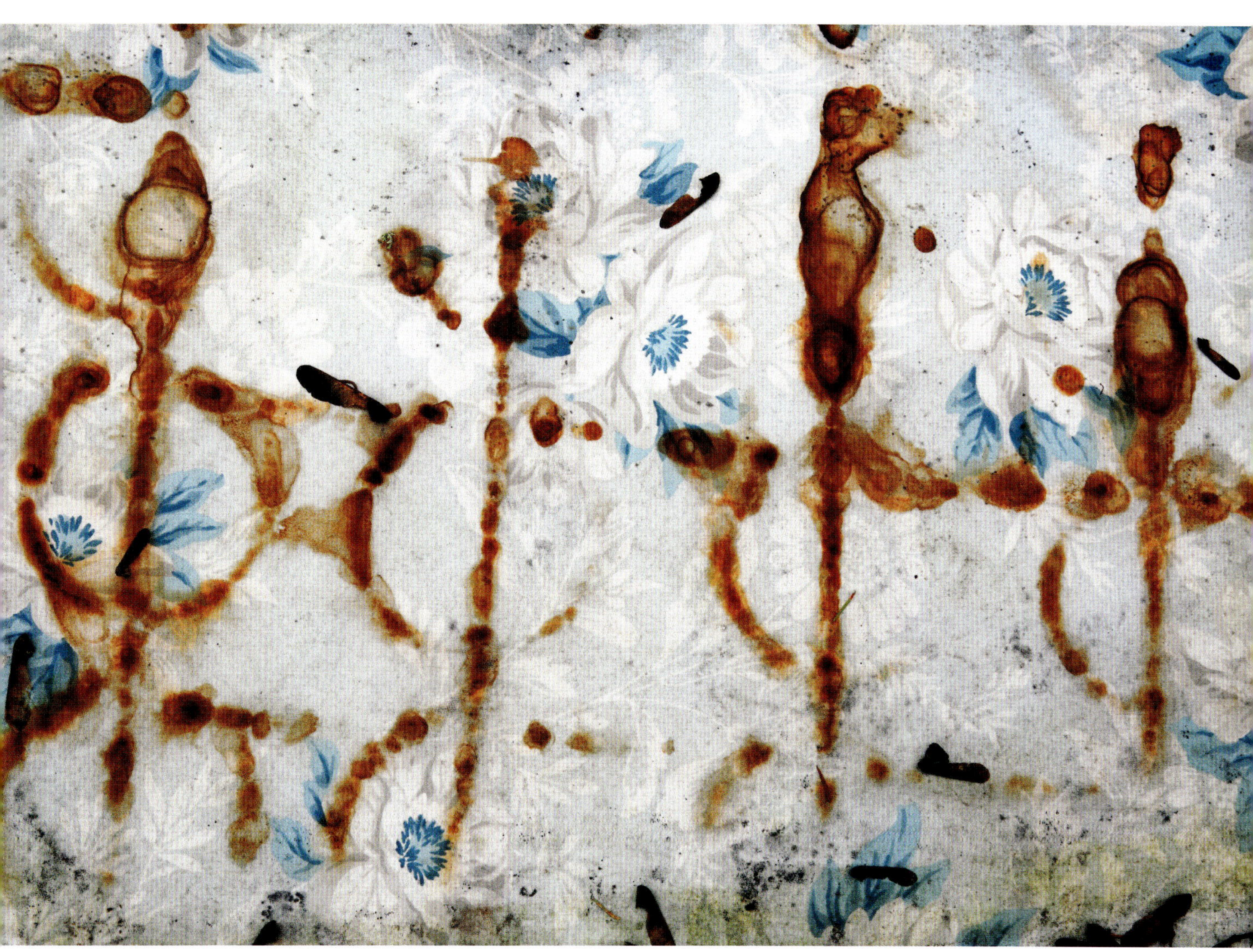

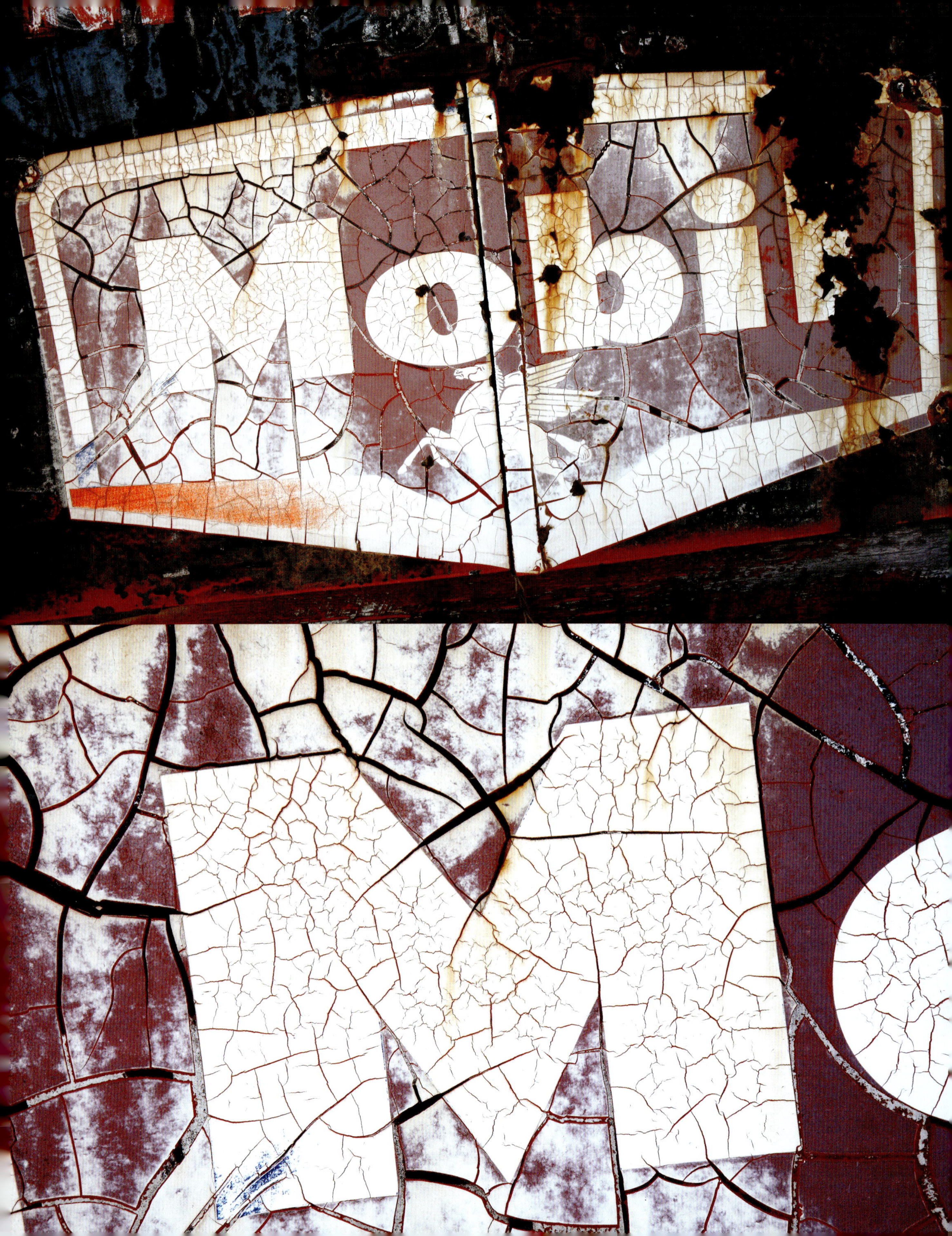
Mobi

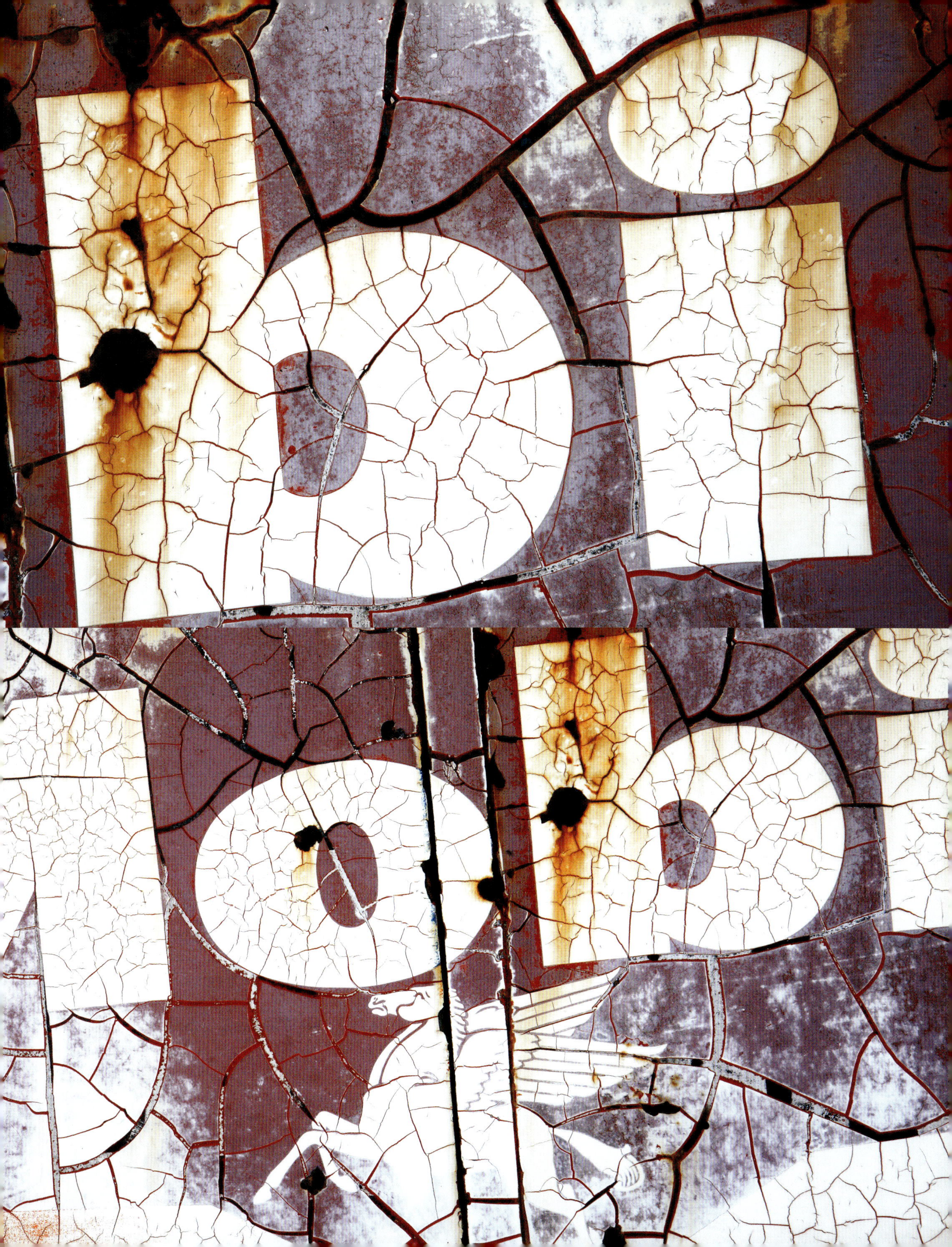

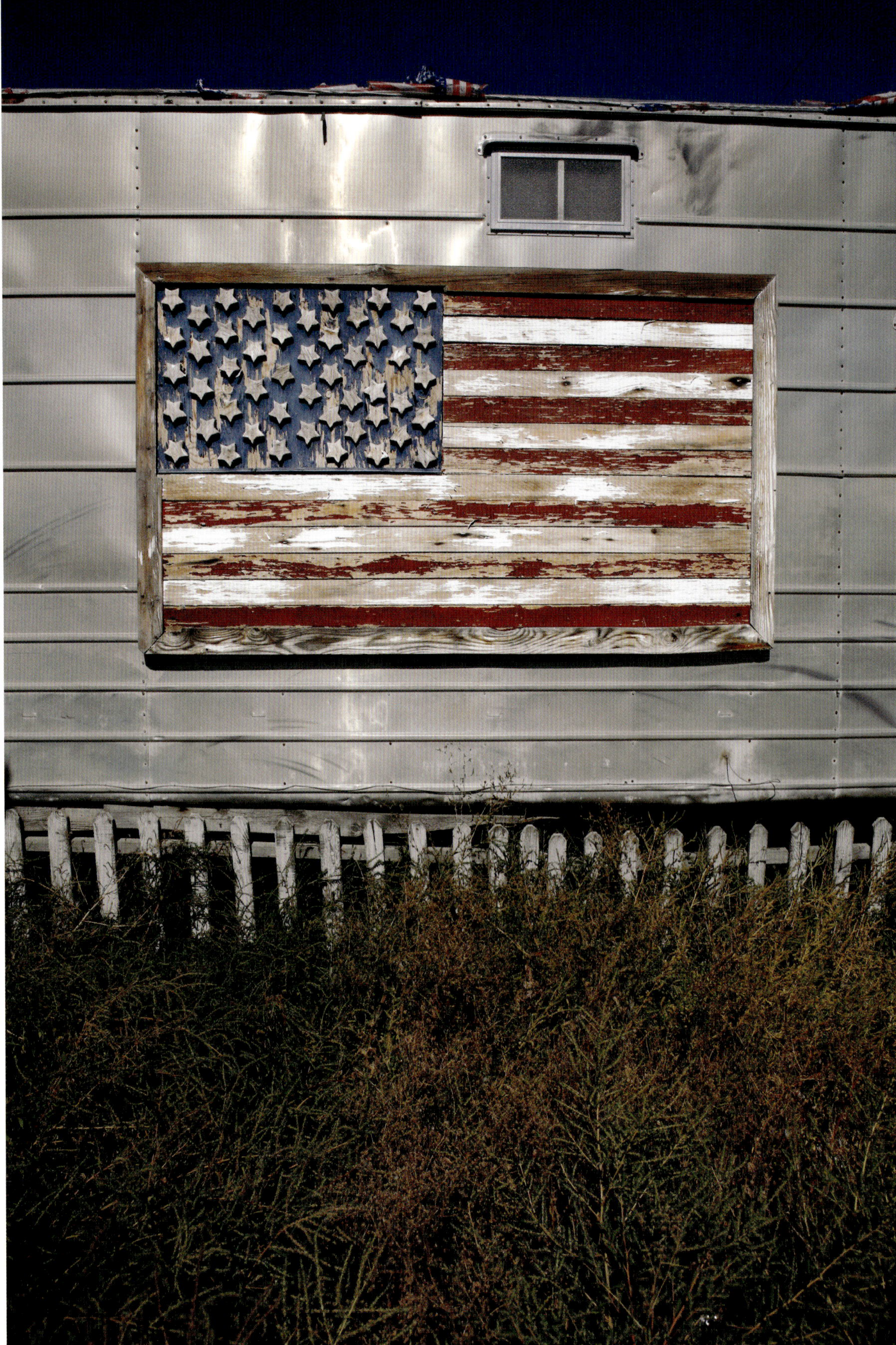

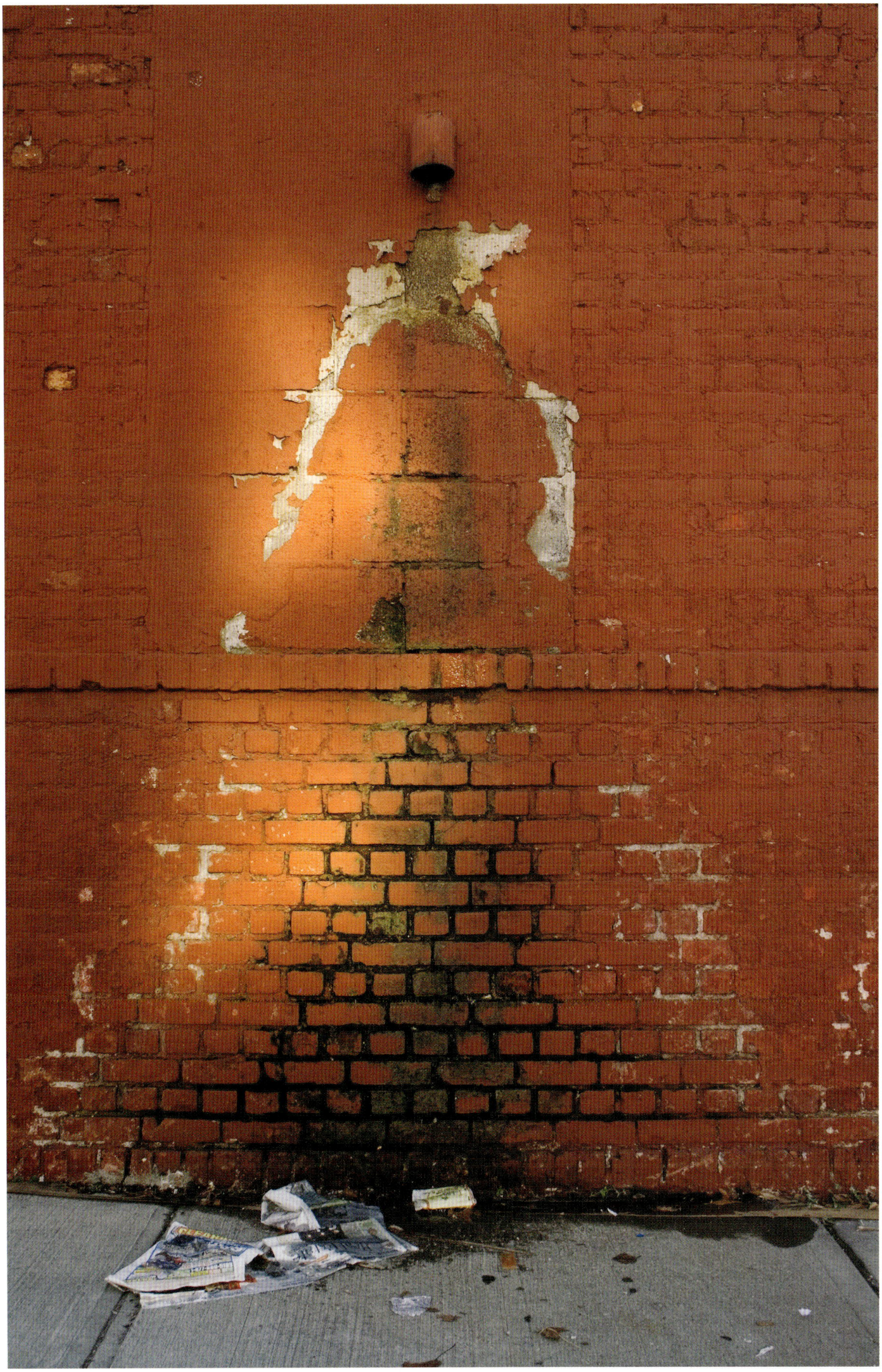

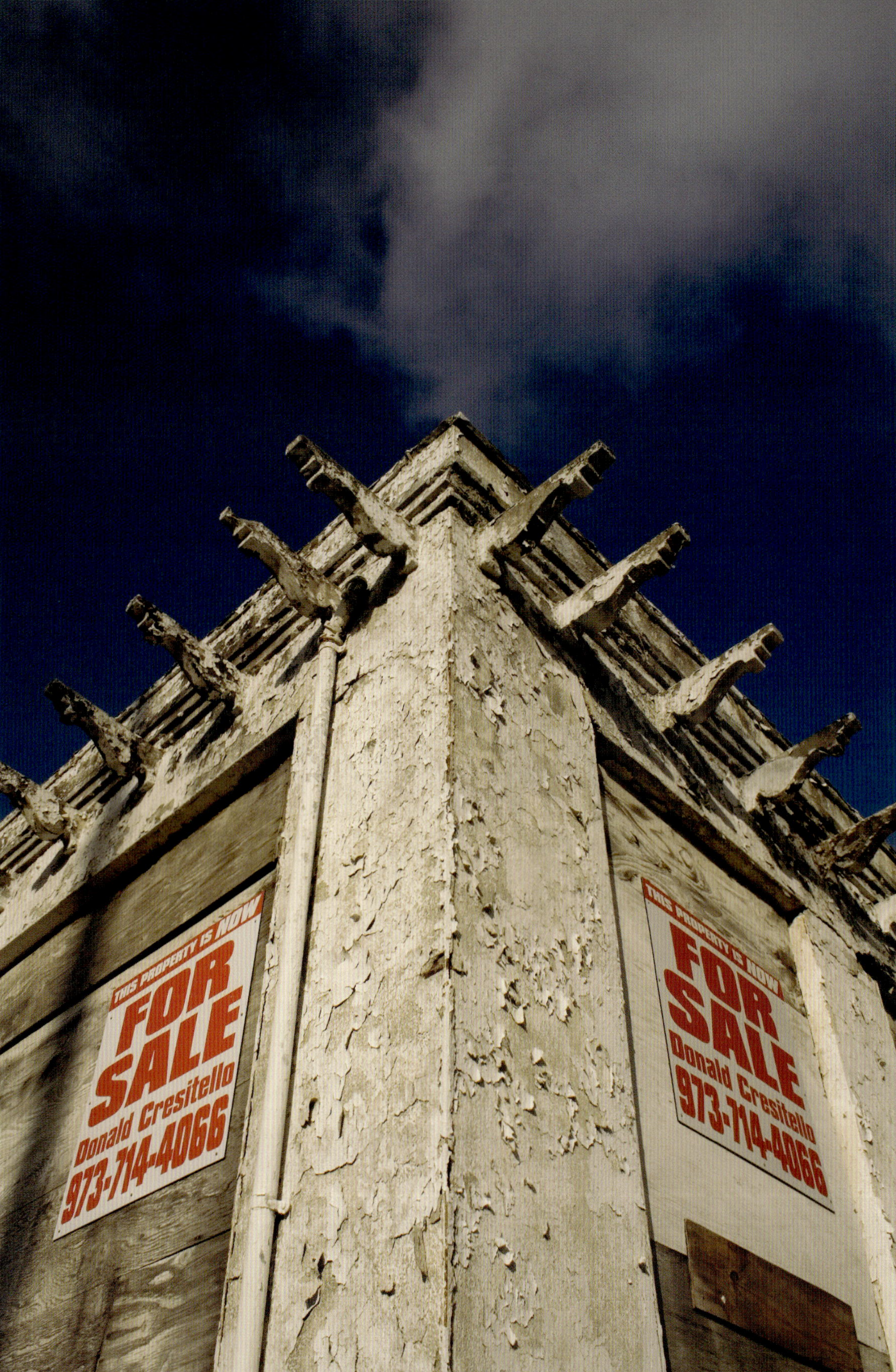
THIS PROPERTY IS NOW
FOR SALE
Donald Cresitello
973-714-4066
THIS PROPERTY IS NOW
FOR SALE
Donald Cresitello
973-714-4066

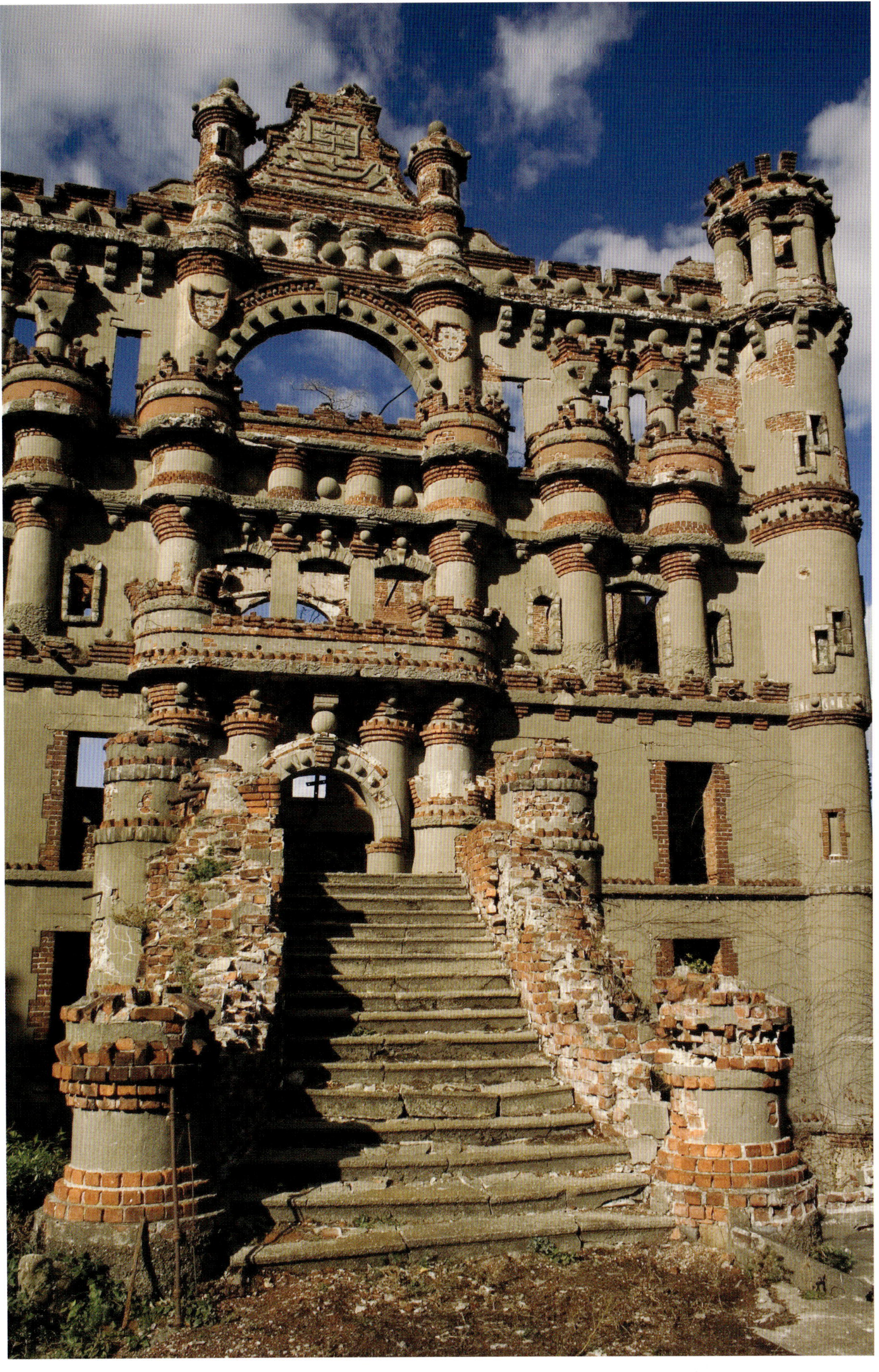

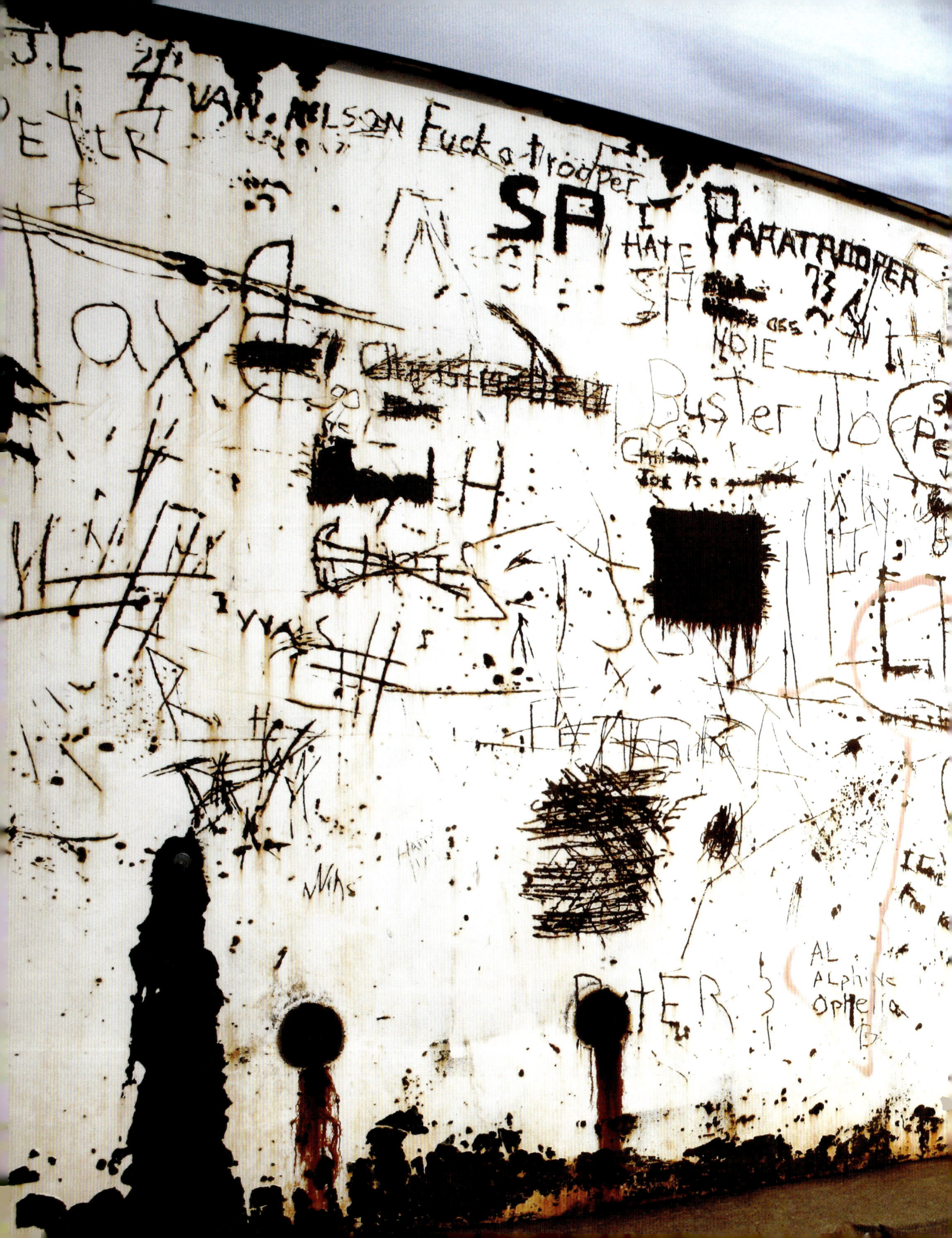

J.L
Fuck a trooper
SP
I HATE
PARATROOPER
Buster
PETER
AL
Ophelia

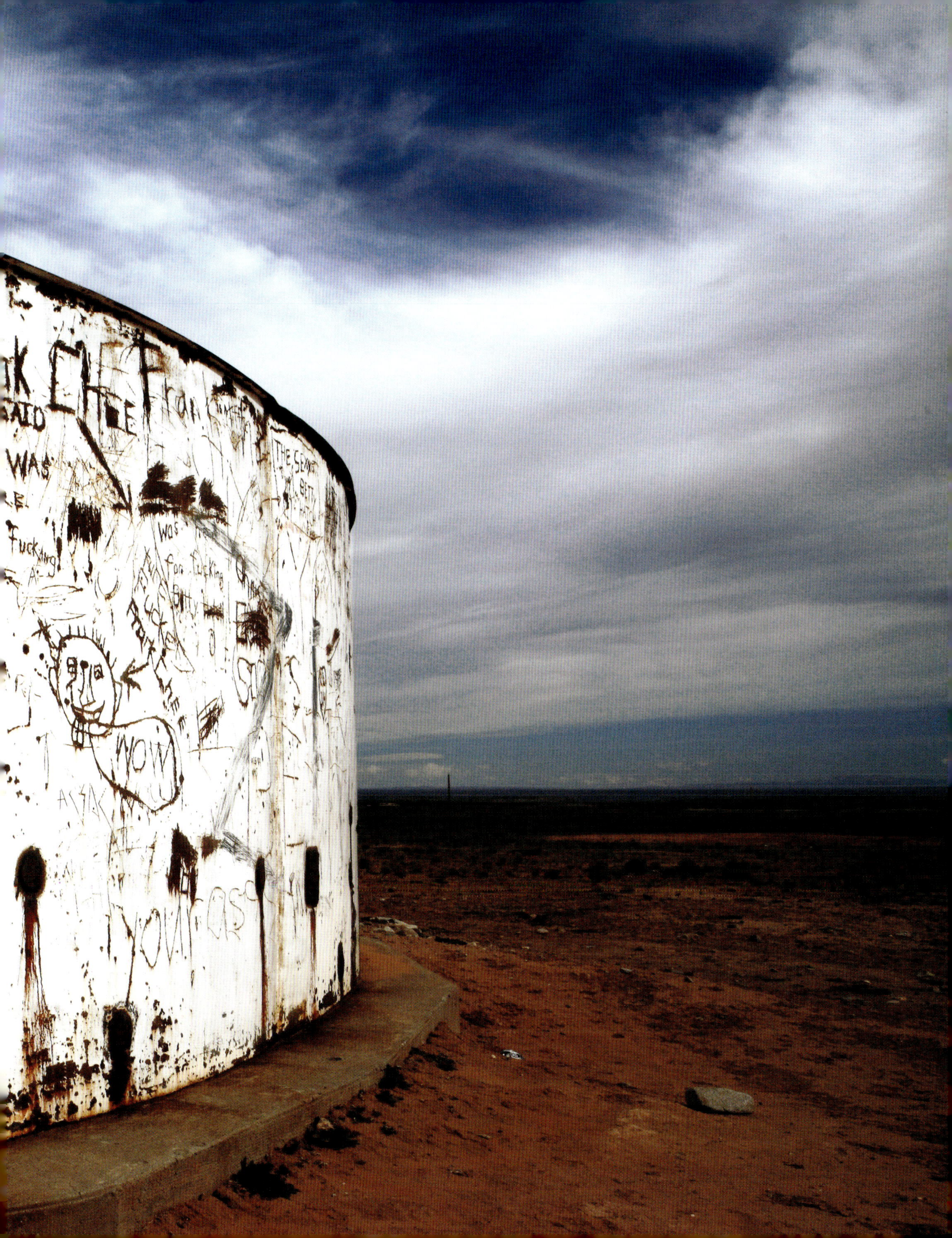
WOW

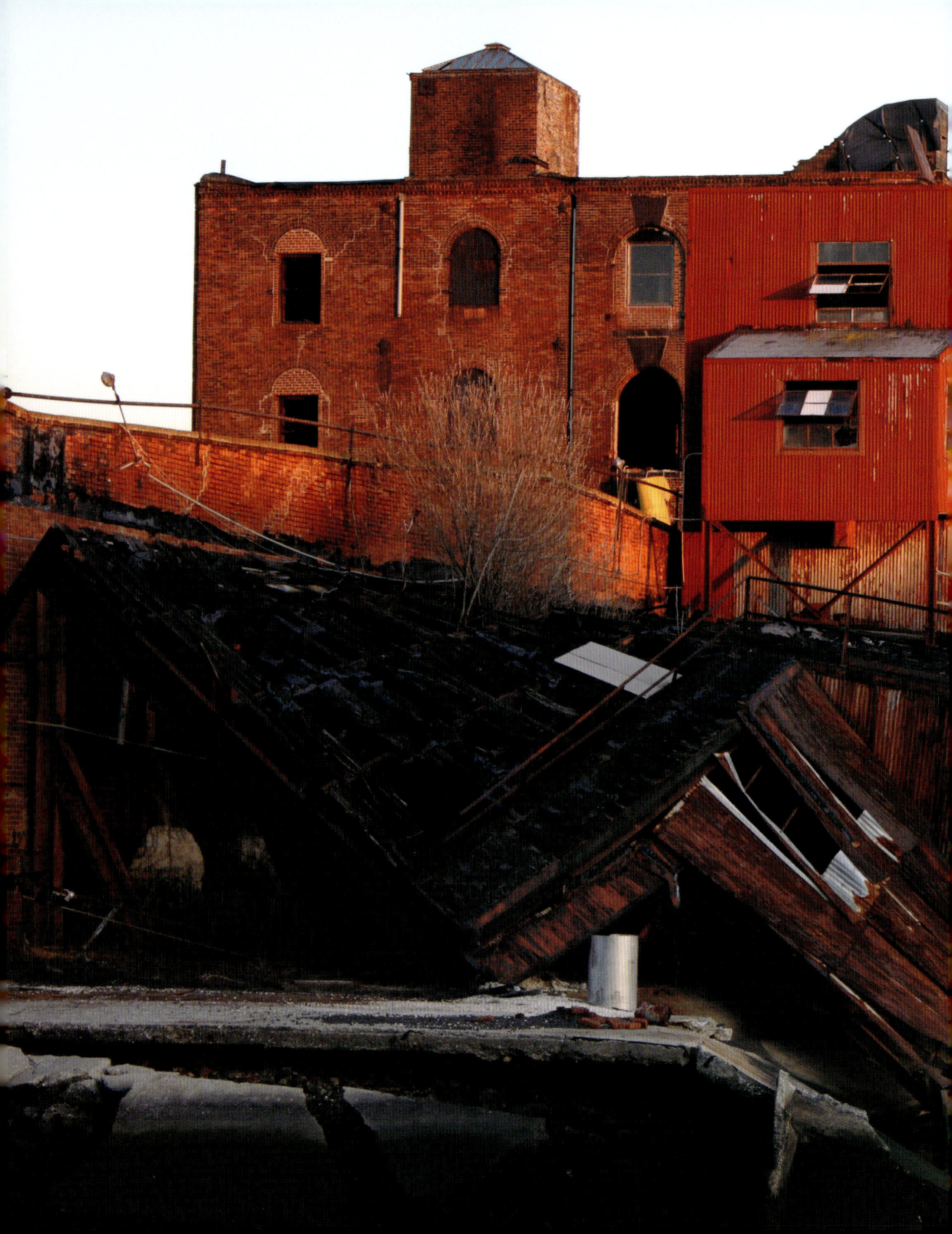

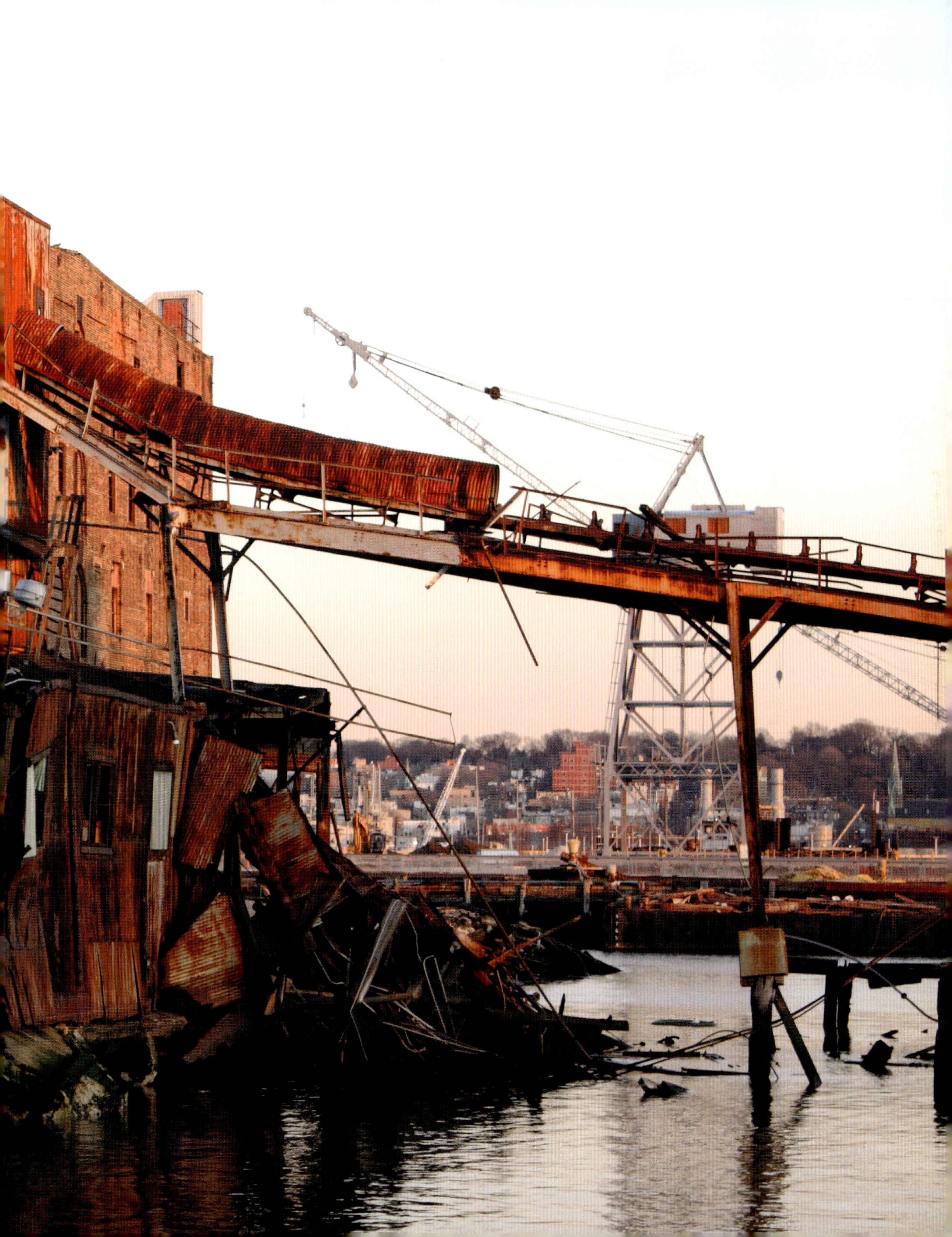

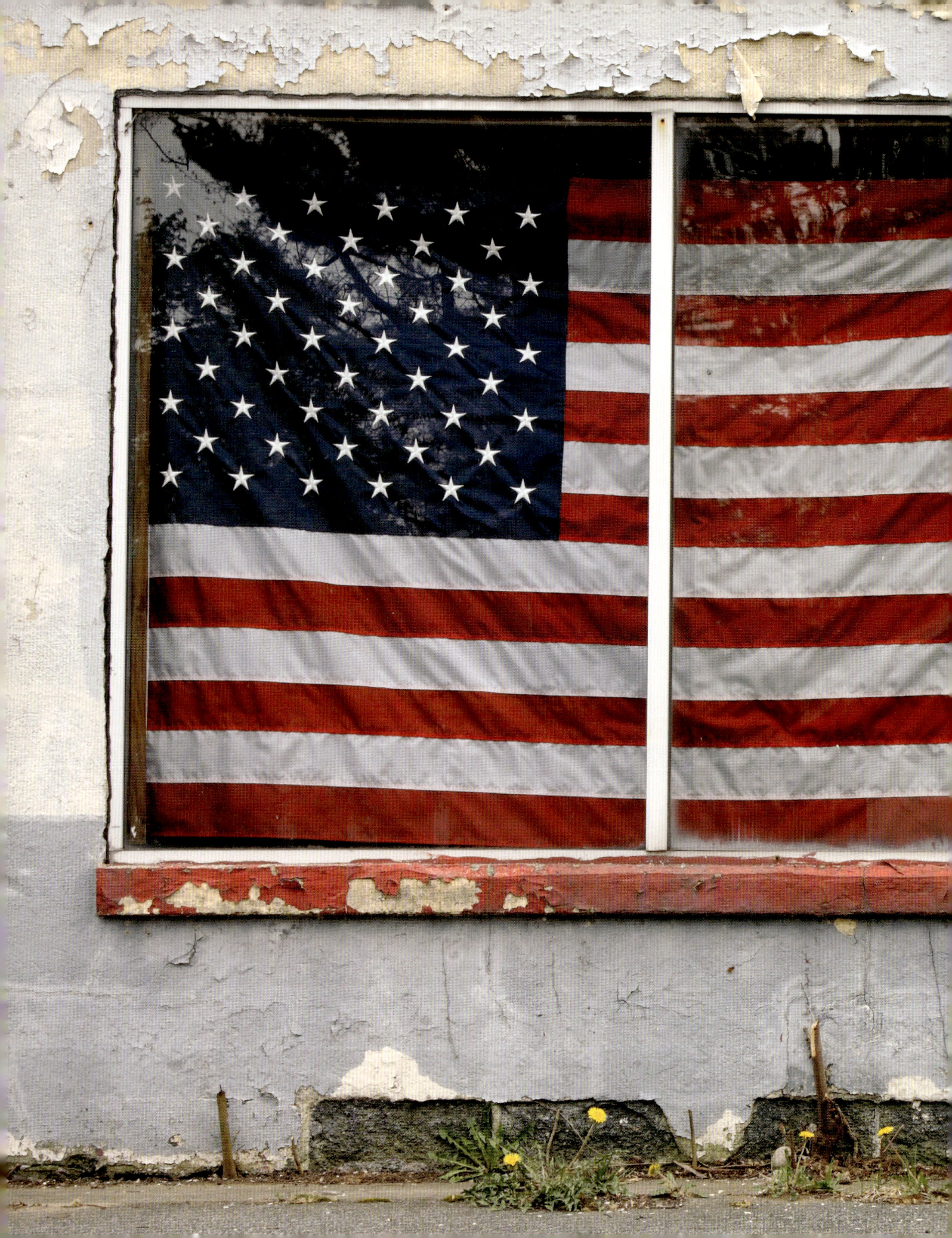

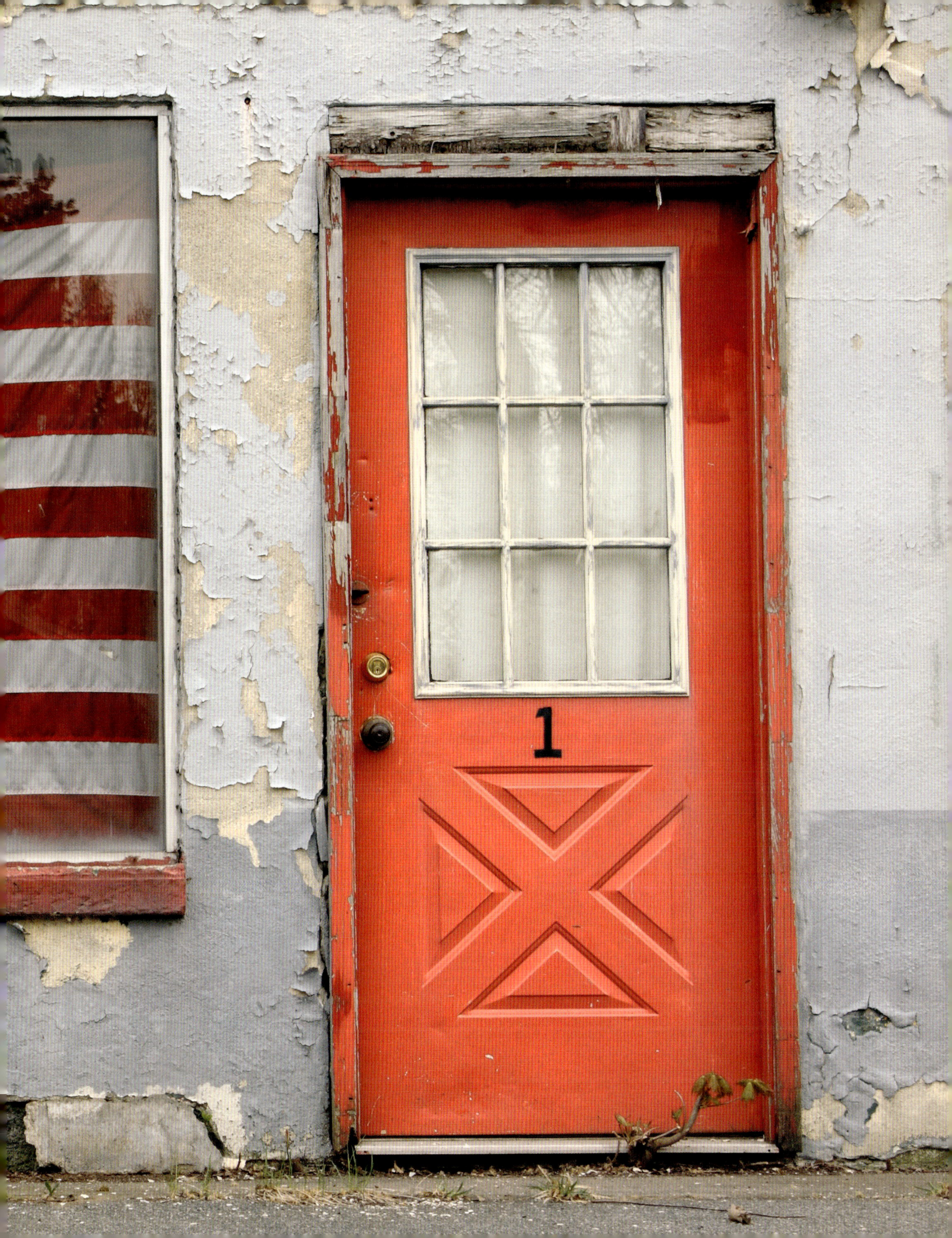
1

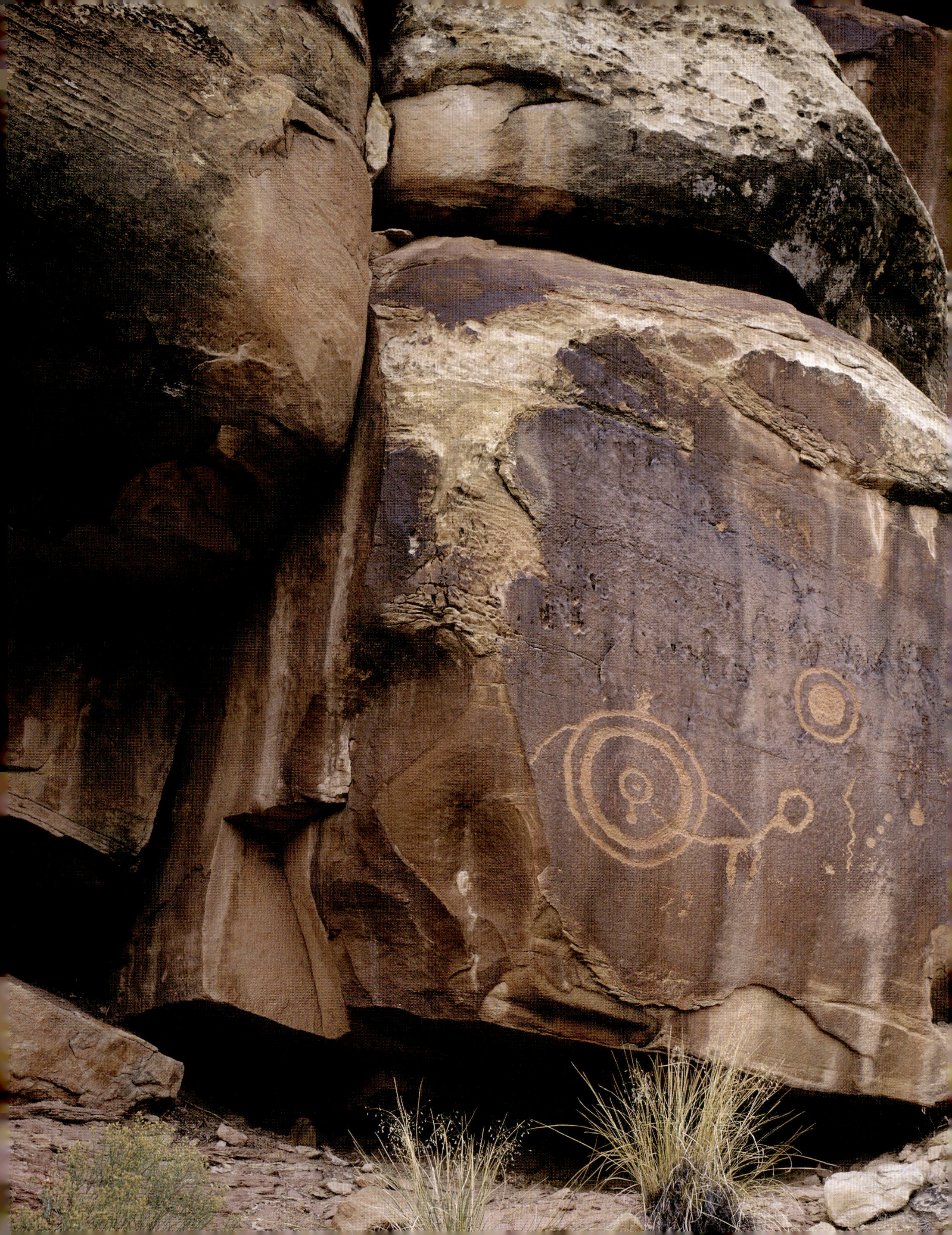

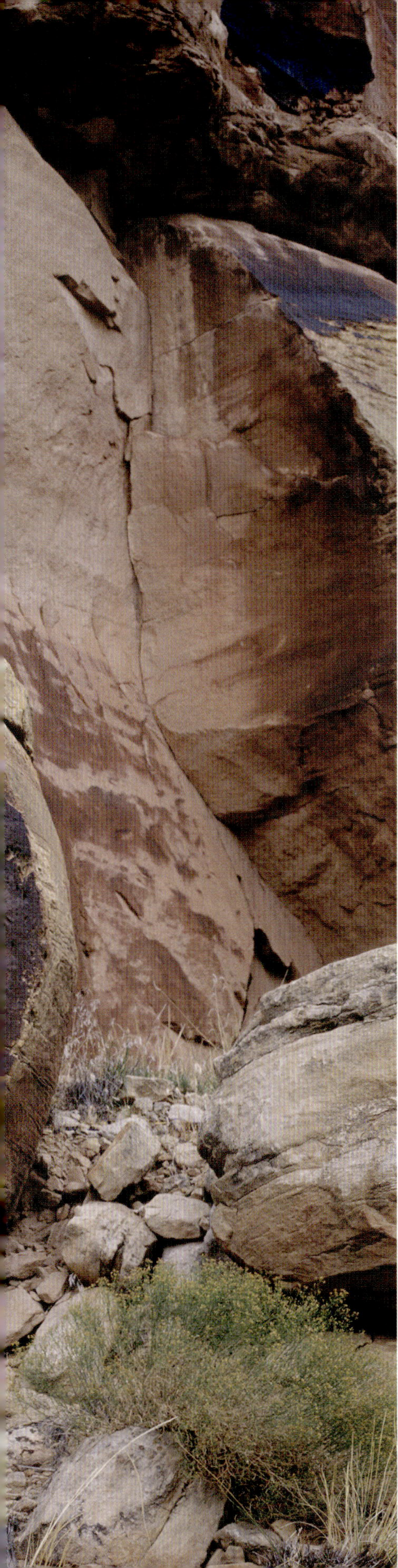

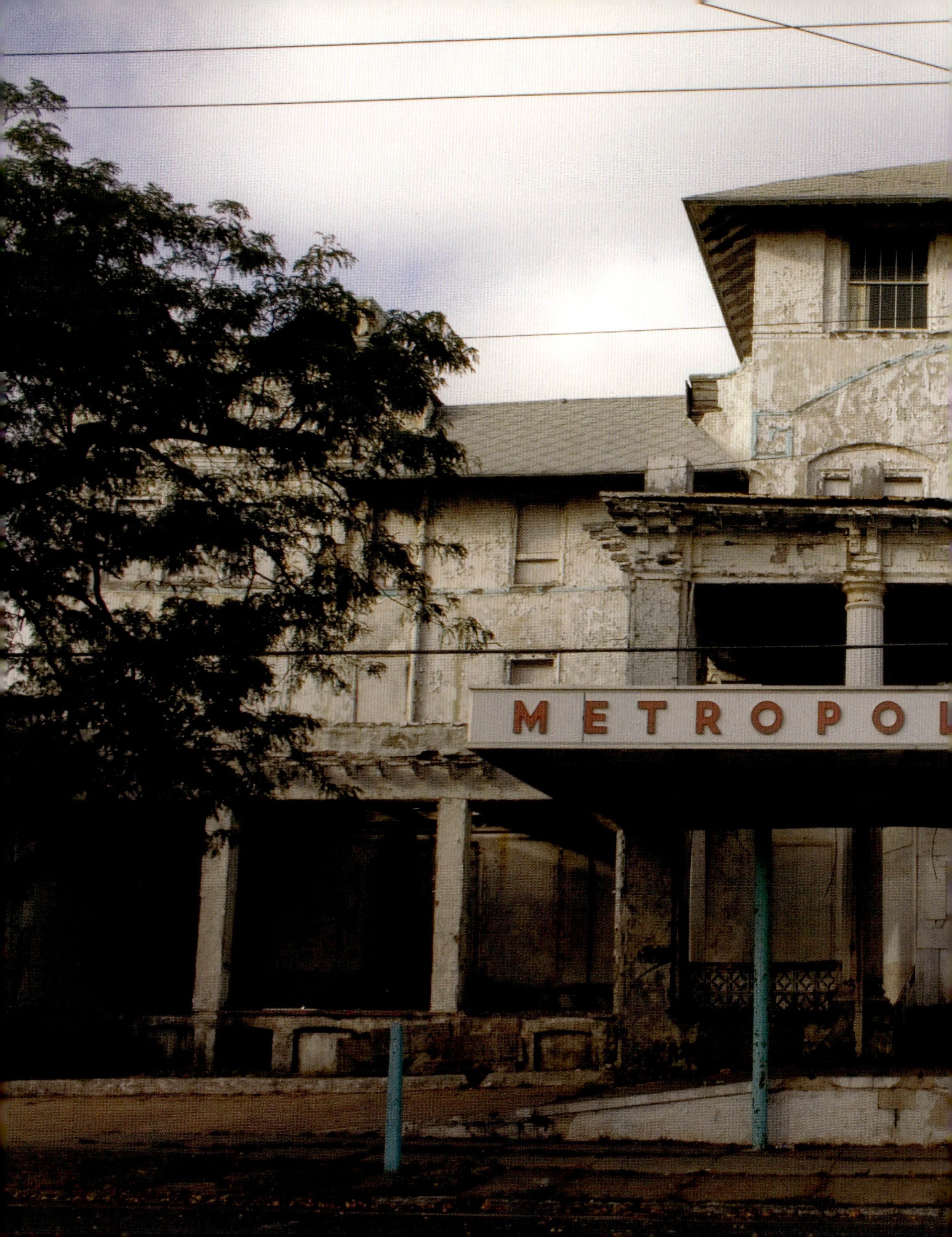
METROPOL

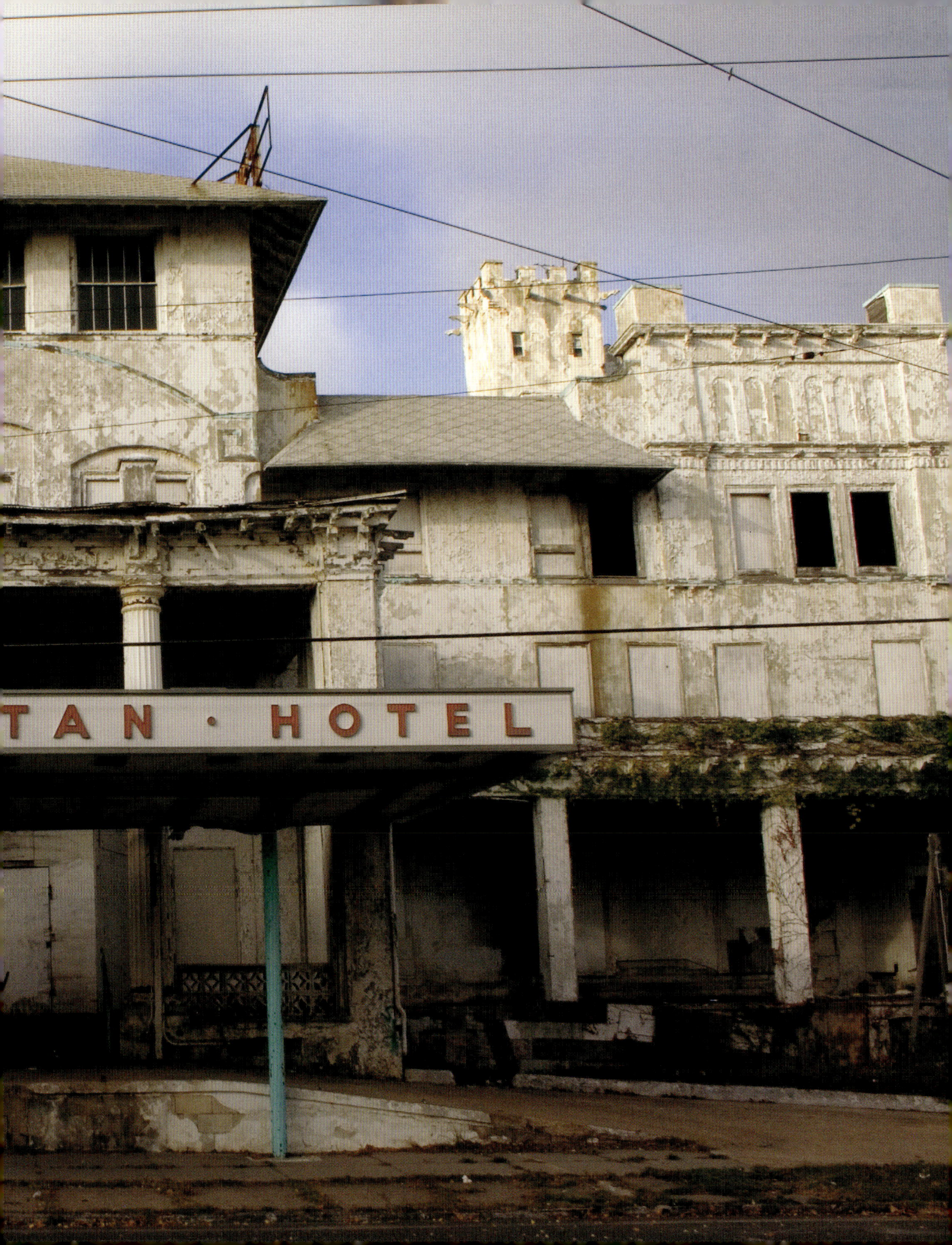
TAN · HOTEL

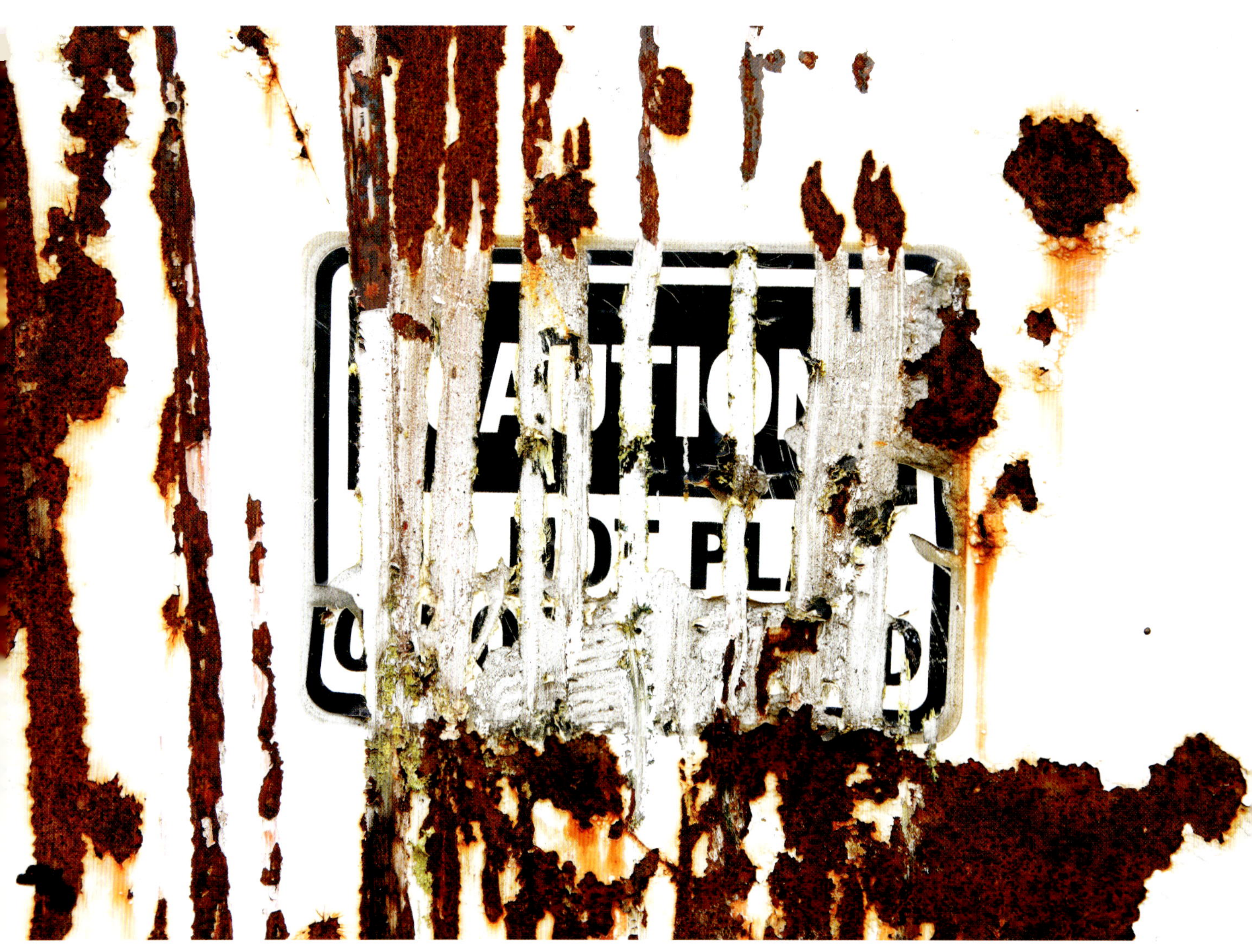
AUTION
PLA

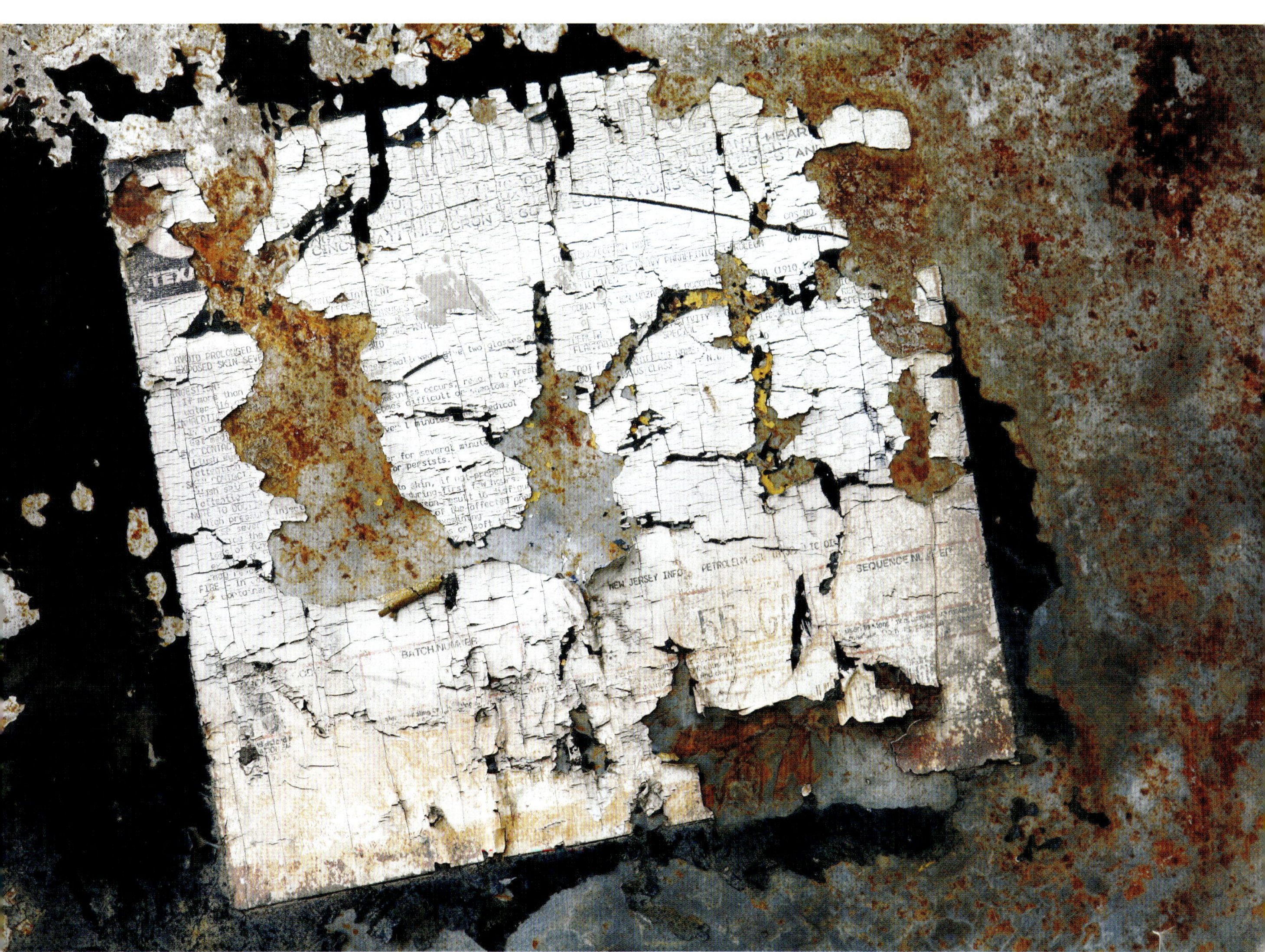
AVOID PROLONGED
EXPOSED SKIN
NEW JERSEY INFO
PETROLEUM
BATCH NUMBER

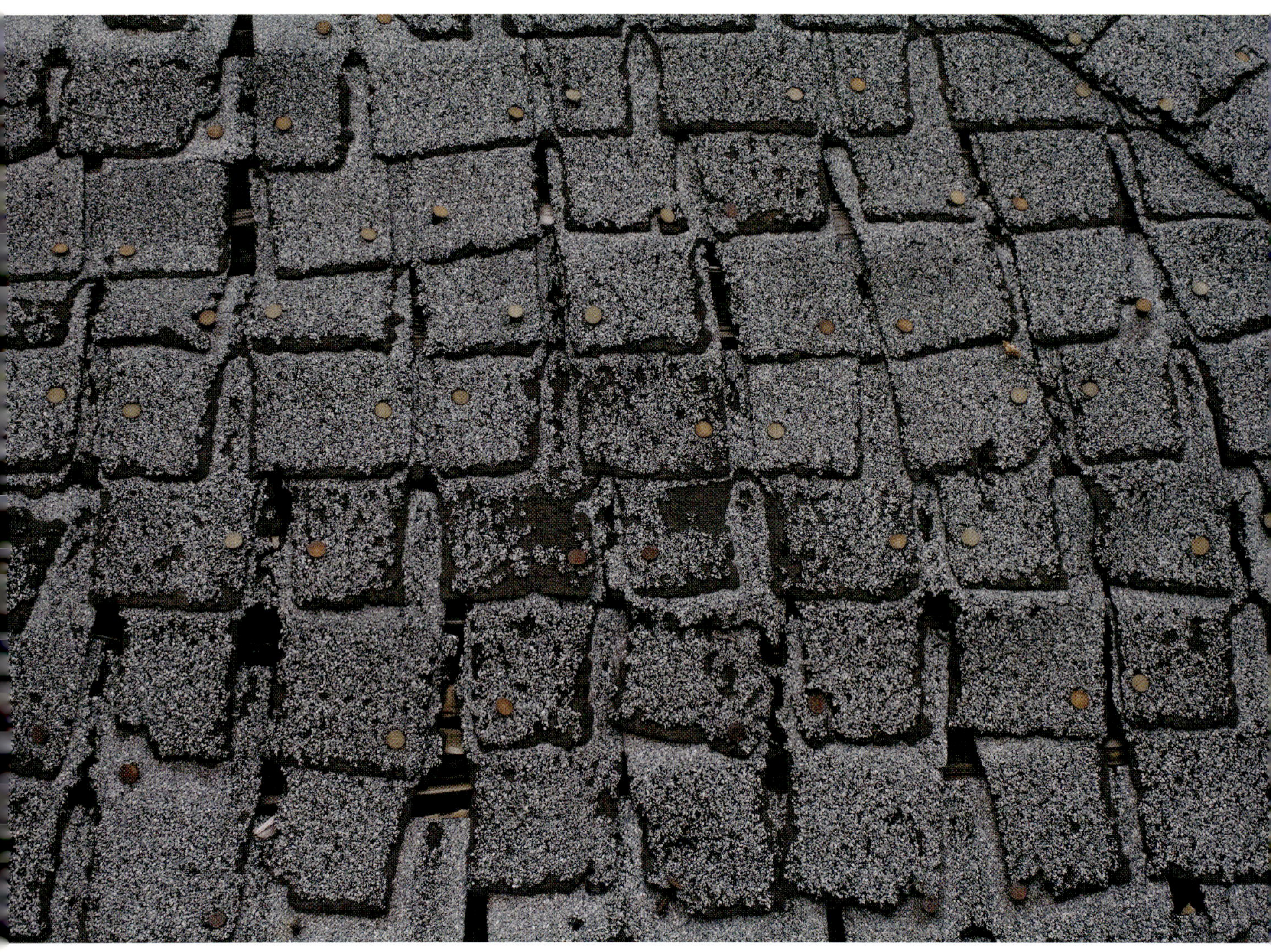

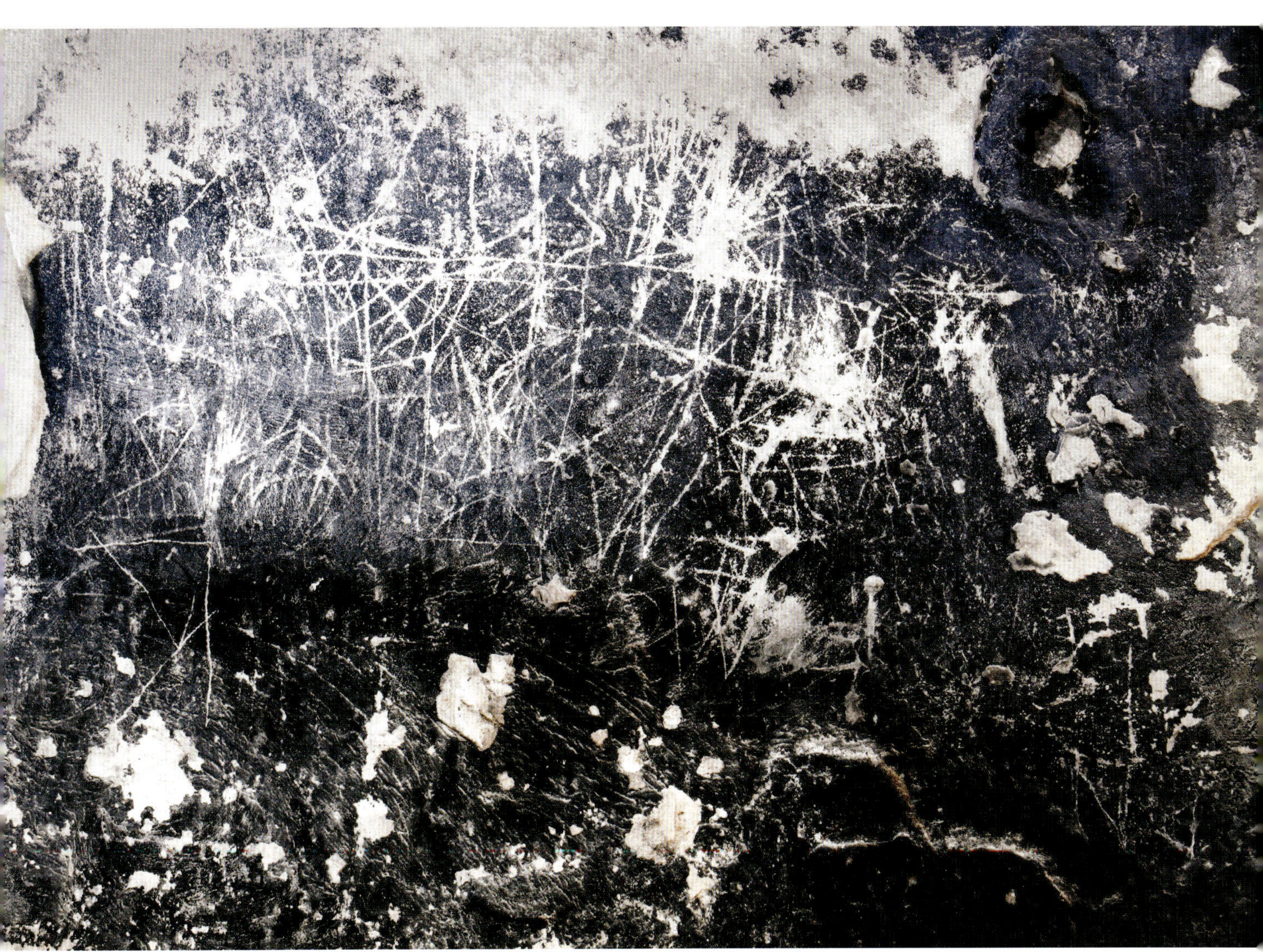

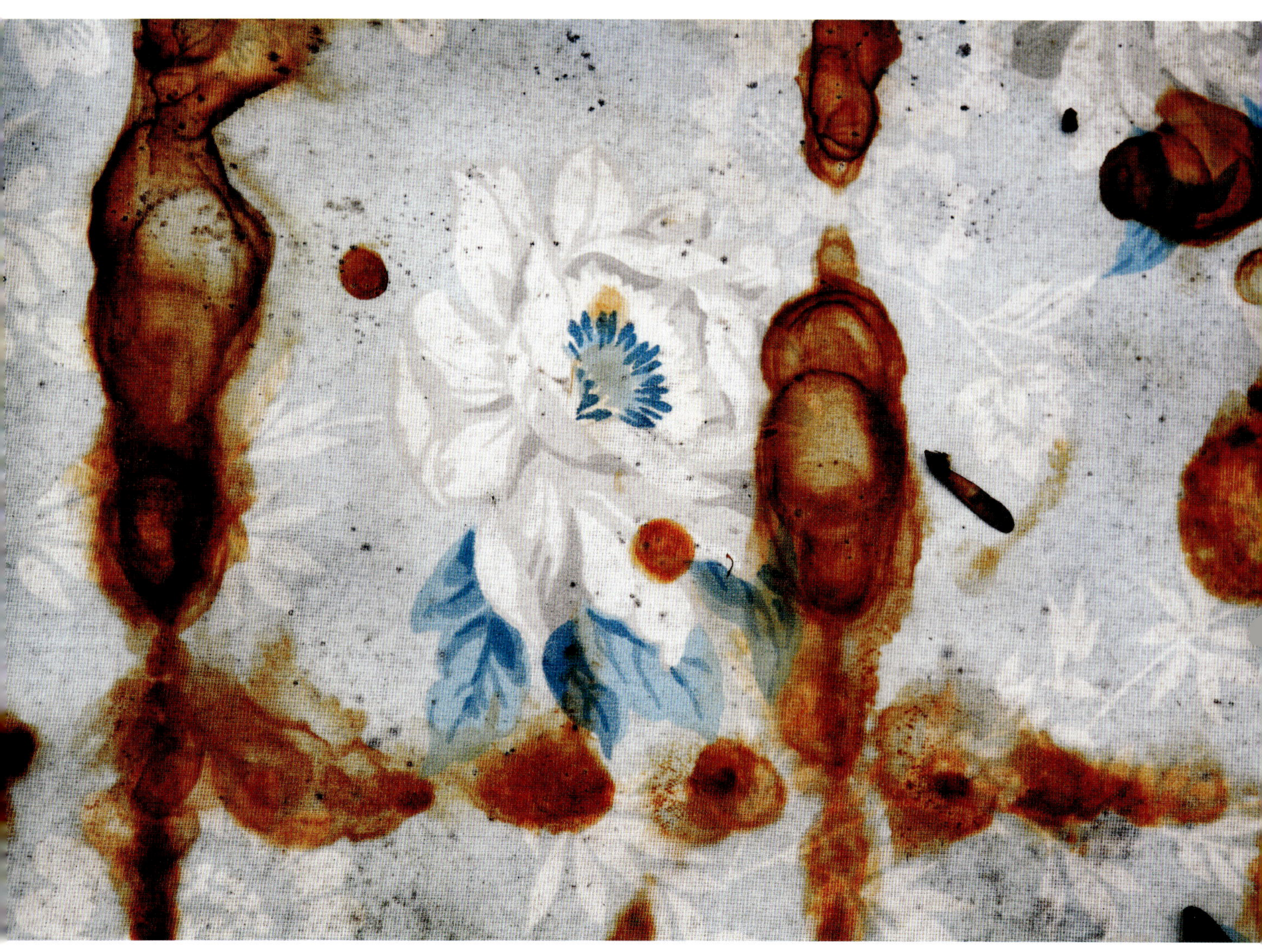

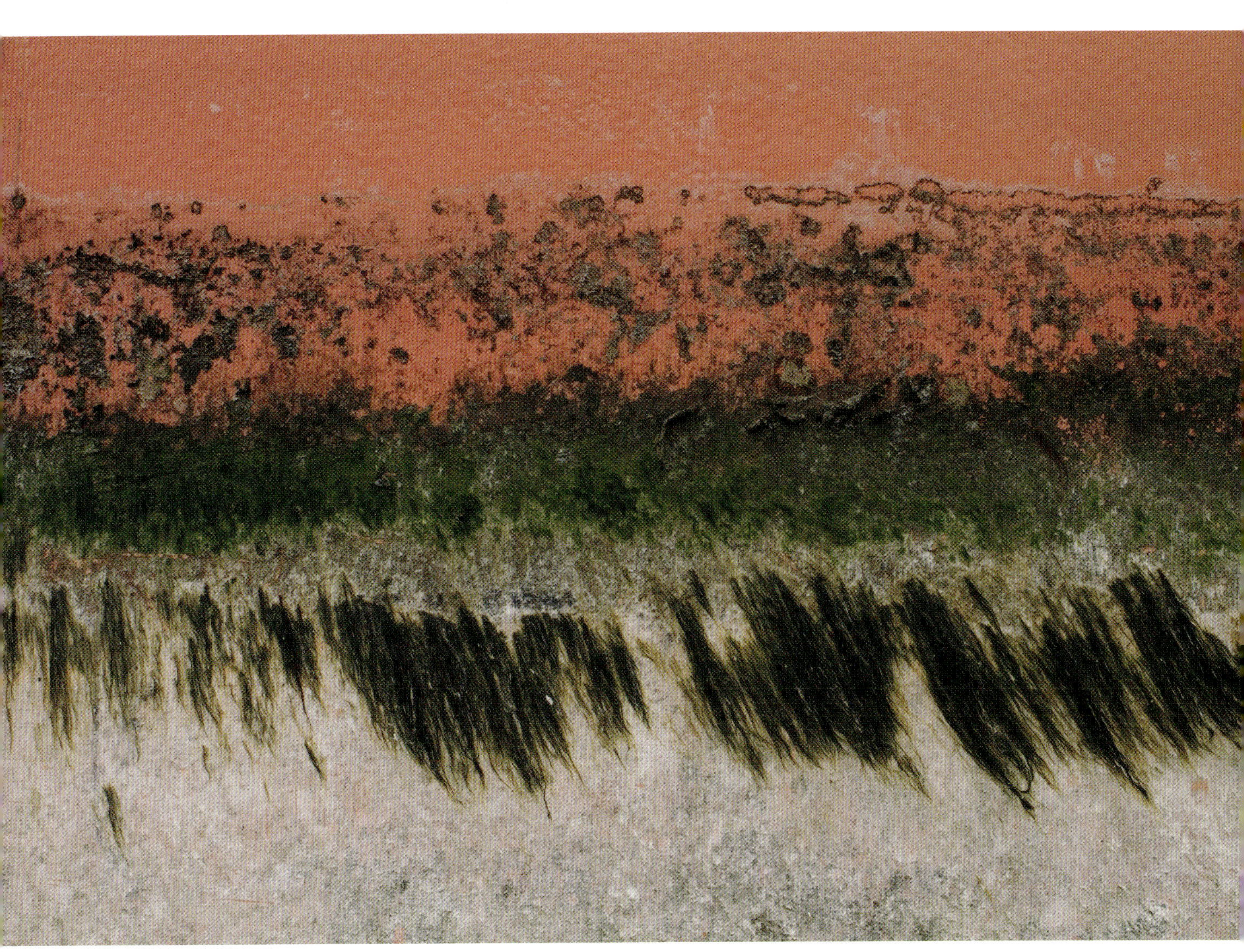

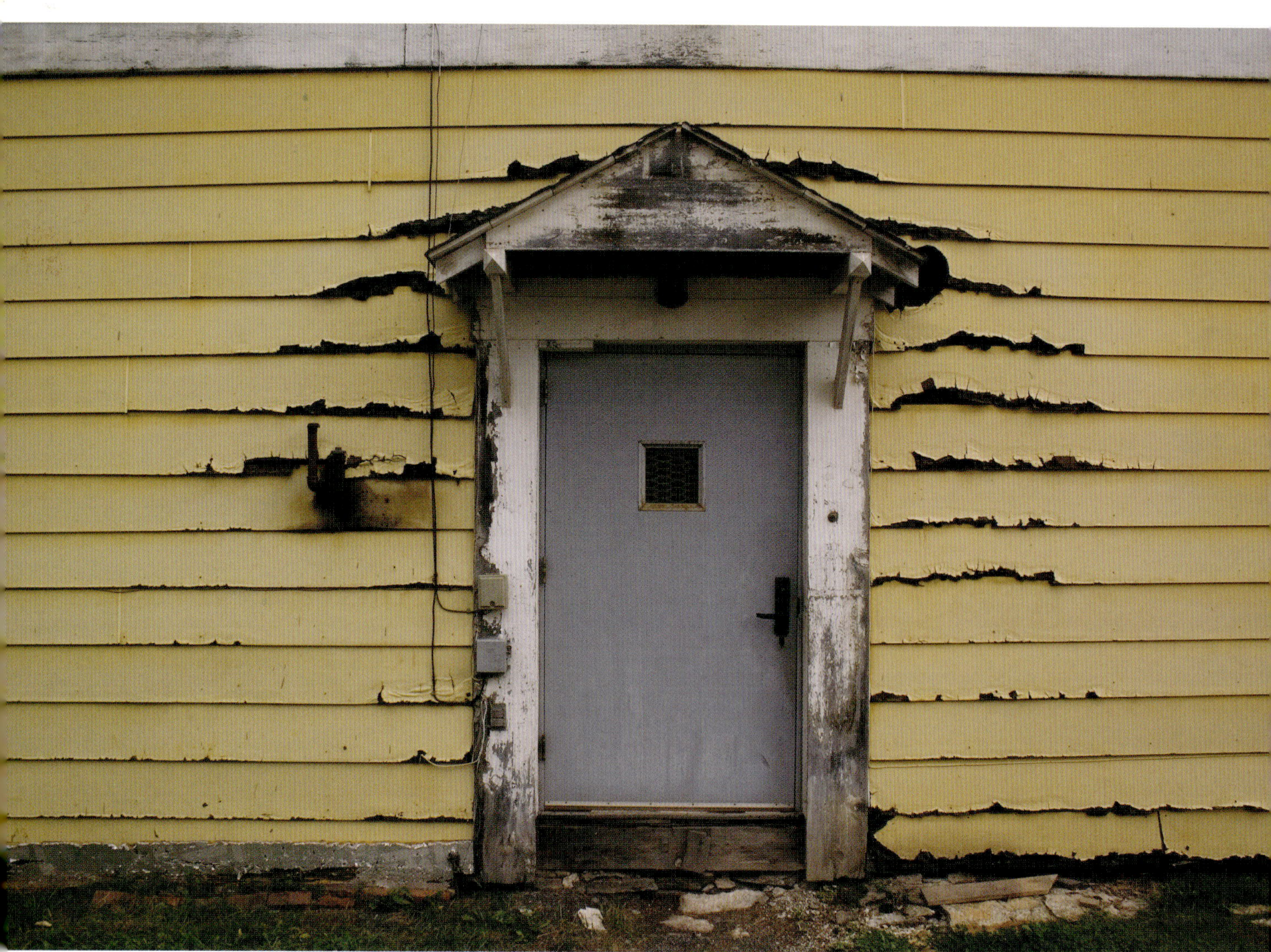

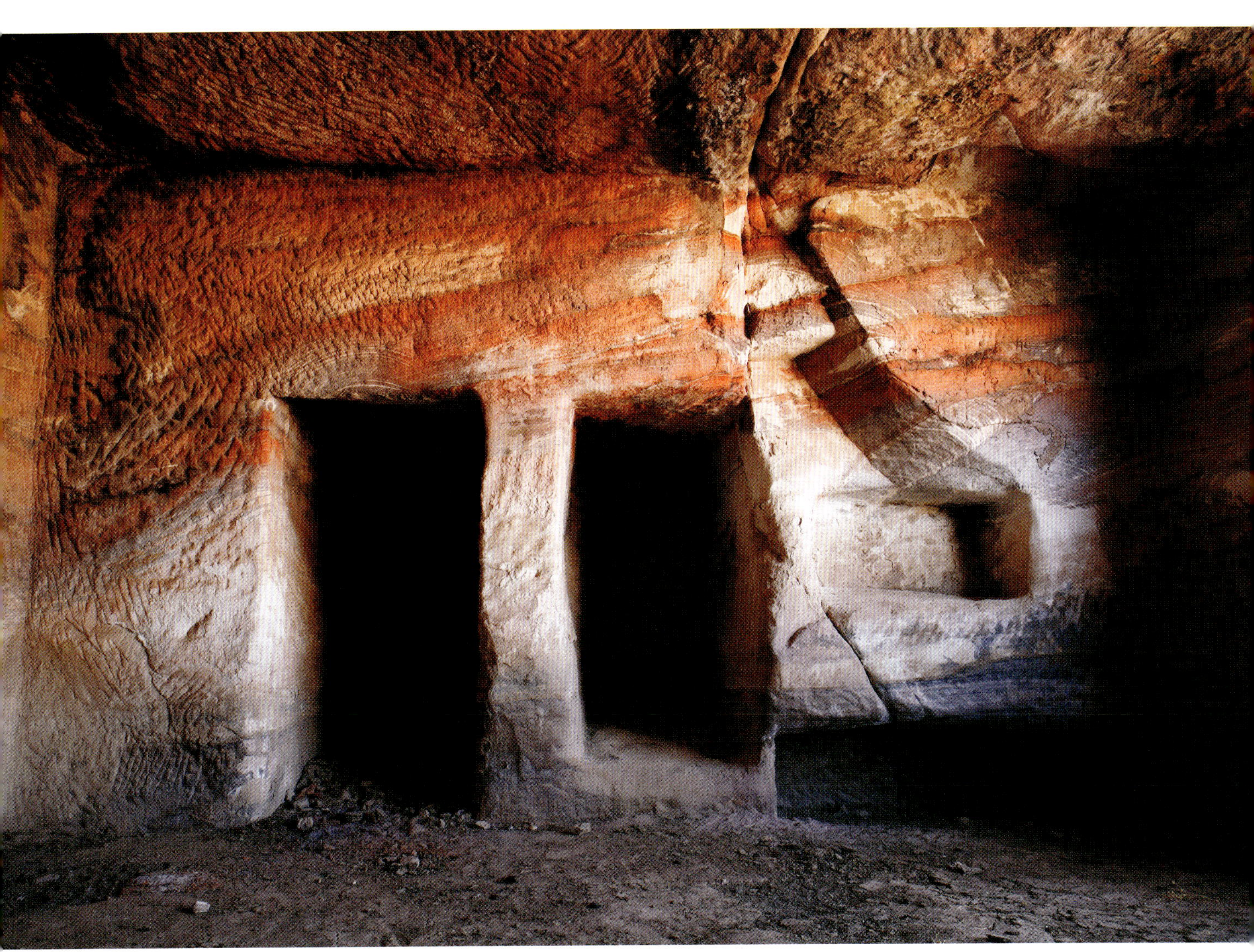

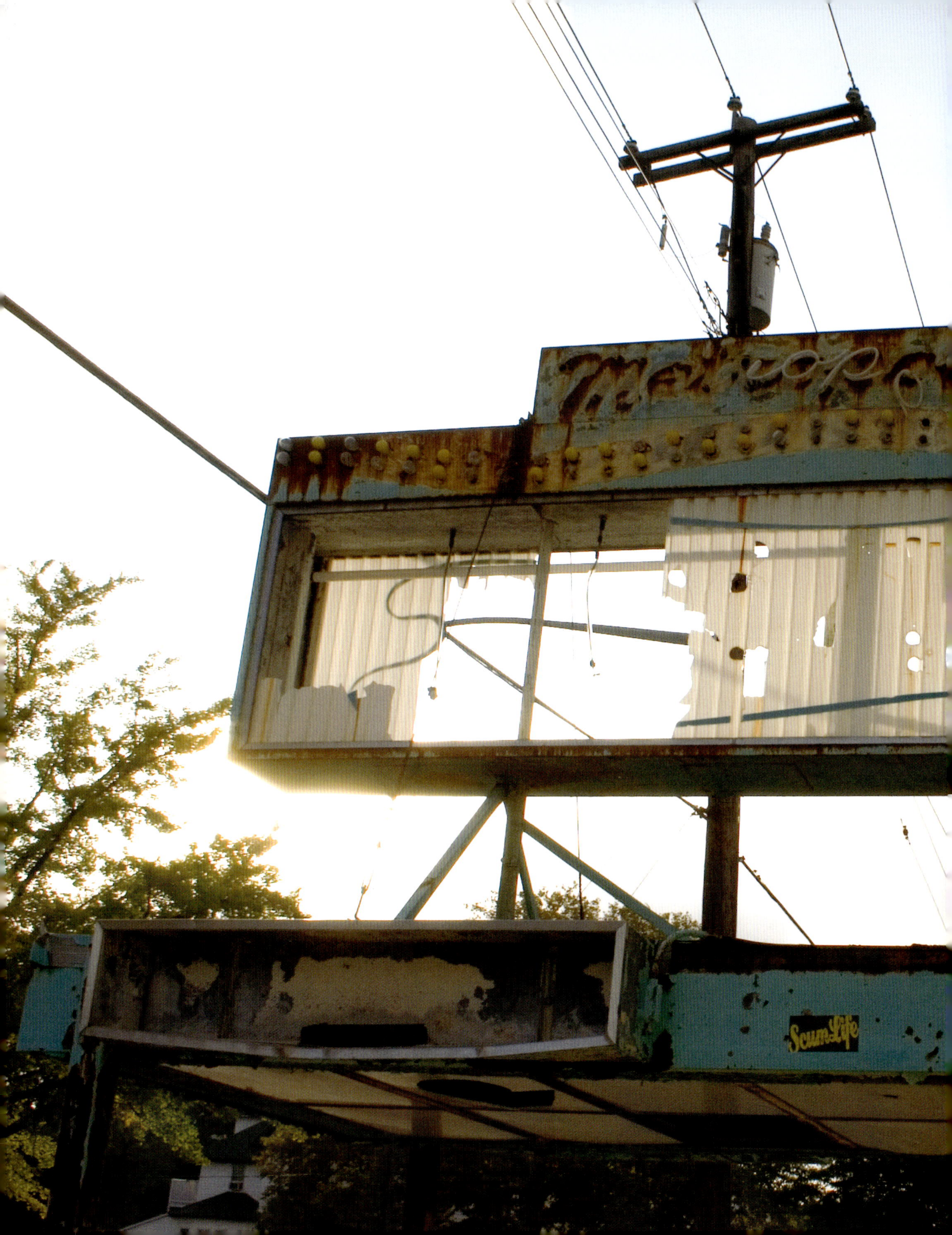
ScumLife

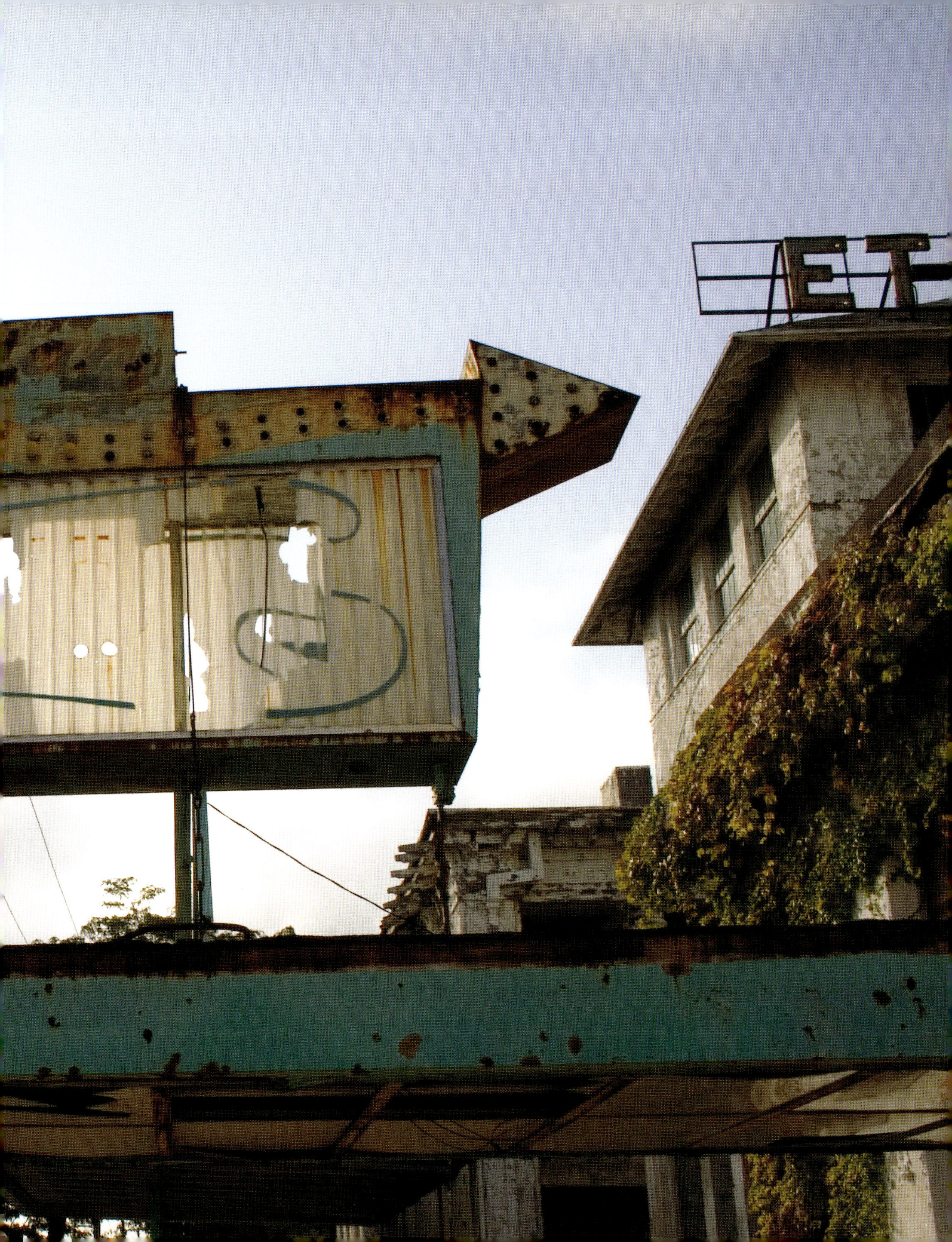
ET

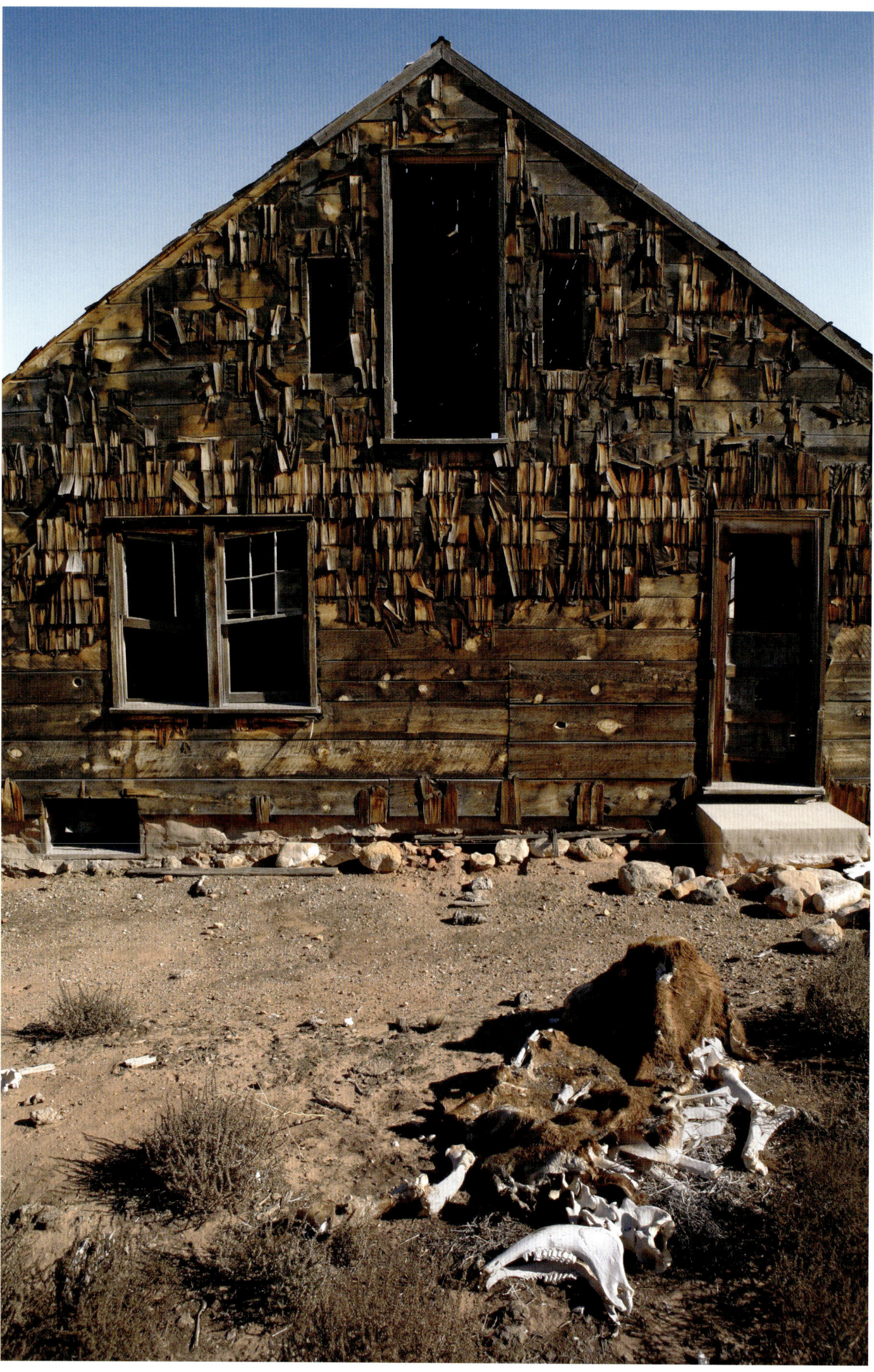

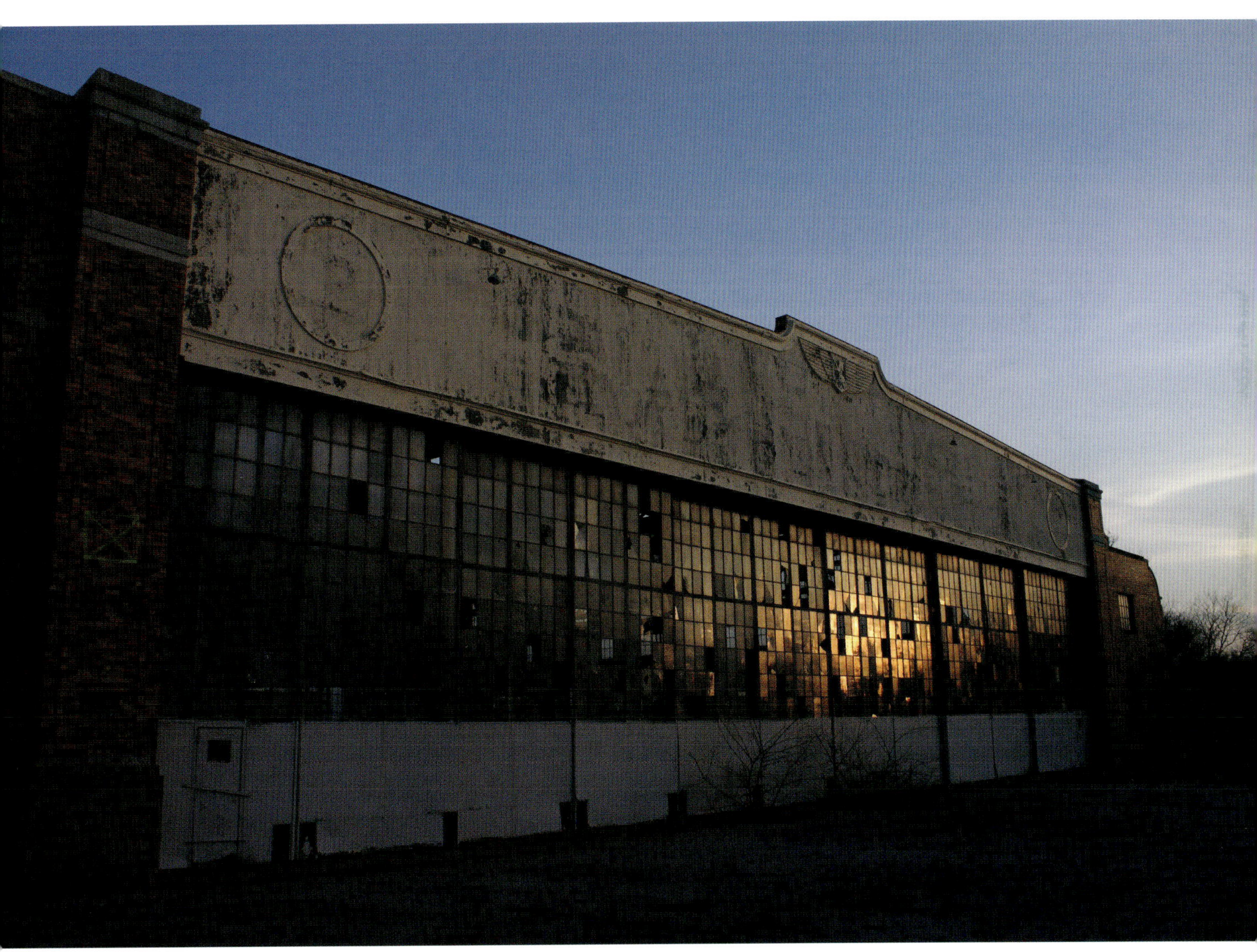

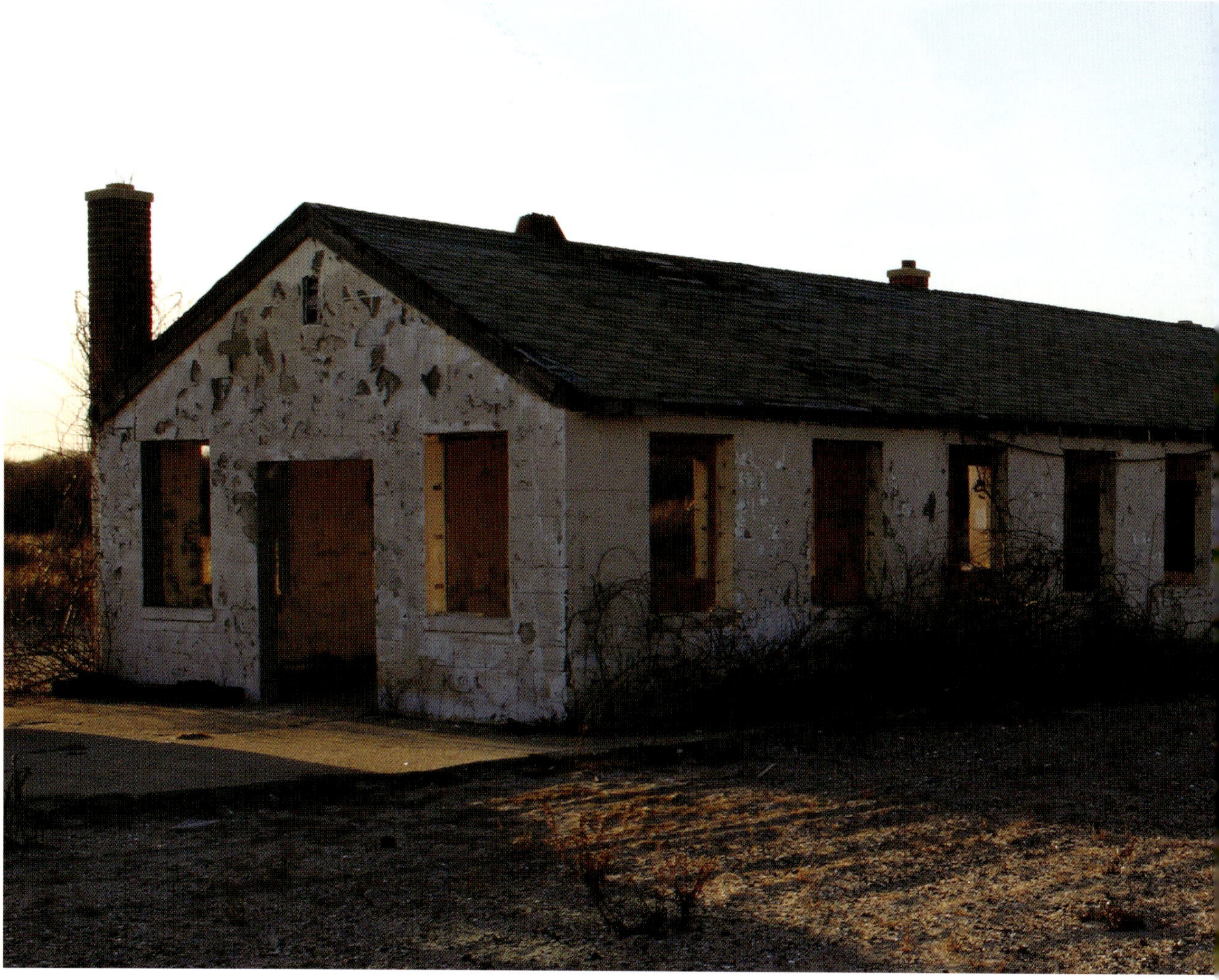

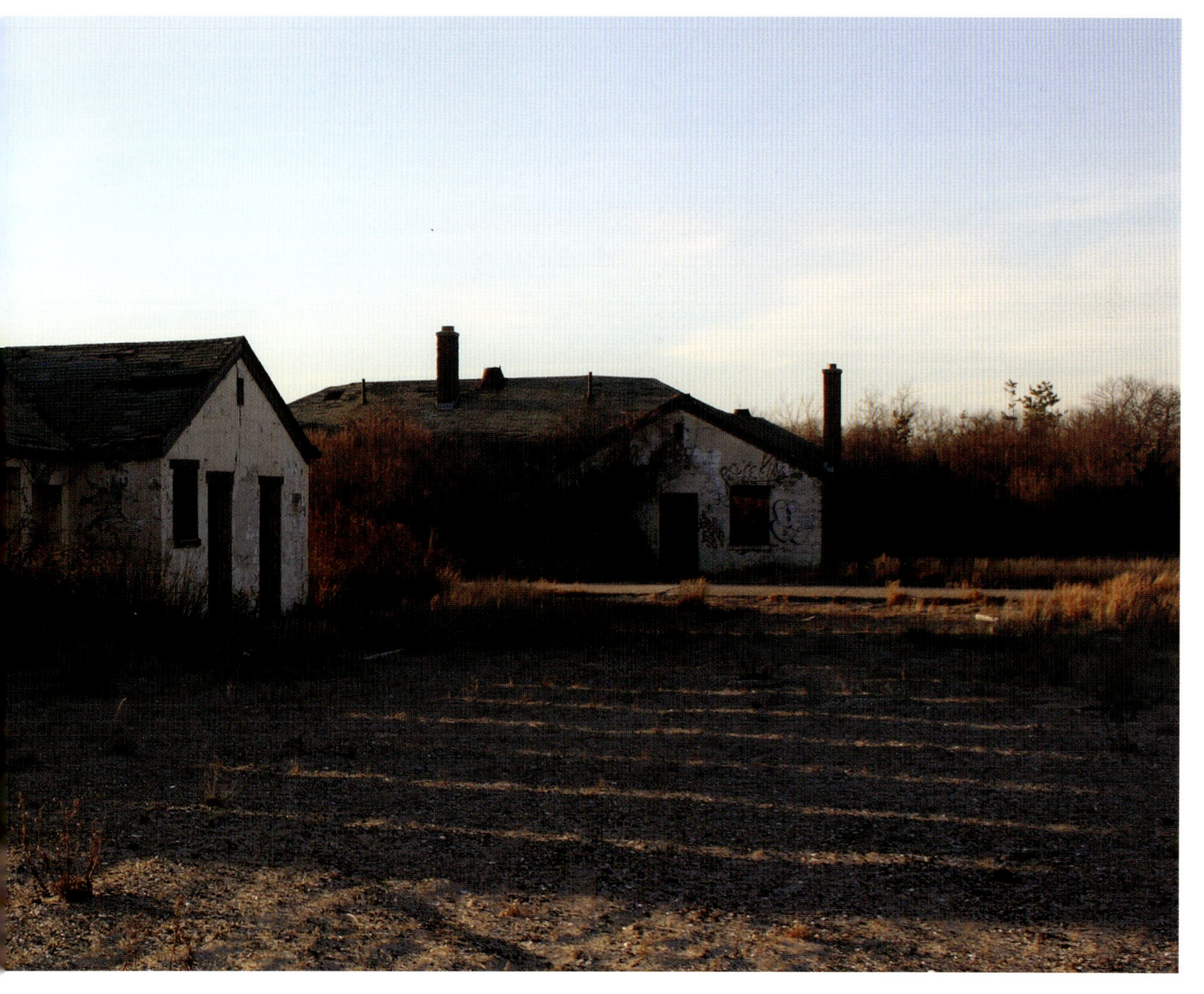

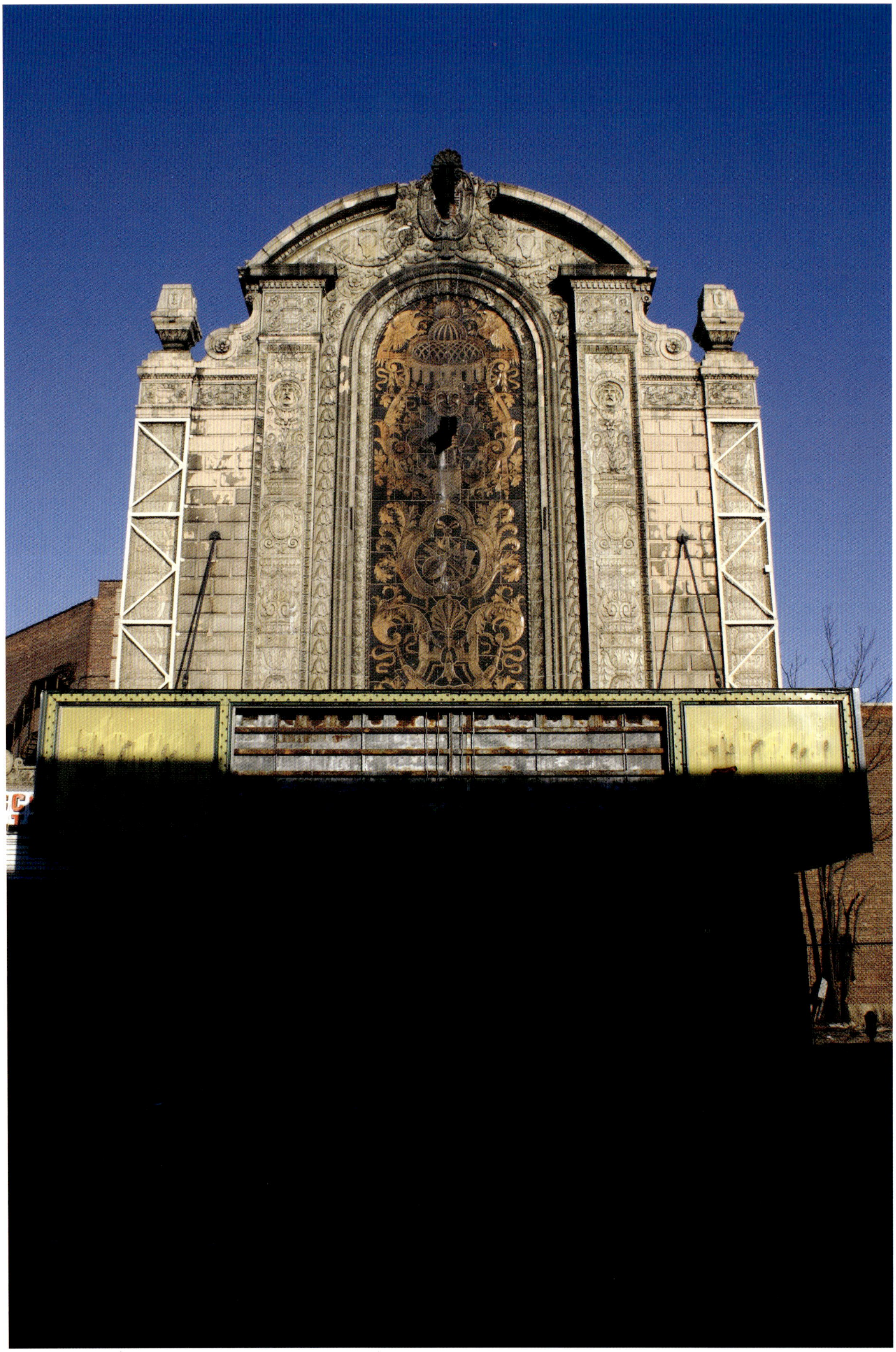

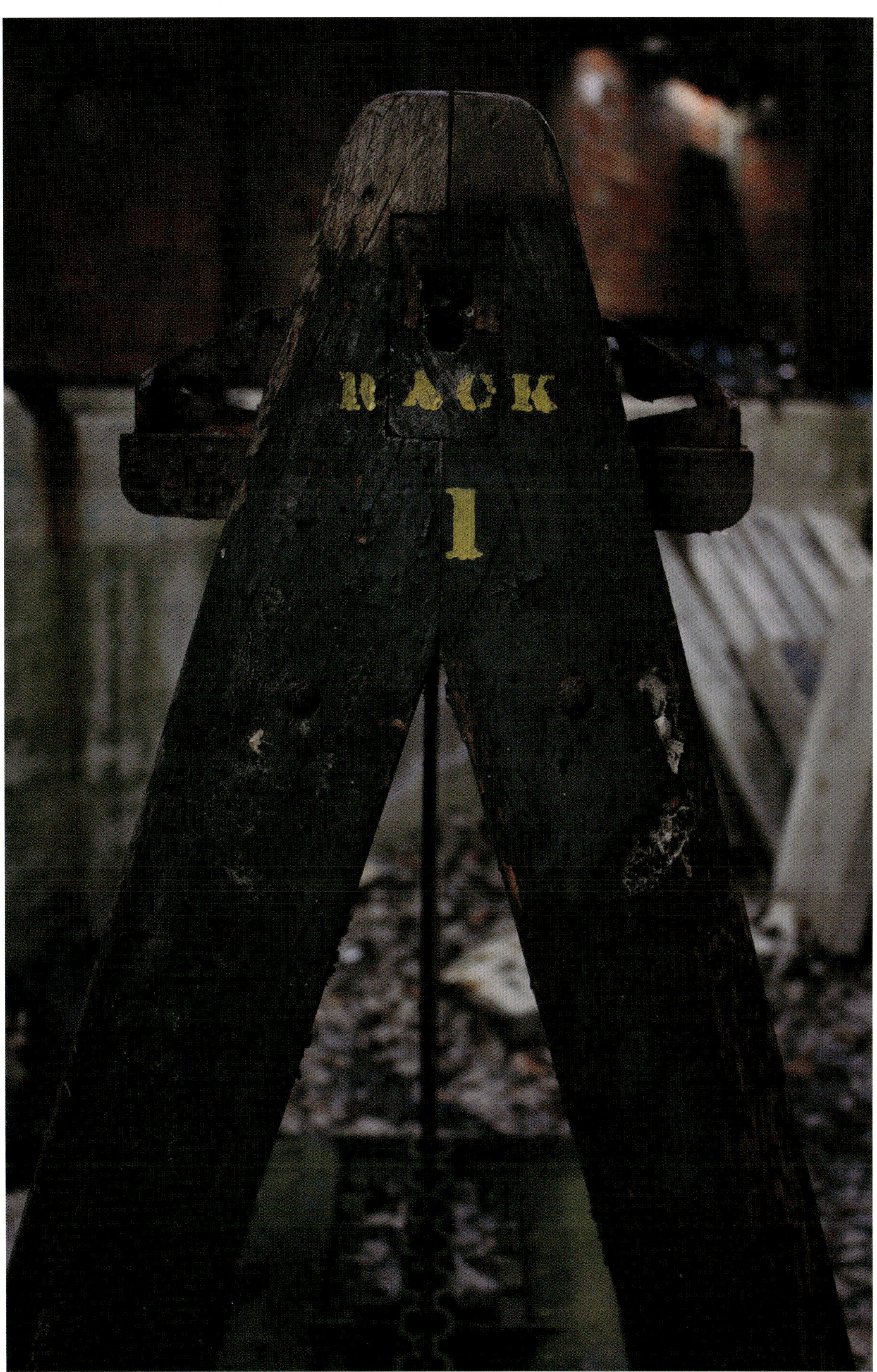
RACK
1

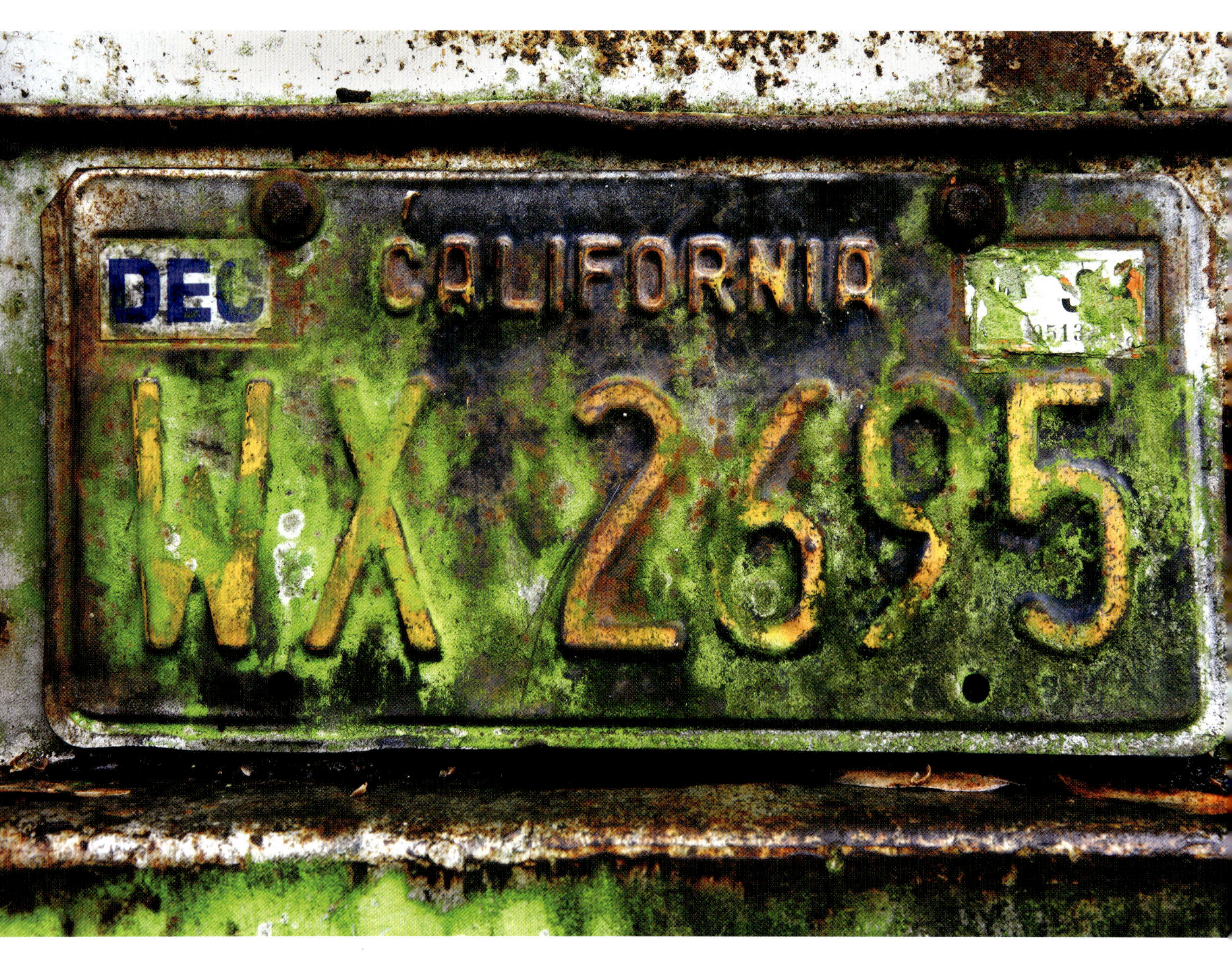
DEC
CALIFORNIA
WX 2695

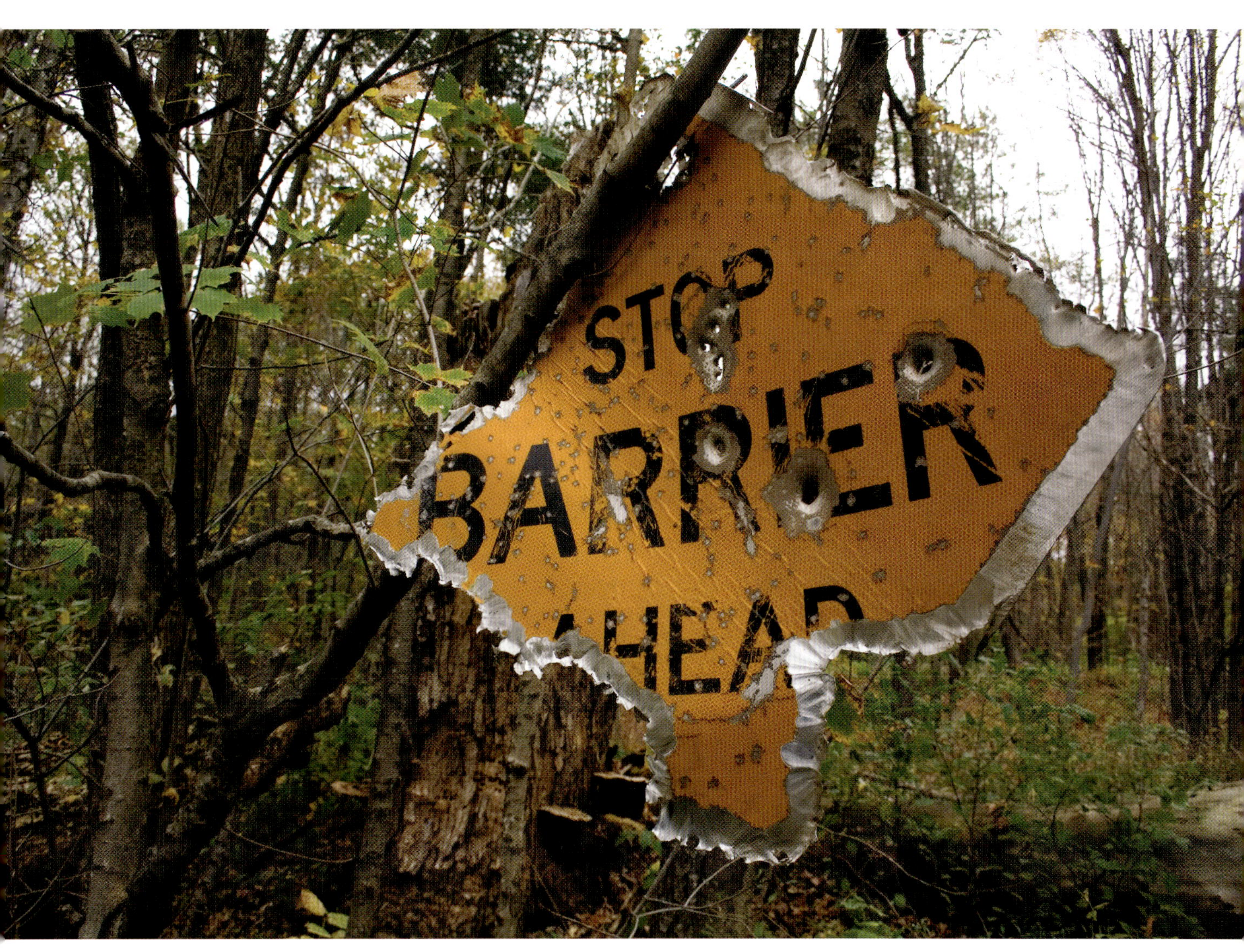
STOP
BARRIER

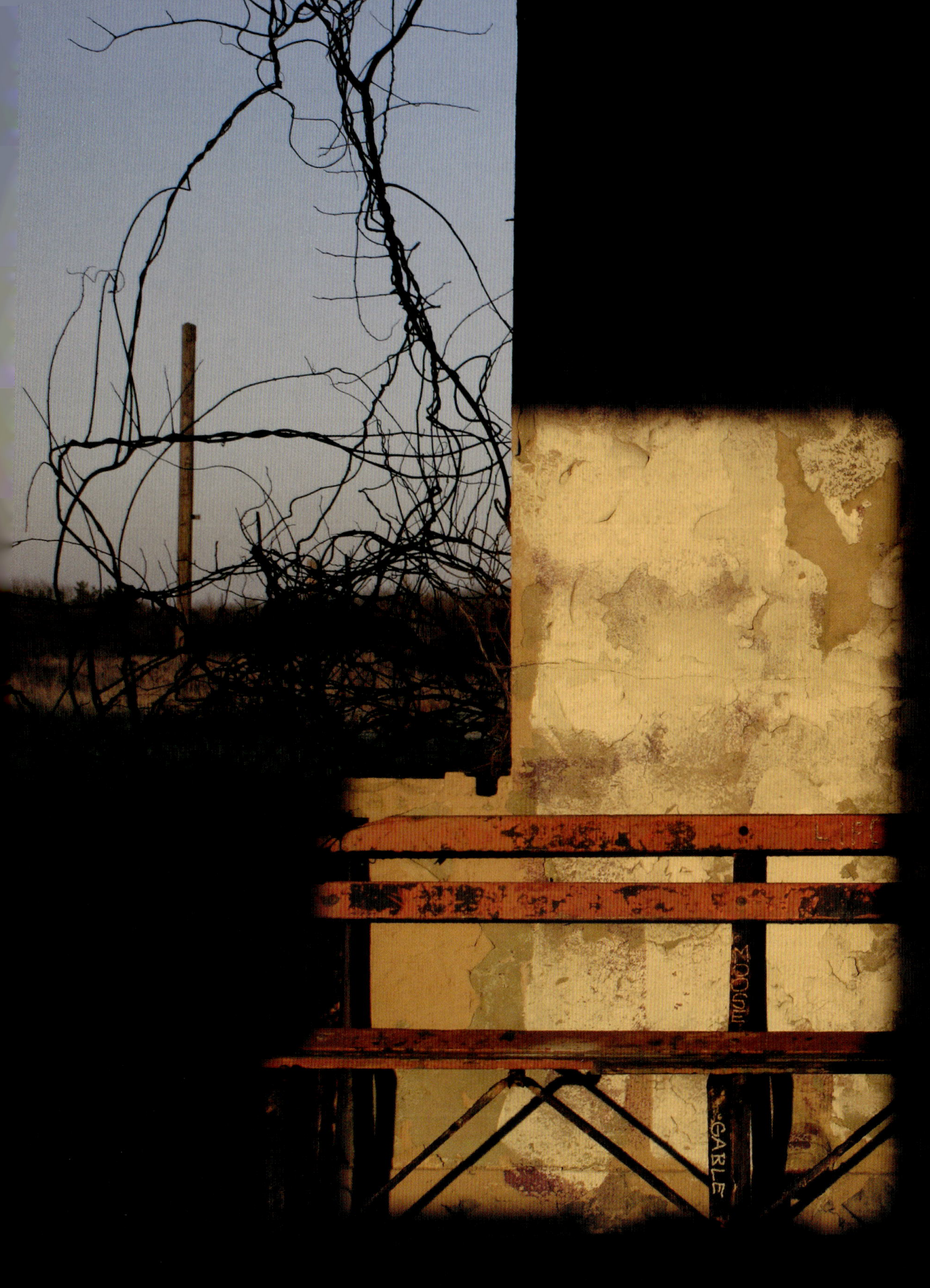
MOOSE
GABLE

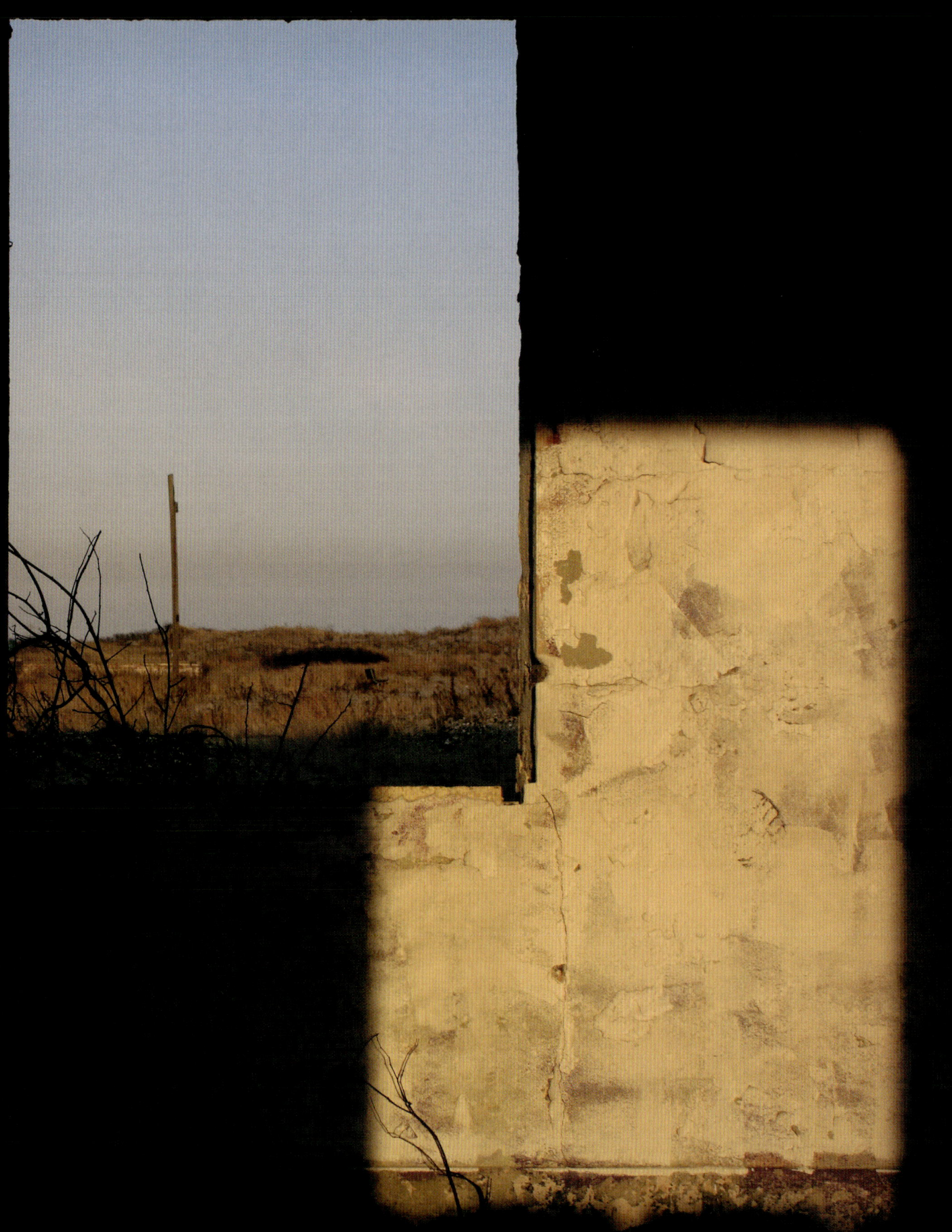

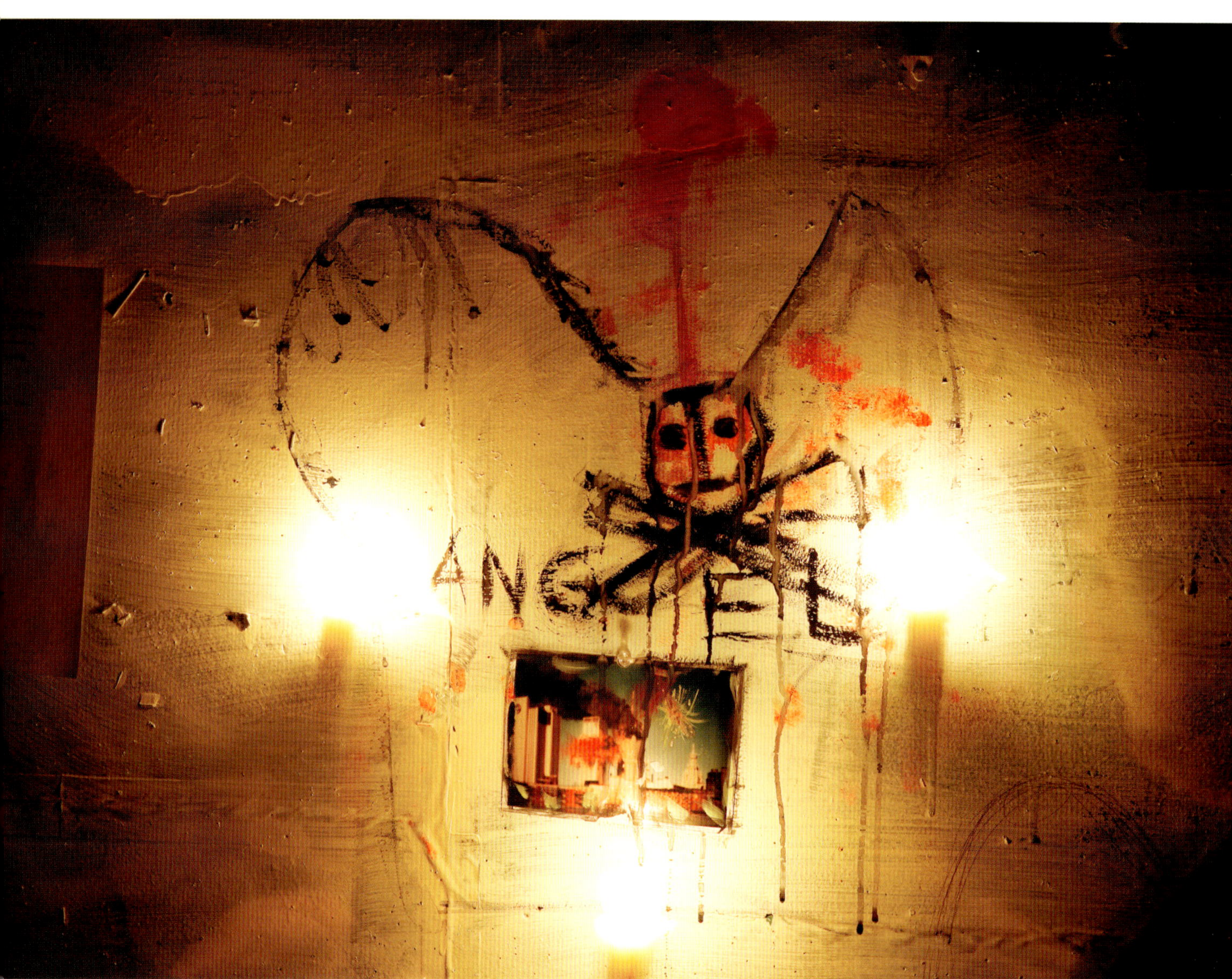
ANGEL

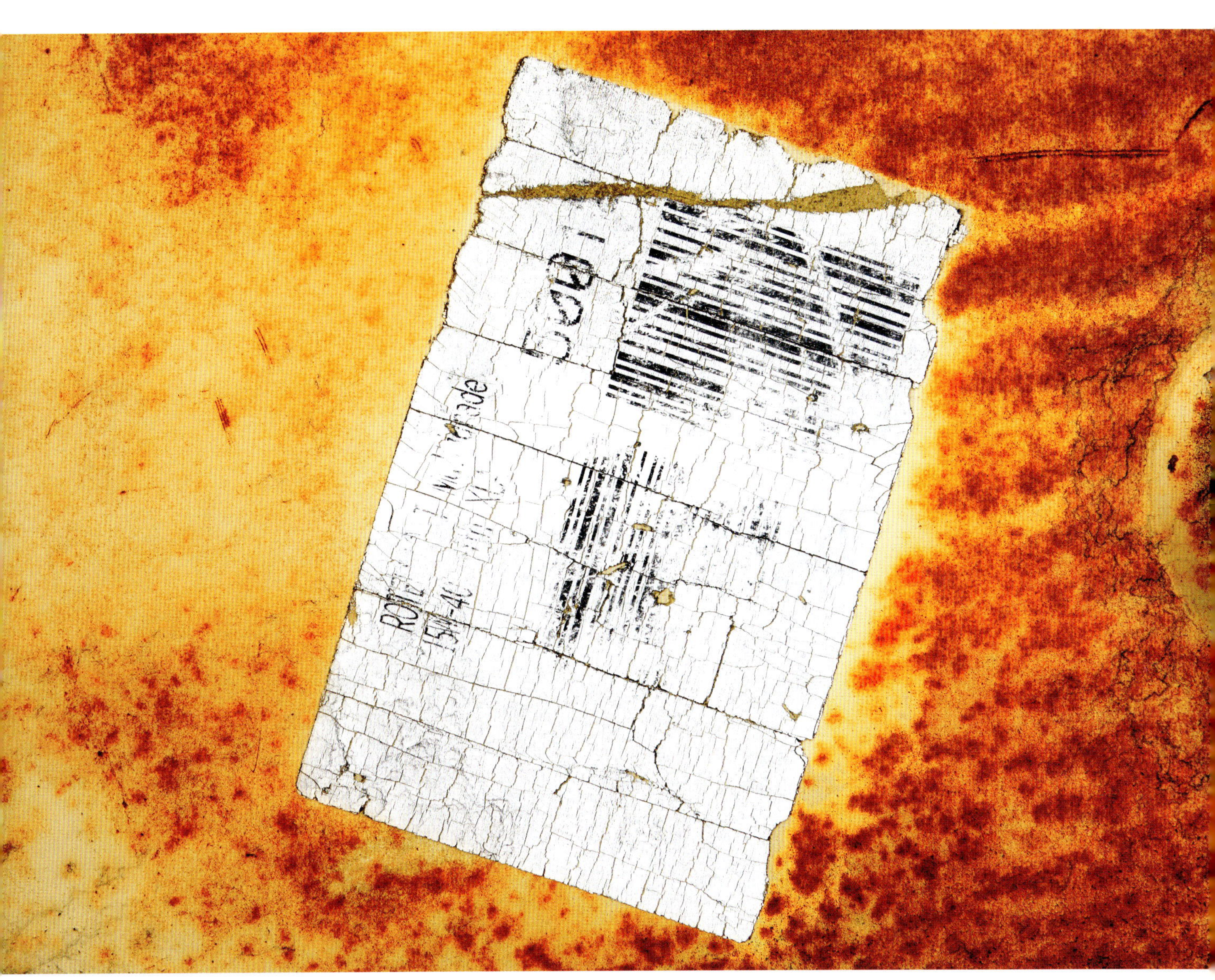

MAJEED

ON DECA

Decay is just another senseless borderline between the whisper of the ghosts of past days and the roar of painfully recovered memories. It is the heavy boots of time and the luster in the countless tiny eyes of rats. Time, rats, time, rats… so goes the unbearably slow pace of decay turning dust into ash and ash into nothing. But Man, the son of decay (often misspelled as "clay"), has invented a wonderful set of wild lies, including culture, history and the self to rationalize the fear of decay in the vain hope of breaking its logos. He imprisoned time in small ticking boxes and banished the luster of all the world's rats' eyes into the realm of metaphor. Nevertheless, all that humanity did was shackle itself to decay. Hourly, time sticks its tongue out from the small ticking boxes mocking humans' impatient denial of decay. But it is there, everywhere. It is there in the big eyes of famine-struck children in Africa. It is there lurking glaringly in the eyes of criminals, war-mongers, politicians and all of the fake statues of liberty in the third world.

Are all human perceptions then but pale shadows of decay? A gathering of dancing shadows drifting aimlessly in the endless corridors of human memory? What remains are the pale reflections of decay's shadows: in the shattered mirror of human life: the broken joy of what once was a smile and the deep trails of time's ticking wheels on a severely wrinkled face. Here are the crumbled and faded shadows of yesterday's footprints.

But then isn't the invocation of decay a celebration of human hypocrisy? The same time-shattered face can be an ugly spectacle and/or a mirror of wisdom and experience. It depends on the viewer and the object in question. Such semantics of human hypocrisy (or is it indecision, or denial?) can elevate the bitter sum of human tyranny and suffering to that of a cherished historical relic. Rome's Coliseum: What do the swarms of tourists look at and preserve in their photos and videos but the irresistible appeal of decay to the innermost darkness in the human soul?

The shinning heroics of war also render this fine, confused line. They are no more than a thin curtain screening the ultimate degradation of humanity into the abyss of decay. Medals, decorations, codes of honor are the glory of decay in the human world. Every war, every medal, every military parade is a celebration of the eternal imprisonment of humanity in decay's all-encompassing arena: tombstones mark the endless trails of the murdered, disfigured, orphaned, homeless, dishonored: the betrayal of all that is human.

Decay is so familiar because it puts on a human face and walks with a big, funny smile that disdains our desperate clinging to free will and the stock exchange. That familiarity might breed contempt but decay as a human mask surely breeds names and epithets that foreground human language and perception. The world and eternity are really linguistic constructs of decay; this "d" proliferates every mortal second of the human lexicon: decay, decline, decomposition, degeneration, deterioration, dust, devil, death, defense, democracy. Are the d-days of human history but commemorations of this familiarity? Isn't decay the actual proprietor of all the prisons, hospitals, cemeteries and other institutions of civilized human society? Find me a mortal who won't shake hands with decay… because I could not stop for decay he gently stopped for me. What remains in the wake of decay but the shuttered remains of broken sunrays, a handful of maggots and the hollow echo "Say the struggle availth not!"

So the prophecy goes (said in a deadly serious, but fake, Hollywood tone): "Desperately helpless stands the Son of Man on the plains of Mount Armageddon defiantly facing the armies of Decay with few weapons left: the laughter of children, the chirrup of sparrows and the faith in tomorrow's sunset."

Nathan Anderson met Majeed in Amman, Jordan, in 2006. An Iraqi university teacher, too proud to abandon his work and his people, was taking a brief respite before returning to the war-ravaged country he calls home. Since meeting, Anderson and Majeed have corresponded frequently via email.

War is a reality that most of us only ingest through a media filter. But war, like decay, exists in an unfiltered state. Turning a blind eye to either devalues existence.

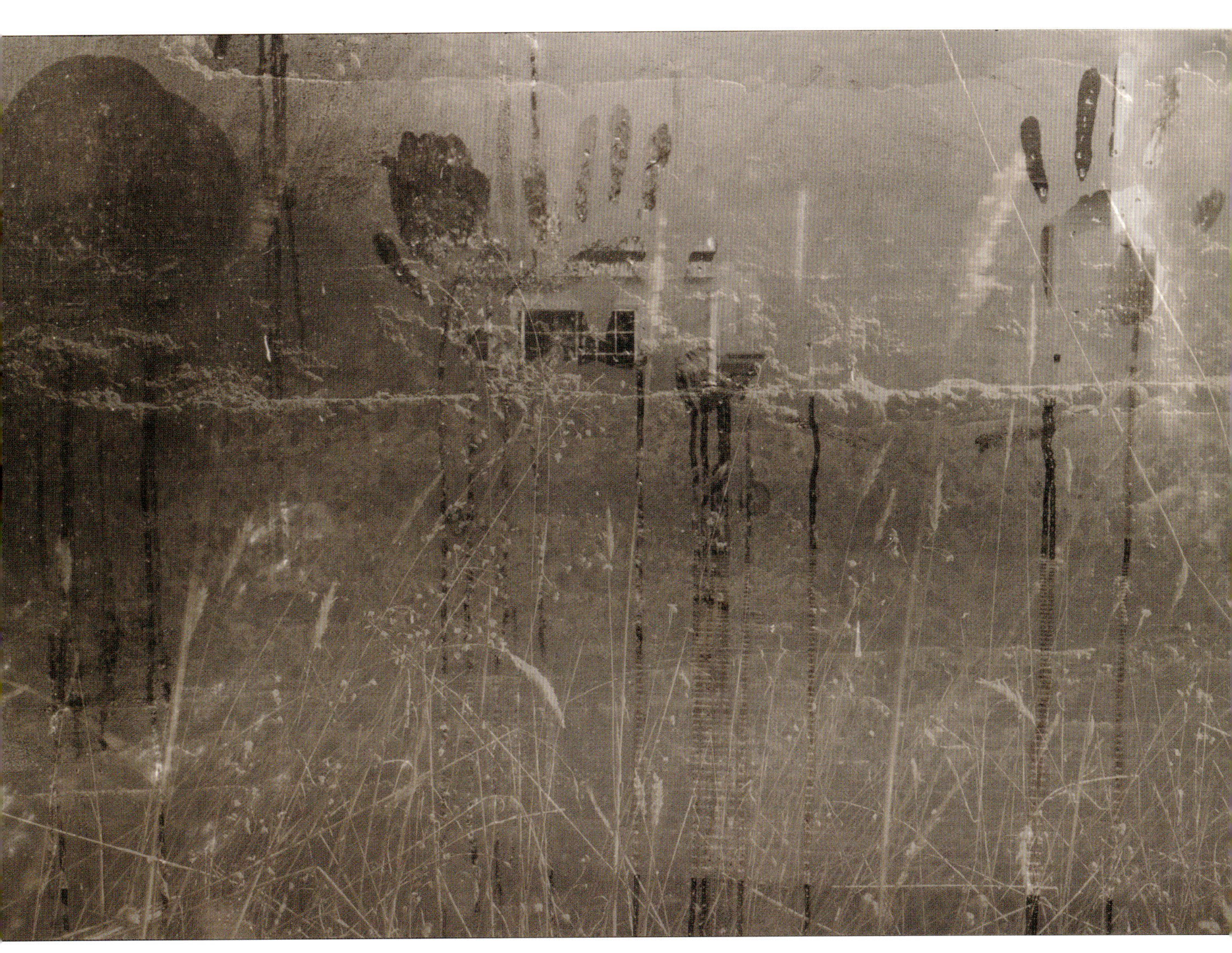

J.K. PUTNAM

IMAGE C

NATHAN TROI ANDERSON

10-11, 12, 17, 19(2), 11, 20-21, 28, 29, 30-31, 32, 33, 38-39, 40-41, 46-47, 48, 49, 50, 51, 56, 57, 58, 59, 62, 63, 68, 69, 70, 71, 72, 73, 78-79, 82, 83, 84-85, 86-87, 91, 94, 96-97, 98, 99, 100-101, 102, 104-105, 106-107, 112-113, 116, 117, 118, 119, 120, 123, 126, 132, 136, 137, 138-139, 141

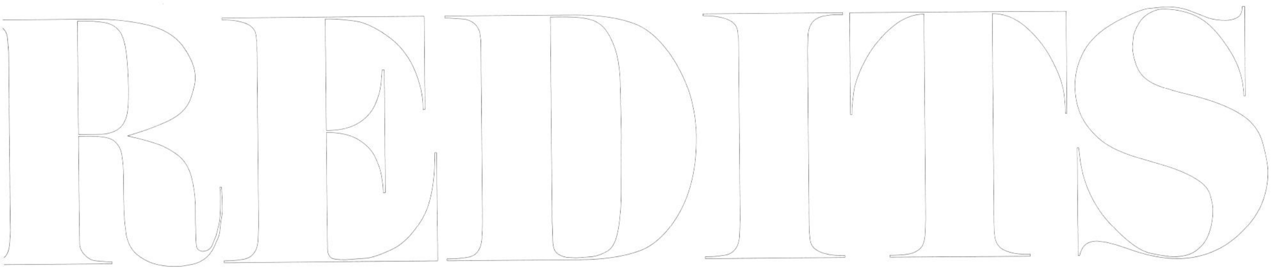

J.K.P. would like to thank Christopher D Salyers for his vision, support and work on this book. He would also like to thank the following places for being where they are and offering all they have to offer: The Olympic Peninsula, The North Cascades, Everglades National Park, Boca Grand, The Thousand Islands, The Catskills, Asbury Park, Fort Tilden, Bannerman's Island, Caleb Smith State Park, the trails I hike on, the streets I walk down and Brooklyn. A final thank you to Allison for being there for every click of the shutter.

Decay is J.K. Putnam's ninth collaboration with Mark Batty Publisher. Other titles include *Green Design* and *CBGB: Decades of Graffiti*. J.K.P. began taking pictures with his father's hand-me-down Nikkormat. That camera has long been replaced by his grandfather's Nikkormat, a Lomo Fish-Eye and a Canon 40D. When not taking pictures of the rotting world, he spends his time and patience photographing wildlife. J.K.P. lives and works in Gowanus, Brooklyn, New York.
www.jkputnamphotography.com

Nathan Troi Anderson is a photographer working out of Cortez, Colorado. He is the author of *Shadows of Time* (Mark Batty Publisher, 2006).

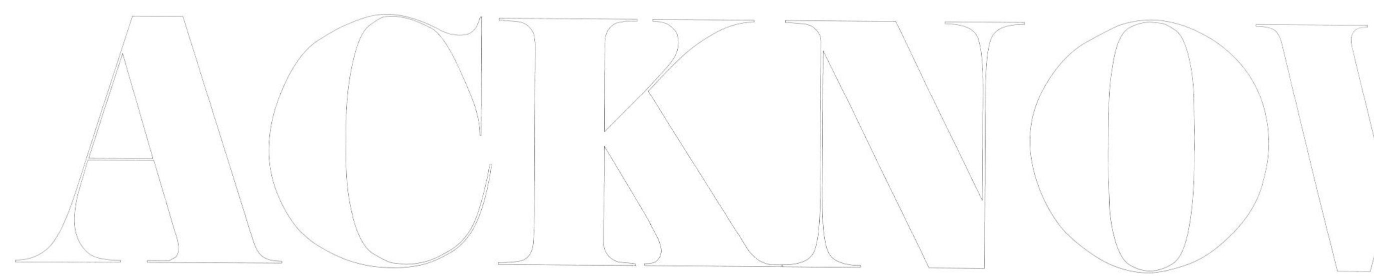

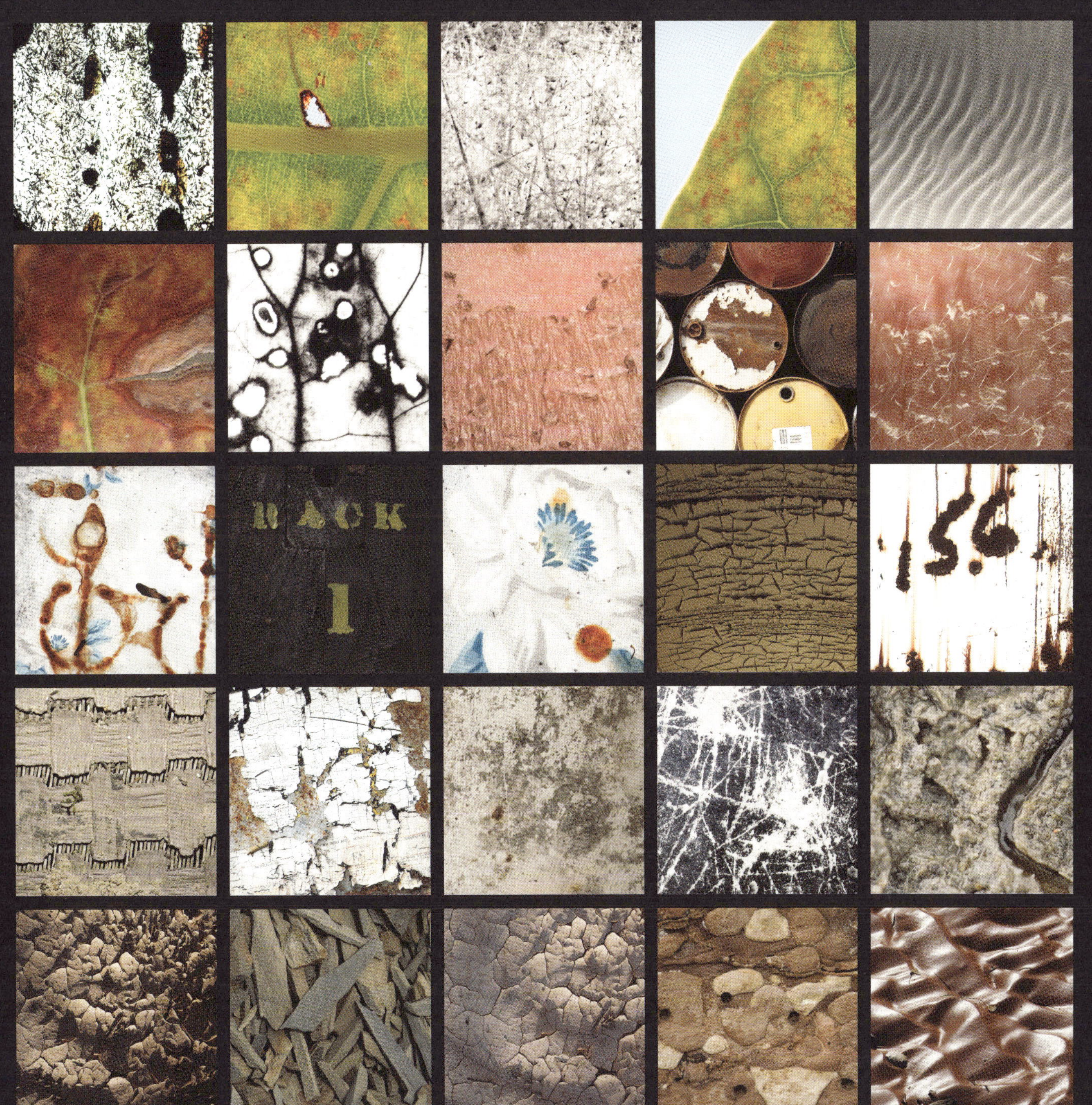
RACK
1

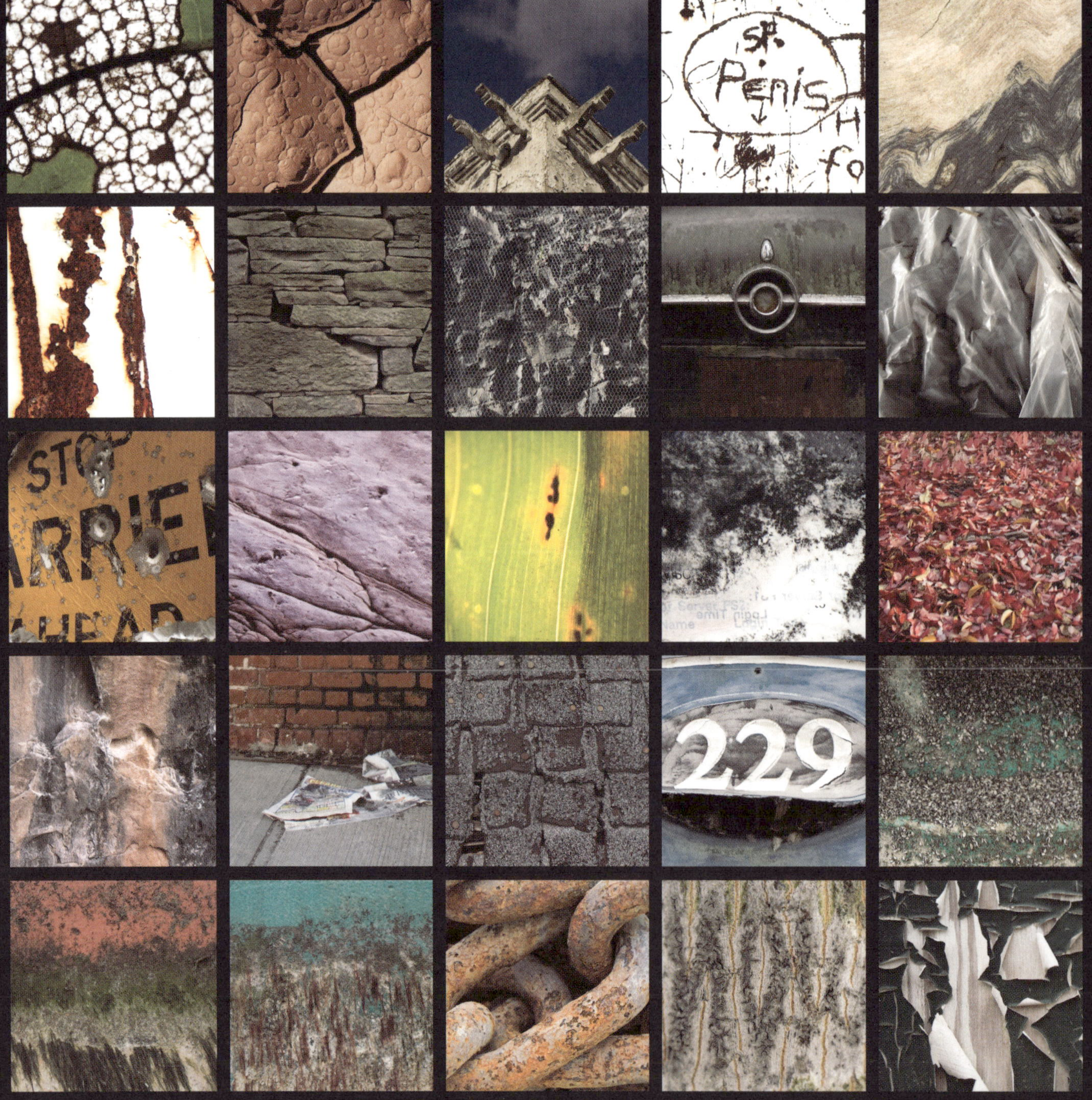
Penis
229